Corpus Use in Italian Language Pedagogy

Corpus Use in Italian Language Pedagogy: Exploring the Effects of Data-Driven Learning provides a comprehensive overview of corpus use in Italian L2 Pedagogy. The author addresses Italian language corpus resources, their potential uses in pedagogical settings, and the range of research methods available to evaluate their effectiveness. Overall, this book:

- provides a comprehensive account of Italian corpora and corpus-based research on Italian that can inform the design, implementation and evaluation of DDL practices in Italian learning and teaching contexts;
- traces the history of DDL, by describing its origins and discussing its theoretical underpinnings, in relation to both linguistics and pedagogy;
- examines the state-of-the-art in DDL research, in light of the available empirical evidence on both etic and emic dimensions, while placing particular emphasis on the methodological gaps;
- illustrates the main methodological challenges in researching DDL, from corpus resource selection to empirical evaluation of its pedagogical effectiveness, and describes how they can be overcome;
- demonstrates, by means of an in-depth case study, how the guidelines provided above can be applied when researching DDL effects in a specific second language learning and teaching context;
- discusses the overall challenges the field faces today, while outlining some desirable avenues for future research and pedagogical practice.

This book will not only be of interest to those conducting research in corpus linguistics and teaching in the Italian domain, but also to those working with other languages.

Luciana Forti is a researcher and lecturer in Applied Linguistics at the University for Foreigners of Perugia, Italy.

'This book is the first comprehensive synthesis of resources, teaching applications, and empirical research devoted to data-driven learning of Italian. Deeply rooted in the field's history, supplemented with detailed theoretical and methodological considerations, and exemplified by a longitudinal empirical study, Luciana Forti's book is an invaluable reference resource, model, and inspiration for expanding corpus-based research and teaching beyond English..'

Nina Vyatkina, *University of Kansas, USA*

'This book represents an invaluable contribution to the data-driven learning approach for Italian: researchers, teachers and students will find much to inform their work with Italian and other less-represented languages. Luciana Forti confirms her role as an important researcher in data-driven learning, especially for Italian as a foreign language. The author shows a solid understanding of research methodology in the field and an ability to transmit this via practical examples of her own research, whether qualitative or quantitative, emic or etic. The book recognises the challenges of dealing with DDL for languages that are under-researched and currently under-resourced, but provides a wealth of suggestions to meet that challenge'.

Alex Boulton, *CNRS & University of Lorraine, France*

Routledge Applied Corpus Linguistics

Series Editor: Michael McCarthy

Michael McCarthy is Emeritus Professor of Applied Linguistics at the University of Nottingham, UK, Adjunct Professor of Applied Linguistics at the University of Limerick, Ireland and Visiting Professor in Applied Linguistics at Newcastle University, U K. He is co-editor of the Routledge Handbook of Corpus Linguistics, editor of the Routledge Domains of Discourse series and co-editor of the Routledge Corpus Linguistics Guides series.

Series Editor: Anne O'Keeffe

Anne O'Keeffe is Senior Lecturer in Applied Linguistics and Director of the Inter-Varietal Applied Corpus Studies (IVACS) Research Centre at Mary Immaculate College, University of Limerick, Ireland. She is co-editor of the Routledge Handbook of Corpus Linguistics and co-editor of the Routledge Corpus Linguistics Guides series.

Series Co-Founder: Ronald Carter

Ronald Carter (1947–2018) was Research Professor of Modern English Language in the School of English at the University of Nottingham, UK. He was also the co-editor of the Routledge Corpus Linguistics Guides series, Routledge Introductions to Applied Linguistics series and Routledge English Language Introductions series.

Editorial Panel: IVACS (Inter-Varietal Applied Corpus Studies Group), based at Mary Immaculate College, University of Limerick, is an international research network linking corpus linguistic researchers interested in exploring and comparing language in different contexts of use.

The Routledge Applied Corpus Linguistics Series is a series of monograph studies exhibiting cutting-edge research in the field of corpus linguistics and its applications to real-world language problems. Corpus linguistics is one of the most dynamic and rapidly developing areas in the field of language studies, and it is difficult to see a future for empirical language research where results are not replicable by reference to corpus data. This series showcases the latest research in the field of applied language studies where corpus findings are at the forefront, introducing new and unique methodologies and applications which open up new avenues for research.

Other Titles in this Series

Native and Non-Native Teacher Talk in the EFL Classroom
A Corpus-informed Study
Eric Nicaise

Corpus-Based Analysis of Ideological Bias
Migration in the British Press
Anna Islentyeva

Academic Writing and Reader Engagement
Contrasting Questions in English, French, and Spanish Corpora
Niall Curry

Corpus Linguistics and Cross-Disciplinary Action Research
A Study of Talk in the Mathematics Classroom
Joanna Baumgart

Representing Schizophrenia in the Media
A Corpus-Based Approach to UK Press Coverage
James Balfour

The Linguistic Challenge of the Transition to Secondary School
A Corpus Study of Academic Language
Alice Deignan, Duygu Candarli and Florence Oxley

Investigating a Corpus of Historical Oral Testimonies
The Linguistic Construction of Certainty
Chris Fitzgerald

Corpus Use in Italian Language Pedagogy
Exploring the Effects of Data-Driven Learning
Luciana Forti

Inter-Varietal Applied Corpus Studies

More information about this series can be found at www.routledge.com/series/RACL

Corpus Use in Italian Language Pedagogy

Exploring the Effects of Data-Driven Learning

Luciana Forti

LONDON AND NEW YORK

First published 2023
by Routledge
4 Park Square, Milton Park, Abingdon, Oxon OX14 4RN

and by Routledge
605 Third Avenue, New York, NY 10158

Routledge is an imprint of the Taylor & Francis Group, an informa business

© 2023 Luciana Forti

The right of Luciana Forti to be identified as author of this work has been asserted in accordance with sections 77 and 78 of the Copyright, Designs and Patents Act 1988.

All rights reserved. No part of this book may be reprinted or reproduced or utilised in any form or by any electronic, mechanical, or other means, now known or hereafter invented, including photocopying and recording, or in any information storage or retrieval system, without permission in writing from the publishers.

Trademark notice: Product or corporate names may be trademarks or registered trademarks, and are used only for identification and explanation without intent to infringe.

British Library Cataloguin g-in-Publication Data
A catalogue record for this book is available from the British Library

Library of Congress Cataloging-in-Publication Data
Names: Forti, Luciana, author.
Title: Corpus use in Italian language pedagogy : exploring the
effects of data-driven learning / Luciana Forti.
Description: First edition. | Abingdon, Oxon ;
New York, NY : Routledge, 2023. |
Series: Routledge applied corpus linguistics |
Includes bibliographical references and index.
Identifiers: LCCN 2022043894 | ISBN 9780367683634 (hardback) |
ISBN 9780367683917 (paperback) | ISBN 9781003137320 (ebook)
Subjects: LCSH: Italian language–Study and teaching–
Foreign speakers. | Corpora (Linguistics)
Classification: LCC PC1065 .F67 2023 |
DDC 458.0071–dc23/eng/20221028
LC record available at https://lccn.loc.gov/2022043894

ISBN: 978-0-367-68363-4 (hbk)
ISBN: 978-0-367-68391-7 (pbk)
ISBN: 978-1-003-13732-0 (ebk)

DOI: 10.4324/9781003137320

Typeset in Sabon
by Newgen Publishing UK

Contents

List of figures xi
List of tables xii
Foreword xiv
Acknowledgements xvii

1 Introduction 1
   1.1 *Corpora, second language pedagogy and data-driven learning (DDL)* 1
   1.2 *The need for and the challenge of conducting rigorous empirical DDL research* 4
   1.3 *Researching DDL for learning Italian* 6
   1.4 *This book* 8
   References 9

2 Data-driven learning: origins, theoretical underpinnings, and development through time 12
   2.1 *Origins of DDL* 12
   2.2 *DDL pedagogy* 15
   2.3 *Theories underpinning DDL pedagogy* 18
      2.3.1 Theories of language 18
      2.3.2 Theories on language learning and teaching 21
   2.4 *The evolution of DDL through time* 25
   2.5 *DDL in Italian L2 learning and teaching* 28
   2.6 *DDL debates* 32
   2.7 *Chapter summary and conclusions* 34
   References 36

3 Delving into the research evidence on data-driven learning effects 42
   3.1 *Does DDL work?* 42
   3.2 *How do learners and teachers respond to DDL?* 49

viii   Contents

    3.3   *Italian L2 and the research evidence on DDL effects* 54
    3.4   *Chapter summary and conclusions* 56
    References 57

4 **Methods in researching data-driven learning effects** 59
    4.1   *The nature of knowledge in researching DDL effects* 59
    4.2   *The nature of scientific knowledge in researching DDL effects* 63
    4.3   *Choosing the learners and the learning context* 64
    4.4   *Designing the DDL activities* 69
    4.5   *Collecting empirical data on DDL effects* 72
    4.6   *Developing the study design* 75
    4.7   *Coding, analysing, and interpreting the data* 78
    4.8   *Chapter summary and conclusions* 80
    References 81

5 **Italian L2: corpus resources and language learning research** 85
    5.1   *A brief history of Italian corpus linguistics* 85
    5.2   *Italian corpus linguistics in the Italian L2 landscape* 90
    5.3   *Developing data-driven learning practices for Italian: resources and affordances* 93
        5.3.1   Italian L1 corpora 93
        5.3.2   Italian L2 corpora 99
        5.3.3   DIY corpora 104
    5.4   *Chapter summary and conclusions* 105
    References 107

6 **Language gains and learner attitudes in data-driven learning: study design** 112
    6.1   *Phraseology: a central component in the development of second language proficiency* 112
        6.1.1   What is phraseology? 112
        6.1.2   The role of phraseology in second language learning 115
        6.1.3   What we know about phraseological competence development in second language learning 116
            6.1.3.1   The international perspective 116
            6.1.3.2   The view from studies on L1 and L2 Italian 119
    6.2   *Rationale, research questions, and hypotheses of the study* 120
    6.3   *Method* 122
        6.3.1   Study design 122
        6.3.2   Population and participant sample 122
        6.3.3   Operationalising the DDL construct 124
            6.3.3.1   Identification of learning aims 124
            6.3.3.2   Development of learning materials 125

      6.3.4   A data collection tool for the etic dimension: the phraseological competence test 128
      6.3.5   A data collection tool for the emic dimension: the student questionnaire 129
      6.3.6   Data analysis 130
  6.4   *Chapter summary and conclusions* 133
  References 134

7 How data-driven learning impacts language gains   140
  7.1   *Overall DDL effects over time* 140
      7.1.1   Descriptive overview 140
      7.1.2   Modelling DDL effects over time 142
  7.2   *DDL effects through the lens of semantic transparency and L1 congruency* 148
      7.2.1   Semantic transparency 148
      7.2.2   L1 congruency 149
  7.3   *DDL effects and dimensions of phraseological knowledge* 152
  7.4   *Discussion of findings* 156
  7.5   *Chapter summary and conclusions* 163
  References 163

8 How learners react to data-driven learning   166
  8.1   *Data collection and analysis* 166
  8.2   *Working on word combinations: learner perceptions from DDL and non-DDL groups* 167
      8.2.1   Likert-scale items 167
      8.2.2   Open-ended questions 168
  8.3   *Working on word combinations through DDL activities: learner perceptions from DDL groups* 174
  8.4   *Discussion of findings* 175
  8.5   *Chapter summary and conclusions* 184
  References 185

9 Conclusions and future prospects   187
  9.1   *Investigating DDL effects on Italian L2 phraseological competence development: a summary* 187
  9.2   *The need to connect DDL research with SLA research evidence* 189
  9.3   *The need to connect DDL research with SLA theories* 190
  9.4   *Reflecting on DDL empirical research methods* 193
  9.5   *Contributing to Italian language learning studies and pedagogy* 195
  9.6   *Looking ahead* 196
  References 197

*Appendix A: Sample experimental lesson plan and
  activities (week 4)* 200
*Appendix B: Sample control lesson plan and activities
  (week 4)* 216
Appendix C: Phraseological competence test 230
*Appendix D: End-of-course student questionnaire
  (DDL group)* 235
*Appendix E: End-of-course student questionnaire
  (non-DDL group)* 238
Index 240

Figures

1.1	Pedagogical uses of corpus data	3
2.1	SkELL: concordance of *viso*	16
2.2	SkELL: word sketch of *viso*	17
2.3	DDL for (mainly) English language learning: study counts by publication date	26
2.4	DDL for Italian language learning: study counts by publication date	29
4.1	Population and sample	65
5.1	Temporal distribution of corpus-related publication types in BELI	92
6.1	Judgment sampling conducted for the study	124
7.1	Measures of central tendency related to correct answers in DDL and non-DDL group	141
7.2	Identification of outliers in control group	143
7.3	Overall DDL effects: plot of fixed effects across conditions	146
7.4	Overall DDL effects: plot of fixed effects in each condition	147
7.5	DDL effects related to semantic transparency: plot of fixed effects	150
7.6	DDL effects related to L1 congruency: plot of fixed effects	153
7.7	DDL effects related to dimensions of phraseological knowledge: plot of fixed effects	155
8.1	Perceptions of DDL groups on phraseology-based language course (likert scale items). Item 5. Reading groups of sentences containing the same combination confused me	175
8.2	Perceptions of DDL groups on phraseology-based language course (likert scale items). Item 6. The observation of groups of sentences containing the same combination has helped me to understand how to use that combination in the future	176
8.3	Perceptions of DDL groups on phraseology-based language course (likert scale items). Item 7. The groups of sentences will help me make fewer errors in the future	177
8.4	Perceptions of DDL groups on phraseology-based language course (likert scale items). Item 8. A new smartphone application with groups of sentences for word combinations would be useless	178

Tables

3.1	Summary of meta-analyses on DDL	47
4.1	Main types of probability sampling methods	67
4.2	Main types of non-probability sampling methods	68
5.1	Occurrences of corpus-related keywords in BELI over time	91
5.2	Main corpora of L1 Italian (in chronological order of publication)	94
5.3	Main corpora of L2 Italian (in chronological order of publication)	102
6.1	Working definitions of *pharseological unit*	113
6.2	Study design	123
6.3	Summary statistics of participant sample	125
6.4	Learning aims of the study: Weekly sets of verb + noun (object) combinations	126
6.5	List of semantically transparent and semantically opaque combinations	132
6.6	List of congruent and incongruent combinations	132
7.1	Outliers across subjects	144
7.2	Overall DDL effects: fixed effects and interactions of final model	145
7.3	Overall DDL effects: random effects values of final model	147
7.4	Overall DDL effects: R^2 values of final model	147
7.5	DDL effects related to semantic transparency: fixed effects and interactions of final model	149
7.6	DDL effects related to semantic transparency: random effects of final model	150
7.7	DDL effects related to semantic transparency: R^2 values of final model	150
7.8	DDL effects related to L1 congruency: fixed effects and interactions of final model	152
7.9	DDL effects related to L1 congruency: random effects values of final model	153
7.10	DDL effects related to L1 congruency: R^2 values of final model	153

7.11	DDL effects related to dimensions of phraseological knowledge: fixed effects and interactions of final model	154
7.12	DDL effects related to dimensions of phraseological knowledge: random effect values of final model	156
7.13	DDL effects related to dimensions of phraseological knowledge: R^2 values of final model	156
8.1	Perceptions of DDL vs. non-DDL groups on phraseology-based language course (likert-scale items) – Item 1	167
8.2	Perceptions of DDL vs. non-DDL groups on phraseology-based language course (likert-scale items) – Item 2	168
8.3	Perceptions of DDL vs. non-DDL groups on phraseology-based language course (likert-scale items) – Item 3	169
8.4	Perceptions of DDL vs. non-DDL groups on phraseology-based language course (likert-scale items) – Item 4	169
8.5	Perceptions of DDL vs. non-DDL groups on phraseology-based language course (open-ended questions). Question 1	170
8.6	Perceptions of DDL vs. non-DDL groups on phraseology-based language course (open-ended questions). Question 2	171
8.7	Perceptions of DDL vs. non-DDL groups on phraseology-based language course (open-ended questions). Question 3	172
8.8	Perceptions of DDL vs. non-DDL groups on phraseology-based language course (open-ended questions). Question 4	173

Foreword

As its title may suggest, the broad areas that Luciana Forti covers in this book are mainly two: the role of data-driven learning in second language pedagogy – with a specific focus on L2 Italian learning contexts – and the ways in which the use of corpora is influencing (Italian) L2 pedagogy. In both cases, the book is a remarkable resource for readers involved in language learning, and notably for those who wish to explore further how to exploit corpora in teaching and in research on second language learning. Analyses and evaluations on the effectiveness of DDL, which throughout the volume have the role of problematising the use of corpora in education, are very timely, in any second language learning context. What really enhances and complements the value of the volume, however, and makes it a key reference tool in approaching these areas, is the choice of placing these analyses and evaluations in the L2 Italian context.

There are several reasons for this. First, it is acknowledged that research on the use of corpora in teaching and learning – an area dominated by studies on English – is not as widespread for Romance languages. This is especially true for Italian: although sporadic studies have been published in the past 25 years, research on Italian in this area has never been systematic, so that today it is not possible to refer to an actual strand of research on the use of corpora in the teaching of Italian. This is part of a general and historically rooted trend in pedagogical research on Italian, which struggles to be empirical, and too rarely is experimental. Second, even the use of corpora in linguistic research on Italian – albeit not specifically pedagogical – can hardly establish itself as an autonomous area of research, in a context dominated by other traditions of studies, mainly historical. Additionally, and despite what has just been described, there is a growing and widespread demand among researchers and teachers of L2 Italian for resources, tools and training on pedagogical uses of corpora. For all these reasons, this volume is extraordinarily well-timed in attempting to answer the question 'What do corpora have to offer in the field of Italian language learning and teaching?', and can serve both as a valuable gap-filling resource and as a catalyst for addressing these teachers' demands.

Another strength of the book, that Luciana Forti develops with great care, stems from the twofold nature of its intended audience. The areas of interest of its two main target audiences – researchers interested in language learning and teachers of Italian as a second language – only rarely overlap and coexist. More often, each of the two groups complains, on the contrary, of a lack of integration with the other's achievements: from this point of view, the language teachers' side is little aware and takes even less account of the research results, while the researchers' side is not sufficiently grounded in language teachers' practices and needs. This gap between teaching and research is certainly not new in the field of applied linguistics, nor is it exclusive to the context of L2 Italian. An informed use of corpus-related methodologies like DDL may provide an effective way to bridge this historical gap, and at least to tend towards a closer integration between the two areas.

Luciana Forti makes this attempt consciously and systematically throughout the book, focusing the readers' attention on the three key issues of theory, corpora and methods. A thought-provoking discussion of the main linguistic and language learning theories underpinning the DDL pedagogy provides the reader with the necessary background to design research on DDL or to plan teaching interventions based on the use of corpora. In this sense, the book tries to bridge the other well-known gap between DDL research and second language acquisition debates, and is therefore a highly valuable resource for anyone interested in DDL, even outside the context of L2 Italian. Once the different theoretical frameworks have been discussed, corpora and their pedagogical use become the common thread running through the entire volume. The key topic of the role of corpora in second language learning is approached from different, complementary perspectives. From a simply informative point of view – which is, however, not trivial, given the context described above – by providing a rationale of the currently available corpora of Italian, and from a more methodological approach, by discussing crucial DDL topics such as the different modalities of interaction with the corpus (paper-based, computer-based, mixed), or the teacher and learner attitudes towards corpus use. Corpora are therefore the core theme of the entire volume, binding all its different parts together and acting as an interface between theoretical frameworks – whether acquisitional or involving language learning – and DDL-related methodological choices. Methods are indeed the third key theme of the book, the one to which the author devotes the largest space. An entire chapter (Chapter 4) is devoted to a discussion of methodological choices involved in research on DDL, and three others (Chapters 6–8) present an experimental study on a teaching approach to Italian collocations through DDL, which is described and discussed in great detail. This case study aims on the one hand to concretely exemplify the methodological choices that research on DDL entails, and on the other hand to identify and possibly fill some of the gaps that remain to be addressed in that field. The study is particularly relevant in this sense, as it adopts a longitudinal approach, which has rarely been taken so far, and analyses data on the effects of DDL using sophisticated multidimensional statistical techniques.

Luciana Forti addresses the issues I have briefly outlined with thoroughness and clarity, and this is certainly another value of this volume. Her style is sober, essential and straightforward, and is combined with great methodological accuracy, thus endowing the book with solidity and rigour.

By offering researchers and teachers a comprehensive toolbox for research on DDL and for the informed use of corpora in language teaching, the volume serves as a foundation and a catalyst for future studies and teaching practices. What makes this book different from other introductory works on DDL and corpora in language teaching is that it provides a broad and complete overview of Italian corpus resources, as well as an in-depth longitudinal case study on the use of DDL in the teaching of Italian. All in all, because of this specific context in which it is grounded, it is a truly irreplaceable resource for researchers and teachers involved in L2 Italian.

Stefania Spina

Acknowledgements

This book stems from my PhD thesis entitled *Developing phraseological competence in Italian L2: A study on the effects of data-driven learning*. It would not have been possible without the support of Stefania Spina, who supervised my PhD work and encouraged me to publish an extended version of it. I am grateful to Stefania also for kindly accepting to write the Foreword to the book. Many thanks to my PhD thesis reviewers, Fanny Meunier and Dana Gablasova, and examiners, Silvia Bernardini, Alex Boulton and Henry Tyne, all of whom invited me to consider publishing my work. I would like to express my deepest gratitude to Anne O'Keeffe and Mike McCarthy, series editors for this monograph, who provided me with incessant encouragement and guidance throughout the various stages of writing. A special thank you goes to Paola Giunchi, the first professor to witness my interest in corpora and language pedagogy when I was a BA student at Sapienza University of Rome, and who has ceaselessly supported me throughout the years. Attending conferences such as EuroCALL, TaLC and LCR had a huge impact on my work because of the wonderful colleagues and mentors I had the honour of meeting there. I thank them all. I am also indebted to the community of scholars working at UCLouvain and Lancaster University, where I had the privilege of spending two enriching research stays. Finally, I would like to thank all the friends, colleagues and family members who infused me with their enthusiasm about this book project, making the journey all the more meaningful.

Luciana Forti

1 Introduction

This chapter gives an overview of the main gaps this book seeks to fill. It first sets the scene by identifying the domain of data-driven learning, within the broader area of corpus use in second/foreign language pedagogy. Then, it zooms in on the need for and the challenge of conducting sound empirical DDL research, as a way to increase our awareness of its effects, while providing more resources to foster its normalisation within learning and teaching contexts. Some of the additional challenges that characterise DDL research in the field of Italian L2 are also introduced.

1.1 Corpora, second language pedagogy and data-driven learning (DDL)

When engaging in learning a second or foreign language, both teachers and learners long for relevant, authentic, and motivating linguistic input. Corpora, large machine-readable collections of (sampled to be) authentically produced language (McEnery et al., 2006, p. 5), are able to provide such input. While being designed to describe actual language usage in the most accurate way possible, corpora are nevertheless a sample related to a population, in other words a subset of a larger set of data (a more in-depth illustration of these notions may be found in Chapter 4). Sampling criteria reflect the motivation for building a specific corpus in the first place. For instance, they can be built to reflect varieties of text types (e.g., everyday language, newspaper articles, academic texts in general, academic texts from a specific field, etc.), varieties of speaker categories (e.g., L1 speakers, L2 speakers) and/or a specific communicative channel (i.e. written, spoke, mediated) (Tono, 2003). These variables can be variously intersected to reflect the needs of a language teaching and learning context, ranging in specificity from the highly specific to the highly generic.

Corpora also provide invaluable information that can help inform the definition of syllabus and curriculum design, pedagogical lexicography, language testing and coursebook development (Curry et al., 2021; Gablasova, 2021; Paquot, 2012; McCarten, 2010). Mirroring actual language use, whether by first or second language speakers, corpus tools can let teachers

DOI: 10.4324/9781003137320-1

see which structures are most frequently used by first language speakers in certain contexts, and also help them navigate through learners' most recurring errors. Corpus data can also inform the development of coursebooks and be an important aid in pedagogical lexicography. Language testing can also greatly benefit from corpora, not only because they can be used as vast repositories of authentic examples, but also because corpora can lead to the development of new testing formats involving various types of corpus data, including but not limited to concordance lines.

A number of ways in which second language pedagogy can benefit from corpora are summarised in Figure 1.1. Here we see a broad distinction between direct and indirect uses. In direct uses, corpus data are explicitly and immediately visible to the learners, who can access them either via a computer or through printouts. In both of these cases, corpus data may come in the form of concordance lines or other types of data (e.g., word sketches, frequency lists, etc.). Direct uses of corpus data are generally associated with the expression *data-driven learning*. In indirect use, corpus data is not explicitly and immediately visible to the learners. It may be used in syllabi and curriculum development, pedagogical lexicography, language testing and coursebooks, even in connection with specific findings deriving from corpus linguistics (CL) or learner corpus research (LCR).

Figure 1.1 does not aim to be exhaustive of the different ways in which the pedagogical uses of corpora can be conceptualised, nor does it seek to define strict boundaries between the various categories (e.g., the visibility of the data is possible also in an indirect approach), but merely attempts to systematise some of the most recurring conceptualisations found in the literature, that relate to the pedagogical uses of corpus data. The direct vs. indirect dichotomy was first introduced by Geoffrey Leech, who based this distinction on whether the corpus data are or are not visible to learners (Leech, 1997, p. 5). However, using corpus data indirectly does not always lead to making corpus data invisible to the learners. If faced with a language test, based on a multiple-choice format which is informed by learner corpus data (i.e. choosing among the options provided), the learner will see the data deriving from the corpus, but will not be aware of the fact that it comes from a corpus. This aspect will, in fact, not be explicit as it would be in the case of, say, a hands-on concordance-based activity. For this reason, in Figure 1.1, we associate the notion of 'visibility of the data', with that of 'explicitness' of such visibility.

This direct vs. indirect dichotomy is reaffirmed by Römer (2008, p. 113), who clarifies the association between direct pedagogical uses of corpus data and the notion of data-driven learning, just as Tim Johns envisioned when advocating an interaction between corpus data and the learner that would be as direct as possible, 'cutting out the middleman as far as possible' (Johns, 1991, p. 30). These notions of direct and indirect uses of corpus data are also adopted in Granger (2009) and Meunier (2010) when discussing how learner corpus research can be used in SLA and teaching practices.

Introduction 3

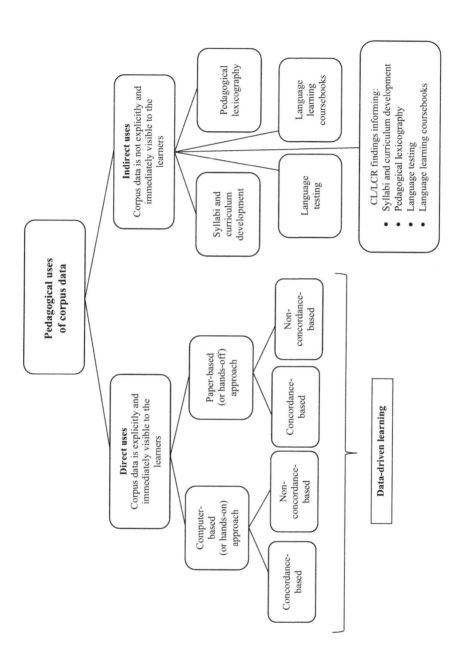

Figure 1.1 Pedagogical uses of corpus data.

Granger, in particular, extends these notions by adding the variable of immediacy: Granger, in fact, identifies an immediate and a delayed pedagogical use of learner corpus data in language learning and teaching. The former relates to direct uses, the latter to indirect uses. The immediate or delayed uses of corpus data identified by Granger in relation to LCR can easily be extended to the definition of corpus use in the general domain of second language pedagogy.

Over the years, the terminology describing DDL has been characterised by a certain degree of variation. This is especially true with regard to the terms 'direct' and 'indirect'. While originally referring to the different ways in which corpus data can be used in second language pedagogy as a whole, including but not limited to DDL, this meaning of the dichotomy has gradually been applied to DDL only. The term 'direct' has been associated with the meaning of 'computer-based' or 'hard version' of DDL, while the term 'indirect' has been associated with the meaning of 'paper-based' or 'soft version' of DDL (Boulton, 2017; Gabrielatos, 2005; Yoon & Hirvela, 2004). The idea behind this terminological shift seems to be that the terms 'direct' and 'indirect' are perceived as more suitable to describe the degrees of explicitness in DDL instruction (Yoon & Hirvela, 2004, p. 260; Yoon & Jo, 2014, p. 97). A frequently referred to definition of DDL is the one proposed by Gilquin and Granger (2010, p. 359), who describe it as the use of 'the tools and techniques of corpus linguistics for pedagogical purposes'. This definition has the advantage of being broad enough to cover all the more specific definitions and classifications that have been applied to DDL over the years. Nevertheless, clearly defining what we mean by DDL is instrumental in conducting rigorous empirical research, as we will start to see in the next section.

1.2 The need for and the challenge of conducting rigorous empirical DDL research

How can language learning benefit from DDL? Can corpora really reach 'the parts that other teaching can't reach' (Boulton, 2008)? The steadily growing number of studies on DDL effects has provided the basis for several meta-analyses and research syntheses. The aim of these reviews has been to provide an aggregated understanding of DDL effects, from the perspective of learning gains and teacher/learner attitudes. The year 2015, in particular, marked the publication of the first two meta-analyses, focused on the quantitative analysis of DDL language gains: Cobb & Boulton (2015) and Mizumoto & Chujo (2015). In 2017, Boulton and Cobb (2017) published a highly comprehensive meta-analysis, comprising 25 categories of moderator variables. These were then incorporated in Lee et al. (2018), with a specific focus on vocabulary learning. In terms of learner attitudes Chambers (2007) analyses 12 studies seeking to synthesise positive and less positive reactions to DDL. Research syntheses on DDL have also taken the form of historical overviews, such as Boulton (2017). Additional research syntheses have been published, providing a coding analysis and a historical overview, based on 30 years of DDL (Boulton, 2021; Boulton & Vyatkina, 2021).

Apart from their aggregated findings on DDL effectiveness, what these syntheses point at are the areas in need as far as our knowledge base of DDL goes. First and foremost, almost all the studies included in the cited syntheses are based on studies reporting on DDL for learners of English. This is due partly to the still very few studies on languages other than English, and to the tendency to consider only the DDL literature published in English. Furthermore, while stressing the increased effectiveness of DDL when the learners are exposed to the approach on an on-going basis, studies collecting data on language learning outcomes cover a limited time span, with no more than three data collection points, including delayed tests. In addition to this, the links between DDL research and SLA are still under-developed (O'Keeffe, 2020), and very little guidance on how to conduct sound DDL research is available.

And yet, expanding the scope of DDL research, as well as taking it to the next level both theoretically and methodologically is core to its normalisation within teaching and learning practices. We need to know about the longer-term benefits of DDL, about what makes DDL more difficult to be adapted to certain learning contexts and how these difficulties may be overcome. We need to know which parts of teaching DDL is able to reach in more effective ways compared to other teaching approaches. Why should teachers and learners try out DDL? What is so special about it? At a time when DDL is still far from being normalised in teaching and learning contexts (Pérez-Paredes, 2019), and numerous attempts to make DDL viable to teachers and learners are being made (e.g., Friginal, 2018; Poole, 2018; Vyatkina, 2020), research on DDL needs to not only be rigorous but also relevant to teachers' needs. It also needs to align with second language theories, incorporating them into the definition of the variables, and not simply as rationales for supporting investigation into the approach (Flowerdew, 2015; O'Keeffe, 2020).

We can expand our knowledge of DDL effects through the collection, analysis and interpretation of empirical data. The reliability of these phases is proportionate to the level of rigour that is applied. Researching DDL effects rigorously is a highly challenging endeavour, because it requires multidisciplinary expertise. First, we need to be able to design a pedagogical experiment in a way that it will reliably measure what we are interested in. Then, we need to develop our data collection instrument(s), which may be a language test, which will be able to measure language gains with respect to DDL effects. Next, we may wish to include a tool such as a questionnaire, which will be able to elicit learner attitudes with respect to the DDL approach. We also need the pedagogical expertise to design our DDL materials in a way that works in order to measure the variable(s) that we are interested in. Finally, we need the statistical skills to analyse the different kinds of data that we collected. Taken together, we need expertise from (a) social sciences; (b) language testing; (c) questionnaire design; (d) second language pedagogy; and (e) statistics. All these methods converge in the analysis of DDL effects.

An additional challenge consists in the seeming lack of methodological guidelines as to how DDL research should be conducted. What mostly needs to be known can be certainly found in a social sciences methodology book: formulating hypotheses, defining a research design, collecting and analysing the data, interpreting the findings and then reporting them. However, research methodology issues seem to have received limited attention with reference to DDL research. Further challenges include the still limited availability of learner-friendly corpora, especially when languages other than English are concerned. Options are, of course, available in terms of DIY corpora and creation of paper-based materials, and these options can very well counterbalance the lack of corpora built with second language learners in mind, especially in languages other than English. These processes of operationalising DDL for a particular teaching and learning context, while dealing with particular restrictions and limitations, are seldom treated and recognised in a comprehensive way, especially when dealing with languages other than English. This book seeks to bring depth of focus to methodological considerations in the context of using DDL in learning Italian.

1.3 Researching DDL for learning Italian

The first article on how corpora can be used to learn Italian was published in ReCALL in 1993 and authored by Loredana Polezzi (Polezzi, 1993). She showed how DDL principles were implemented into the highly specialised academic context she was working in: Italian language courses tailored for graduate students specialising in Italian renaissance theatre. The language presented needed to be relevant to the learners' needs, and so Polezzi created a corpus from the transcription of her own lectures on Italian renaissance theatre. As we will argue in Chapter 2, this work is still very much worthy of consideration today, well beyond the domain of DDL for Italian language learning purposes. Since then, several articles on how DDL can be integrated in learning and teaching contexts focusing on Italian have been published. This indicates a lineage of DDL for Italian going back over the last 30 years, just like DDL for English. However, the studies on DDL for Italian covering this timeframe are quite sparse, and despite some notable exceptions (Kennedy & Miceli, 2001, 2010, 2016) most are descriptive/theoretical papers advocating the use of corpora in Italian learning and teaching contexts, with no empirical grounding.

The under-representation of Italian in the field of empirical DDL research could alone justify the need to increase the number of studies of this kind. But the need for more research dealing with how DDL can be beneficial in teaching and learning Italian is also motivated by the fact that learner-friendly tools are becoming increasingly more available even for Italian (e.g.,

SkELL). These tools are still to be extensively explored and evaluated with reference to the Italian language. Furthermore, the increased publication of books and online materials explaining how DDL can be incorporated in learning and teaching practices for any language creates a favourable environment for an osmosis into languages other than English. More empirical research on DDL for Italian is also needed as it may foster more publications on DDL for Italian, written in Italian and thus for an audience of teachers working with and in Italian. Finally, the intersection between corpora and language learning, in the domain of Italian language learning studies, has mostly been explored at the academic level, whether in terms of learner corpus research or teacher training sessions. More research on DDL for Italian is needed not only to contribute to the broader field of DDL, and to better understanding how it can be beneficial and which variables influence its effectiveness, but also to make it viable to teachers, while seeking to meet their needs (Forti & Spina, 2019).

The challenges involved in empirically researching DDL effects in general, namely the interdisciplinary nature of the endeavour, the limited availability of materials and guidelines to inform the pedagogical operationalisation of DDL in a way that is suitable for empirical research, and the need to bridge the gap between corpora for linguists and corpora for learners, apply naturally to DDL for Italian also. However, we may identify at the least three challenges in addition to these that feel quite specific of the Italian domain, while possibly being relevant for languages other than English also.

To begin with, it is safe to say that teacher scepticism is one of the main challenges that DDL research focusing on Italian faces. Although this may be considered as a characteristic that is typical of DDL research as a whole, this element seems even more critical in Italian language teaching contexts. The very limited amount of literature on DDL for Italian is an issue, because most of the arguments a researcher will put forward in advocating the use of DDL in Italian teaching contexts will refer to research and experiences dealing with the teaching of English. As a result, this is very unlikely to succeed in persuading teachers about the potentially beneficial effects of DDL in an Italian context. This is a bit of a vicious circle: we need empirical research on DDL for Italian to convince teachers of its benefits, but in order to conduct intervention-based DDL research we need to have convinced teachers of its benefits, so that the intervention can be carried out with their collaboration and in their classrooms.

If we are considering DDL research based on pedagogical interventions, in fact, we need, as researchers, to have access to a teaching context. In the cases where we are not at once researchers as well as teachers, we need a fertile terrain upon which a fruitful collaboration can be built. The only way to do this and help make progress in the field is to identify and face the limitations of the approach together with those who we hope will take on the challenge constructively and collaboratively. Another challenge, somewhat linked to the first one, is the total absence of pedagogical materials and guidelines about corpora for Italian language learning purposes, that are written in Italian. While English is our current international lingua franca, not all language teachers of Italian feel comfortable with the idea of training themselves on materials written in English. The lack of corpus-informed teacher training also has a role in this, as in the case of DDL for English.

Despite the additional challenges posed by conducting DDL research with reference to an Italian language learning context, we are confident in saying that research from this perspective is not only highly desirable but also entirely possible. As will be shown in the next section, this book will take the reader through all the main steps involved in designing and conducting an empirical DDL research study focused on Italian.

1.4 This book

This book demonstrates how DDL research can be conducted within a given theoretical and methodological framework. It does so by focusing specifically on an under-represented language in the field, namely Italian, and by showing the benefits of mixed-methods approaches. In particular, Chapter 2 illustrates the theories pertaining to our view of language, of learning and of language learning that underpin DDL. It also outlines how DDL has evolved over time, both in academic and non-academic settings, and illustrates the criticism and rebuttals that have surrounded its development. Finally, it illustrates how DDL has manifested itself in Italian L2 teaching and learning context. In Chapter 3, we delve into the research evidence supporting the benefits of DDL. We know that the approach is theoretically supported in a number of ways, but does it actually work? Is it actually able to make a difference for language learners? If so, for which learners/languages skills/ language areas is it more beneficial, and why? How have learners and teachers reacted to the approach? Do they like it? What works and what is still an issue and a challenge in empirical DDL research? Chapter 4 identifies the methodological challenges involved in conducting DDL research. It is the chapter where the interdisciplinarity of the endeavour manifests itself to the fullest. How should the design of the experiment be developed? How can DDL be pedagogically operationalised in a way that is at once feasible for the researcher, useful for learners and valid to measure the intended variables? How can data be collected and analysed? These are some of the questions that Chapter 4 addresses, while emphasising throughout the need for and importance of relating each step of the methodological process to the broader SLA and social sciences domains.

The context of Italian L2 teaching and learning is described in Chapter 5. The main themes characterising Italian L2 studies are illustrated, both with and without reference to corpus-based analyses. The relationship between current pedagogical practices and second language learning practices is discussed, as well as the affordances of currently available corpora of Italian in enriching the pedagogical landscape of resources for teaching and learning the language. Chapter 6 illustrates the method adopted in designing a study aimed at investigating the effects of DDL on the development of phraseological competence in a group of Chinese learners of Italian. It identifies and motivates the choice of the learning aim (i.e. verb + noun combinations), it describes the steps taken in identifying the participant sample, it explains how the DDL construct was operationalised pedagogically so as to fit the study design, it illustrates the phases involved in creating the pedagogical materials, and it outlines the procedures that were followed in devising the data collection tools. In Chapter 7, the results of the study pertaining to DDL effects on language gains are presented and discussed. Linguistic properties of the learning aims are taken into account, with specific reference to semantic transparency, L1-L2 congruency and dimensions of phraseological knowledge. Chapter 8 presents and discusses the results of the study pertaining to the effects of DDL on learner attitudes. Several different aspects are explored, including the novelty of working with concordances, the novelty of working with word combinations and the perceived usefulness of the approach in relation to the development of language awareness. Chapter 9 concludes the book by summarising the findings of the empirical study, and then emphasising the importance of connecting DDL research with SLA evidence and broader SLA themes and theories. It also points out the need to reflect on the research methods adopted so far in DDL research, in view of how these can be expanded in scope and deepened in sophistication in the future.

References

Boulton, A. (2008). DDL: Reaching the parts other teaching can't reach? In A. Frankenberg-Garcia (Ed.), *Proceedings of the 8th Teaching and Language Corpora Conference* (pp. 38–44). Associação de Estudos e de Investigação Científica do ISLA-Lisboa.

Boulton, A. (2017). Research timeline. Corpora in language teaching and learning. *Language Teaching*, 50(4), 483–506.

Boulton, A. (2021). Research in data-driven learning. In P. Pérez-Paredes & G. Mark (Eds.), *Beyond the concordance: Corpora in language education* (pp. 9–34). Benjamins.

Boulton, A., & Cobb, T. (2017). Corpus use in language learning: A meta-analysis. *Language Learning*, 67(2), 348–393.

Boulton, A., & Vyatkina, N. (2021). Thirty years of data-driven learning: Taking stock and charting new directions. *Language Learning and Technology*, 25(3), 66–89.

Chambers, A. (2007). Popularising corpus consultation by language learners and teachers. *Language and Computers*, 61(1), 3–16.

Cobb, T., & Boulton, A. (2015). Classroom applications of corpus analysis. In D. Biber & R. Reppen (Eds.), *The Cambridge handbook of English corpus linguistics* (pp. 478–497). Cambridge University Press.

Flowerdew, L. (2015). Data-driven learning and language learning theories: Whither the twain will meet. In A. Leńko-Szymańska & A. Boulton (Eds.). *Multiple affordances of language corpora for data-driven learning* (pp. 15–36). Benjamins.

Forti, L., & Spina, S. (2019). Corpora for linguists vs. corpora for learners: Bridging the gap in Italian L2 learning and teaching. *EL.LE – Educazione Linguistica. Language Education, 8*(2), 349–362.

Friginal, E. (2018). *Corpus linguistics for English teachers: Tools, online resources, and classroom activities.* Routledge.

Gablasova, D. (2021). Corpora for second language assessments. In P. Winke & T. Brunfaut (Eds.), *The Routledge handbook of second language acquisition and language testing* (pp. 45–53). Routledge.

Gabrielatos, C. (2005). Corpora and language teaching: Just a fling or wedding bells? *The Electronic Journal for English as a Second Language, 8*(4), 1–32.

Gilquin, G., & Granger, S. (2010). How can data-driven learning be used in language teaching? In A. O'Keeffe & M. McCarthy (Eds.), *The Routledge handbook of corpus linguistics* (1st ed.) (pp. 350–370). Routledge.

Granger, S. (2009). The contribution of learner corpora to second language acquisition and foreign language teaching: A critical evaluation. In K. Aijmer (Ed.), *Corpora and language teaching* (pp. 13–33). Benjamins.

Johns, T. (1991). Should you be persuaded – Two examples of data driven learning materials. *Classroom Concordancing, English Language Research Journal 4*, 1–16.

Kennedy, C., & Miceli, T. (2001). An evaluation of intermediate students' approaches to corpus investigation. *Language Learning & Technology, 5*(3), 77–90.

Kennedy, C., & Miceli, T. (2010). Corpus-assisted creative writing: Introducing intermediate Italian learners to a corpus as a reference resource. *Language Learning & Technology, 14*(1), 28–44.

Kennedy, C., & Miceli, T. (2016). Cultivating effective corpus use by language learners. *Computer Assisted Language Learning, 30*(1–2), 91–114.

Lee, H., Warschauer, M., & Lee, J. H. (2018). The effects of corpus use on second language vocabulary learning: A multilevel meta-analysis. *Applied Linguistics, 40*(5), 721–753.

Leech, G. (1997). Teaching and language corpora: A convergence. In A. Wichmann, S. Fligelstone, T. McEnery, & G. Knowles (Eds.), *Teaching and Language Corpora* (pp. 1–24). Addison Wesley Longman.

McCarten, J. (2010). Corpus-informed course book design. In A. O'Keeffe & M. McCarthy (Eds.), *The Routledge handbook of corpus linguistics* (pp. 413–427). Routledge.

McEnery, A., Xiao, R., & Tono, Y. (2006). *Corpus-based language studies: An advanced resource book.* Routledge.

Meunier, F. (2010). Learner corpora and english language teaching: Checkup time. *Anglistik: International Journal of English Studies, 21*(1), 209–220.

Mizumoto, A., & Chujo, K. (2015). A meta-analysis of data-driven learning approach in the Japanese EFL classroom. *English Corpus Studies, 22*, 1–18.

O'Keeffe, A. (2020). Data-driven learning – a call for a broader research gaze. *Language Teaching, 54*(2), 259–272.

Paquot, M. (2012). The LEAD dictionary-cum-writing aid: An integrated dictionary and corpus tool. In S. Granger & M. Paquot (Eds.), *Electronic Lexicography* (pp. 163–186). Oxford University Press.

Pérez-Paredes, P. (2019). A systematic review of the uses and spread of corpora and data-driven learning in CALL research during 2011–2015. *Computer Assisted Language Learning*, 35(1–2), 36–61.

Polezzi, L. (1993). Concordancing and the teaching of ab initio Italian language for specific purposes. *ReCALL*, 5(09), 14–18.

Poole, R. (2018). *A guide to using corpora for English language learners*. Edinburgh University Press.

Römer, U. (2008). Corpora and language teaching. In A. Lüdeling & M. Kytö (Eds.), *Corpus linguistics. An international handbook* (pp. 112–131). De Gruyter.

Tono, Y. (2003). Learner corpora: Design, development and applications. In D. Archer, P. Rayson, A. Wilson, & T. McEnery, T. (Eds.), Proceedings of the Corpus Linguistics 2003 Conference. UCREL technical paper number 16 (pp. 800–8009). UCREL, Lancaster University.

Vyatkina, N. (2020). Corpora as open educational resources for language teaching. *Foreign Language Annals*, 52(2), 359–370.

Yoon, H., & Hirvela, A. (2004). ESL student attitudes toward corpus use in L2 writing. *Journal of Second Language Writing*, 13(4), 257–283.

Yoon, H., & Jo, J.W. (2014). Direct and indirect access to corpora: An exploratory case study comparing students' error correction and learning strategy use in L2 writing. *Language Learning & Technology*, 18(1), 96–117.

2 Data-driven learning
Origins, theoretical underpinnings, and development through time

This chapter describes how DDL originated and how it developed thanks to the systematic work conducted by Tim Johns at the University of Birmingham. It then illustrates how the approach is underpinned by a large number of converging theories regarding language and language learning. In detailing the main principles characterising DDL, the chapter provides insight into how language and language learning theories inform the pedagogical practices that are associated with it. An account of its evolution through time is provided by drawing on existing historical syntheses, while also tracing the history of how the approach has been explored in the context of Italian L2 learning and teaching. A specific section is devoted to the arguments against DDL that have received attention over the years. Each of these is addressed with a series of counterarguments, in light of both theoretical and methodological considerations, and also in relation to the most recent advancements in the field.

2.1 Origins of DDL

The origins of DDL can be traced in the relationship between language description and second language pedagogy. Even before the appearance of computer corpora, the compilation of frequency lists of language use was motivated also by pedagogical needs. One of the earliest examples is Edward L. Thorndike's *Teacher's Word Book*, published in 1921, later extended in 1931 and then finally in 1944 with the contribution of Irving Lorge (Thorndike, 1921). This work consists of an alphabetical list of words, followed by quantitative information about their range and their frequency of occurrence. Specific guidance is provided to teachers as to how the book can be used to satisfy specific teaching needs quickly and reliably. In its very first edition, we read:

> This Word Book helps the teacher to decide quickly which treatment is appropriate by telling her just how important any word is. In teaching history or geography or elementary science, almost any book lesson contains one or more words with which some of the pupils will not be

DOI: 10.4324/9781003137320-2

familiar. Which are these, and in which cases should the occasion be used to master the word for future use? Decision obviously depends upon how important the word is. In many cases knowledge of how important the word is, is all that is needed for decision.

(Thorndike, 1921, p. iv)

One interesting aspect in Thorndike's take on the pedagogical value of corpora is that frequency lists such as the one he devised and regularly updated could (and can) be useful not only for second language learning purposes, but also for learning discipline-specific lexis, even in one's first language.

The need for objective language usage data, as a foundation to make pedagogical decisions, is reiterated with the advent of computer corpora. In 1960, Randolph Quirk published a paper entitled *Towards a Description of English Usage*. This paper opens by motivating the need for a better description of actual language use through pedagogical arguments:

It may seem strange to hear of plans for a survey of English usage when one reflects for how long and by how many and with what degree of attention the English language has been studied. The position is, however, that the masses of materials compiled over the years prove quite inadequate to serve as the basis of even elementary teaching-grammars, a fact which has emerged rather suddenly and with particular starkness in recent years, when increasing attempts have been made to improve and extend the teaching of English as a foreign language.

(Quirk, 1960, p. 40)

In striving for ever-more efficient and effective language learning materials, the value of corpora shines through the decades and through the evolution of corpus compilation techniques and corpus linguistics itself. In sharp contrast with rationalist approaches, it adopts an empirical approach to the study of language: real instances of language use are opposed to invented ones, or ones based on subjective impressions related to what is more salient in language and thus worthy of being taught.

The way in which this value of corpora in language pedagogy is first conceived, however, seems to be limited to the indirect uses of corpora, where a more accurate description of actual language usage is used to inform syllabus and curriculum design, dictionaries and manuals, learning activities and language testing (cfr. Figure 1.1). In line with the development of increasingly more learner-centred approaches to language learning, the idea that this more thorough description of language could inform learning practices more directly started to gain terrain. In particular, learners themselves would be put in direct contact with corpus data, in order to explore specific features of language deemed problematic. This is what Sandra McKay reported on in her 1980 article, published in *TESOL Quarterly*, entitled 'Teaching the Syntactic, Semantic and Pragmatic Dimensions of

Verbs' (McKay, 1980). This article is considered the first published article to illustrate a direct approach in using corpora for pedagogical purposes (Boulton, 2017).

She considers the cases of near synonyms *announce* and *declare*. A set of sentences are extracted from the *Stanford Computer Archive of Language Materials*, containing the *Brown University Corpus of Present-Day Edited American English*, and printed on paper. On the basis of these sentences, McKay formulates guiding questions aimed at facilitating the discovery of syntactic, semantic and pragmatic features of the two verbs, shedding light on the differences that set them apart (McKay, 1980, pp. 19–20): '1. List the nouns that follow *announce* and try to characterise the kinds of things that are typically announced. Are they emotions? Programs? Events? Ideas? Human beings? etc. 2. What kinds of nouns are used as the subject of the verb *announce*? 3. What tense is the verb in sentences two and three? Why do you think this tense is used?'. Similar questions are then asked for *declare*. Other examples are provided for the verbs *express* and *expose*. These guided-discovery activities are geared towards allowing the learner to form generalisations on how the verbs are used, based on their occurrence in context. After illustrating the guided-discovery phase, McKay shows examples of traditional controlled practice activities, based on different versions of gap-fill tasks (McKay, 1980, pp. 24–25). Nowhere in the paper, however, is the approach used to put learners in direct contact with corpus data named 'data-driven learning'. This is because the expression derives from the work of Tim Johns.

Tim Johns taught English for Academic Purposes at the English for Overseas Students Unit (EOSU) of the University of Birmingham for 30 years, from 1971 to 2001.[1] In the shared memory of those who knew him and worked with him, he embodied a rare figure at the intersection between the technical developments of corpus linguistics and the pedagogical applications based on such developments. He had close links with Randolph Quirk and John Sinclair, both involved in large projects aimed at describing the English language more thoroughly through corpora, with language learners always in mind. Johns' students would be typically overseas students who needed the necessary English language skills to pursue academic study in the UK. This often meant that they also needed domain-specific English language skills. Johns' day-to-day experience is what forged the first systematic conceptualisations of corpus use in the classroom. In the space of a few years, he published four seminal articles reporting on corpus-based pedagogical practices that he experimented with in the classroom. They are entitled *Micro-concord: A Language Learner's Research Tool* (Johns, 1986), *Whence and whither classroom concordancing?* (Johns, 1988), *From printout to handout: Grammar and vocabulary teaching in the context of Data-driven Learning* (Johns, 1990) and *Should you be persuaded – Two examples of data driven learning materials* (Johns, 1991). He starts off by speaking of a concordance-based methodology (Johns, 1986, p. 158) and ends up by explicitly terming the approach 'data-driven learning' (Johns, 1991). As we shall see in the following sections, the expression 'data-driven learning' goes beyond the identification of an approach based merely on the use of corpus data in the classroom, but rather links such use to precise pedagogical principles, underpinned by specific theories on language and language learning.

2.2 DDL pedagogy

The way in which direct corpus use by language learners was pedagogically operationalised, leading to the development of DDL, introduced a novel combination of *which* language should be presented to learners, and *how* they would be asked to interact with it. This relates to what corpora can offer in relation to linguistic data handling and in terms of learner vs. teacher roles within the pedagogical process. Literally, DDL can be described as 'learning driven by data'. The term *data* refers traditionally to the linguistic information we may find in a corpus. Because the language data needs to be machine-readable, the more powerful the machine is, the larger the collection of data can be. Throughout the decades, this is what has allowed corpus linguists to build increasingly larger corpora, eventually aiming to be representative of a wide range of textual genres and domains. As a result, the first core pedagogical principle of DDL is that language input should be authentic, so as to reflect, though through some degree of approximation, language as used in real-life contexts by real-life proficient speakers. This stance is shared with other pedagogical practices even today, which however ignore DDL. The difference is that DDL not only advocates the use of authentic input but has the opportunity of providing quantitatively and qualitatively significant amounts of input through corpora.

The second core principle characterising DDL lies in how learners are asked to interact with the corpus data. In terms of data presentation, corpora offer valuable tools for input enhancement. With corpora it is possible to extract numerous instances of a word or combination of words, and to visualise the node in a particular way so as to make it more visually salient. Extracting instances from corpora can make input 'condensed' (Gabrielatos, 2005). This is useful in detecting regularities in how the word or combination of words is used in context. These regularities can refer to part-of-speech sequences, meaning differences and lexical co-occurrences. The observation of such regularities, on either side of a node, leads to inferences regarding how the word or word combination works in a given language. And in order to be able to observe regularities, it is necessary to have a set of examples that is numerous enough. For example, the Italian version of SkELL shows 40 examples that are deemed appropriate for a broadly defined intermediate level of language learners. In Figure 2.1 we show the output for the Italian word *viso* ('face'), limited to the first 20 examples. These examples are numerous enough to allow the identification, for instance, of

16 Data-driven learning

Figure 2.1 SkELL: concordance of *viso*.

which co-occurring verbs (*e.g., viso + appare,* 'face' + 'appears') or adjectives (e.g., *viso + luminoso,* 'face' + 'luminous') characterise the word. It even allows the discovery of idiomatic expressions, such *fare buon viso a cattiva sorte* ('to pretend that everything is fine in order to make the best of a difficult situation'). Concordance lines are typically represented in a KWIC (i.e. 'Key Word In Context') format. This format can take the form of either an enbolded and centred node, or as a coloured, non-centred node, as in the case of SkELL. This facilitates observation of semantic and formal regularities on either side of the node. Another way in which input may be enhanced by corpora is visualised in Figure 2.2. Here, the numerosity of examples is not visible in terms of recurring sentences but shielded behind systematised frequency lists. A word sketch such as the one provided in SkELL is able to show learners how a word is used in a variety of syntactic environments.

As for the roles that learners and teachers have in DDL, these reflect in most cases the tenets of learner-centred inductive, bottom-up language learning. Johns himself conceived the learner as a 'detective', famously stating that 'every student is a Sherlock Holmes' (Johns, 1997). The learner would have to sift through the richness of the concordance data to solve a linguistic problem, a usage doubt. In this process, the middleperson would have to be cut out as far as possible (Johns, 1991), so as to put the learners at the centre of their learning process. This way, it is the learner who makes hypotheses about how language works and would go on to experiment with the hypotheses in real-life communication. Only then would they see whether the inference is correct. In the original DDL vision, the learner's journey is

Figure 2.2 SkELL: word sketch of *viso*.

not so different from that of a 'researcher-scientist' (Cobb, 1999): he or she observes, analyses, makes inferences, and then sees whether the inference works. This can also lead to serendipitous findings, and make the learner feel like a 'traveler' (Bernardini, 2000).

The teacher is far from being the ultimate dispenser of absolute knowledge regarding how language works and how it is used. The teacher can either collaborate in the corpus-driven discovery process (Boulton, 2011), guide the learner towards the discovery of regularities which can then provide the basis for inferences (Charles, 2014), or can demonstrate how the process of navigating through the corpus data can be conducted (Frankenberg-Garcia, 2012). In more recent times, however, the consideration that not all languages have corpora that can be easily explored by teachers and learners has pointed at the value of scaffolding, especially for lower-proficiency learners (Meunier, 2020; Corino & Onesti, 2020). Works such as *Reading concordances* (Sinclair, 2003) show quite effectively how a set of guiding questions can be sequenced so as to show the potentially intricate patterning of words in context.

2.3 Theories underpinning DDL pedagogy

The way in which DDL pedagogy developed is deeply intertwined with the conceptualisations of language and language learning which have emerged throughout the decades. Being able to observe multiple instances of language in a systematic manner provided language theories with unprecedented empirical foundation, deepening the divide with rationalist approaches to language analysis based on intuition. The different ways in which the functioning of language has been theorised within the paradigm of empirical linguistics are arguably convergent and variously inform and justify the principles of DDL pedagogy. This is because DDL lends itself to discovering how language works through the lens of those different theories. At the same time, DDL pedagogy incorporates a number of language learning theories that are applied in their own right in pedagogical approaches that do not necessarily coincide with DDL. This makes the theoretical foundation of DDL particularly rich. What the learner and teacher do in typical DDL activities is sustained by the numerous language and language learning theories, as we shall describe in the following two sections.

2.3.1 Theories of language

How are forms, meanings and functions represented in language? From the early 1930s, John Rupert Firth published a number of papers leading towards the formulation of the *contextual theory of meaning* (Firth, 1957, 1962). In order to analyse meaning in language, the context of occurrence of a particular word would need to have a primary role. By observing multiple instances of language, Firth would come to the idea that 'you shall know a word by the company it keeps', hence the view of language as highly patterned and characterised by context-dependent distributional features. Firth's work was highly influential on the work conducted later by John Sinclair (Sinclair, 1991). In the position statement of his *Corpus, Concordance, Collocation*, Sinclair both synthesises and provides a new beginning, to use Ronald Carter's words in the foreword of the volume (Sinclair, 1991, p. xviii), in relation to how language can be conceived in light of the evidence that corpus-based investigation is able to provide us with. He further distinguishes between the highly specific knowledge about language that can derive from intuition, and the broader knowledge about the facts of language deriving from the observation of the multiple ways in which they can occur in context. The authenticity of language as reflected in a corpus could very well be problematic in terms of their interpretation, being 'bizarre and unrepresentative', but this would be no reason for deeming invented examples better for representing language as it actually works (Sinclair, 1991, p. 5). In other words, 'the comprehensive study of language must be based on textual evidence. One does not study all of botany by making artificial flowers' (Sinclair, 1991, p. 6).

Granted that meaning can only derive from text, Sinclair introduces two principles on the basis of which language usage can be interpreted: the open-choice principle and the idiom principle. The former refers to the fact that when producing an utterance, 'words are treated as independent items of meaning. Each of them represents a separate choice' (Sinclair, 1991, p. 175). As a result, 'a large range of choice opens up and the only restraint is grammaticalness' (Sinclair, 1991, p. 109). The latter refers to the cases in which this open-choice is restrained by the tendency of a certain word to co-occur with other words, as 'a language user has available to him or her a large number of semi-preconstructed phrases that constitute single choices, even though they might appear to be analysable into segments' (Sinclair, 1991, p. 110).

Firth's work was also highly influential in relation to the studies conducted by M.A.K. Halliday, who introduced the notion of *lexicogrammar*. According to this notion, grammar and lexis should not be viewed as two separate subsystems of language. Halliday, in fact, claimed that

> There is in every language a level of organization – a single level – which is referred to in everyday speech as the 'the wording'; technically it is lexicogrammar, the combination of grammar and lexis [...]. The point is that grammar and vocabulary are not two different things; they are the same thing seen by different observers.
>
> (Halliday, 1992, p. 63)

In the contributions published in the volume dedicated to the memory of J.R. Firth (Bazell et al., 1966), both Halliday and Sinclair advocate a statistical/probabilistic approach to language description. Halliday highlighted the usefulness of a 'table of the most frequent collocates of specific items, with information about their probabilities, unconditioned and lexically and grammatically conditioned' (Halliday, 1966, p. 160). This stance was echoed by Sinclair, who commented on the fact that 'a very large computer will be strained to the utmost to cope with the data' (Sinclair, 1966, p. 428).

As part of the COBUILD (*Collins Birmingham University International Language Database*) project directed by Sinclair, Susan Hunston and Gill Francis' volume on *Pattern Grammar* emerged (Hunston & Francis, 2000). In this volume, 'the company kept by words' was specified through the identification of part-of-speech sequences which the English language would be found to be filled with. In this sense, the authors spoke of a 'lexical grammar' of the English language, favouring a view of linearity rather than one based on syntactic dependencies. They identify verb, noun and adjective patterns, associating them to specific grammatical functional, as in the following examples (Hunston & Francis, 2000, p. 35):

it **V n to-inf**	e.g. *It hurts me to think of that*	verb pattern
it **v-link N to-inf**	e.g. *It would be a shame to lose touch*	noun pattern
it **v-link ADJ to-inf**	e.g. *It was terrible to see his face*	adjective pattern

The precursor of Hunston and Gill's work is traced in Hornby's *A Guide to Patterns and Usage in English* (Hornby, 1954), which the authors describe at the beginning of their volume as a work that could be superseded only with the advent of computer corpora (Hunston & Francis, 2000, pp. 3–7). Another theoretical strand of research based on the patterning of language is the work by Adele Goldberg (Goldberg, 1995, 2006). She conceptualises patterns in terms of *constructions*, i.e. conventionalised form-meaning pairings. Within the broader domain of constructionist approaches, she investigates how generalisation in language takes place and, more specifically, interprets argument structure in light of constructions. In this approach, the functional dimension of patterns plays a key role. One of the many examples used is that of *sliced* (Goldberg, 1995, p. 171; 2006, p. 7):

(1) *He sliced the bread.*
(2) *Pat sliced the carrots into the salad.*
(3) *Pat sliced Chris a piece of pie.*
(4) *Emeril sliced and diced his way to stardom.*
(5) *Pat sliced the box open.*

In all of these examples, *sliced* is used with a different grammatical function, thus expressing different meanings, 'such as something acting on something else' in example (1), 'something causing something else to move', in example (2), 'someone intending to cause someone to receive something', in example (3), 'someone moving somewhere despite obstacles', in example

(4), and finally 'someone causing something to change state', in example (5) (Goldberg, 2006, p. 7).

The patterning of language is also at the centre of Michael Hoey's research interests (Hoey, 1991, 2005). Hoey considers words as 'primed', that is as characterised by a tendency to co-occur with other words; it is from the property of lexis that grammar then derives. When considering collocation, Hoey defines it as 'a psycholinguistic phenomenon, the evidence for which can be found statistically in computer corpora' (Hoey, 2005, p. 5) and states that 'every word is mentally primed for collocational use' (Hoey, 2005, p. 8). He then formulates a number of hypotheses related to the notion of lexical priming, encompassing its explanatory potential as well as its limitations. He does so on the basis of a corpus-based analysis using a corpus of published articles in the UK *Guardian* newspaper. Hoey's overall purpose is to bridge the gap between what Chomsky had defined as I-language (internalised language) and E-language (externalised language).

This is the very starting point of James R. Taylor's book *The Mental Corpus* (Taylor, 2012). In bridging the gap even further between internalised and externalised language, Taylor conceives the idea of a mental corpus, as a product of the linguistic experiences that each one of us makes. In experiencing language, we form perceptions of language. We are able, for instance, to perceive some word combinations as more likely and familiar than others. Taylor offers the example of *total failure*, as opposed to *total success*. Both combinations are possible and indeed meaningful, but our experience of language will tell us that the first combination will be more likely than the second one. Our perception will be reflected by searching a corpus. The richness of the mental corpus lies in the fact that it is subject to personal memory, i.e. not all of its contents will be represented with the same vividness through time, and the fact that its contents will be associated with a particularly rich context, given by the specific experience of language that produced the exposure to a given instance of language.

Though with differing takes on the kind of lens that should be used when observing language, all these approaches are grounded in empiricism. The different ways of observing language imply a largely common notion of what language is: the patterned structures that are observable in what we say, write, read and hear and their cognitive counterparts. Offering corpus data in the form of DDL activities to language learners allows them to gain insight into these structures, without separating lexis from grammar. At the same, the activities will be informed by the numerous converging language learning theories that will be described in the following paragraph.

2.3.2 *Theories on language learning and teaching*

How does language learning work? Is it something that we learn implicitly through suitable exposure to an appropriate input, is it something we learn via explicit instruction or is there some form of interplay between explicit instruction and implicit knowledge of a second or foreign language? These are the key questions informing the implicit vs. explicit interface debate in SLA. As recently argued by O'Keeffe (2020), this debate has clear implications in terms of how DDL can be operationalised pedagogically and in terms of its likelihood in leading to beneficial learning effects.

According to the strong interface position, conscious explicit learning can be transformed into subconscious implicit learning; the weak interface position maintains that some portion of explicit learning might be transformed into subconscious implicit learning; finally, the non-interface position sees no interaction between the two learning systems, as these are conceived as separate, with the result of considering explicit learning unrelated to the development of the implicit learning of language.

If the goal of any second language pedagogy is to ultimately foster the internalisation of language usage patterns, as a way to achieve automaticity and fluency in language use, we can state that DDL will be theoretically underpinned by the strong and weak positions, with varying degrees of teacher-mediation. In both, the notion of *noticing* is central. According to the *Noticing Hypothesis* (Schmidt, 1990, 2001, 2012), input can be transformed into intake only when the learner consciously notices the linguistic features that characterise it. Conscious noticing has been linked to notions such as *attention* and *awareness*. Making learners notice something about language, as a pre-condition of learning, will be equated with drawing their attention to something specific, raising their awareness about it. Learners can be drawn to what in language is particularly frequent (Ellis, 2002) and/or salient (Gass et al., 2018). They can be guided towards the recognition of a particular pattern, based on form-meaning mappings. Noticing, through specific attention and the development of awareness, is the aim of DDL activities. The way in which this process is done can, however, imply different teacher-learner roles.

In *Constructivist learning theory*, 'knowledge encoded from data by learners themselves will be more flexible, transferable, and useful than knowledge encoded for them by experts and transmitted to them by an instructor or other delivery agent' (Cobb, 1999, p. 15). This approach informed the development of DDL in the practices conducted by Tim Johns. The 'kibbitzers', still visible online today,[2] are examples of problem-solving challenges that learners would engage in through the exploration of a corpus: What is the difference between *incessant* and *steadfast*? Is *data* singular or plural? Which verbs does *job* collocate with? The presence and involvement of the teacher is kept to a minimum: both the choice of the problem to solve, as well as the path towards solving it are largely left to the learners, with the teacher taking on the role of a facilitator or guide, indicating, for example, issues in the learners' academic writing, which can be addressed with a corpus. By exploring corpora, learners not only develop autonomy but also a set of transferrable problem-solving skills.

A more mediated view of learning which has informed DDL practices derives from *Sociocultural theory* (Vygotsky, 1934). In addressing the problem of how thought and speech are related, Vygotsky considers cognitive processes such as language learning as essentially based on mediation achieved through language. By expressing and sharing thoughts verbally about what is being learned, either with a teacher, with peers, or with the self, we engage in metacognitive and metalinguistic activities that nurture our understanding of language. This way, what we notice and become aware of can be the result of guidance through a process of 'scaffolding'. One of the earliest descriptions of this notion can be found in Wood et al. (1976, p. 90), where it is defined as a

> process that enables a child or novice to solve a problem, carry out a task or achieve a goal which would be beyond his unassisted efforts. This scaffolding consists essentially of the adult 'controlling' those elements of the task that are initially beyond the learner's capacity, thus permitting him to concentrate upon and complete only those elements that are within his range of competence. The task thus proceeds to a successful conclusion.

On the basis of Vygotsky's argument, Swain underscores the importance of 'languaging', defined as when language is used 'to mediate problem solutions, whether the problem is about which word to use, or how best to structure a sentence so it means what you want it to mean, or how to best explain the results of an experiment' (Swain, 2006, p. 96).

In O'Keeffe (2020), clear links are made with reference to how the constructivist and sociocultural learning paradigms can be seen as forming a cline that relates specifically to DDL pedagogical practices. In the more constructivist approaches, DDL is mostly student-led, corpus data is not particularly curated, there is no specific target form and no pre-instruction of form, whereas in the more sociocultural approaches, DDL is mostly based on self-regulation and teacher- and/or peer-mediated, corpus data tends to be curated, there is a focus on specific target forms, that are pre-instructed (O'Keeffe, 2020, pp. 261–263). The key factors that determine the pedagogical operationalisation of DDL along this cline are the level of competence, the L1 and the language form being considered; these are the factors that will influence the degree of mediation and, thus, the kinds of cognitive processes involved in the DDL activity.

Different aspects of the way in which DDL is pedagogically operationalised tie in with different theories and teaching methods beyond DDL itself. From the perspective of how linguistic input is visually presented, noticing can be thus fostered at various degrees of mediation and scaffolding. One way in which this can be done is through *input enhancement* (Chapelle, 2003). Learners can be guided towards the recognition of specific patterns by a concordance with a centred and enbolded node, displayed in the KWIC format.

They can be further aided by colour-coded part-of-speech patterns, as is possible in COCA, the *Corpus of Contemporary American English*. From the perspective of what engagement with concordances may mean cognitively, one theoretical stance relevant to DDL is the *Involvement load hypothesis* (Laufer & Hulstijn, 2001). According to this hypothesis, learners are able to more easily learn a certain language item through a concordance, because a concordance will provide 'condensed exposure to language patterns' (Gabrielatos, 2005, p. 8), thus creating the conditions for a higher level of engagement, which will influence memorability. From a more teacher-focused perspective, DDL can also be related to the notion of *normalisation* within existing teaching practices, by integrating it to the point of making it invisible. With specific reference to CALL practices, the theoretical framework developed in Bax (2003) and Chambers and Bax (Chambers & Bax, 2006) has been linked to the overall state of DDL in relation to the language learning and teaching domain (Pérez-Paredes, 2019).

When considering the role of language usage, in relation to both the linguistic exposure that will characterise a learner's experience as well as the opportunities he/she will have to use the language, we can see how DDL aligns well with usage-based theories to language learning (Bybee, 2006; Bybee & Hopper, 2001; Tomasello, 2005). As pointed out in Pérez-Paredes at el. (2020, p. 11): 'Within an instructed context, due to the sometimes limited opportunity for experiencing language across a range of meanings, we are faced with the possibility of incomplete form-meaning mapping in our language classrooms'. In this sense, DDL can offer unique opportunities to characterise the learner's input experience, on the basis of specific learning needs, which can be addressed by interrogating a corpus via minutely constructed queries.

Finally, the view of language as a complex dynamic adaptive system lends itself to the flexible nature of DDL as a source of dynamic and adaptive language exposure for the language learners. Complexity theory was introduced to SLA by Diane Larsen-Freeman (Larsen-Freeman, 1997; Larsen-Freeman & Cameron, 2009; Ortega & Han, 2017), who terms it a 'metatheory', which is reflected in other theories such as the ones described in this section (Larsen-Freeman, 2013, p. 370). At the same time, in acknowledging the non-linear nature of language learning, and the need to consider relationships between variables, it has several methodological implications for DDL effect-oriented research, as we will see in Chapter 4.

Though DDL is sustained by solid theoretical foundations, as highlighted in specific research papers devoted to the topic (Flowerdew, 2015; O'Keeffe, 2020; Papp, 2007; Pérez-Paredes, 2019), including meta-analyses (Boulton & Cobb, 2017; Lee et al., 2018), 'while many empirical studies refer to theoretical and pedagogical foundations, few seek directly to test them, and theory has not been a major driving force leading to new practices' (Boulton & Cobb, 2017, p. 484). This is reiterated and reinforced some years later by O'Keeffe (2020, p. 6): 'some aspects of SLA theory get a mention in DDL research, but these references often form part of the rationale for using DDL or appear as add-ons within the discussion of empirical findings' (O'Keeffe, 2020, p. 6).

2.4 The evolution of DDL through time

The examination of how DDL has evolved through time has mostly focused on empirical studies. From a quantitative perspective, Boulton (2017) reports on a total of 205 empirical studies, whereas Boulton & Vyatkina (2021) identify a total of 489 empirical studies: in the space of just a couple of years, the number of empirical studies has more than doubled. The *Research timeline* published in Boulton (2017) describes a selection of the 205 empirical studies found, together with a number of theoretical, descriptive and survey studies. The resulting selection of 52 studies includes the 25 most cited papers in the field. The author describes each study along a timeline starting with Sandra McKay's *Teaching the syntactic, semantic and pragmatic dimensions of verbs* from 1980 (McKay, 1980) and ending with Chris Tribble's *Teaching and language corpora: Perspectives from a personal journey* (Tribble, 2015). The timeline covers a 25-year period and gives us an idea of the main research questions that researchers have addressed over time: what theories of language and language learning underpin DDL? How can the DDL pedagogy be best described? What are the effects of DDL in relation to learner and teacher attitudes, and to cognitive and behavioural processes during corpus use? What are the pedagogical effects of DDL when using a corpus as a learning aid or a reference resource? How can DDL research be best synthesised? These are the five macro-questions around which Boulton's *Research timeline* is organised.

In their study entitled *Thirty years of data-driven learning: Taking stock and charting new directions*, Nina Vyatkina and Alex Boulton trace the history of DDL through the empirical studies aimed at evaluating corpus use for language learning purposes (Boulton & Vyatkina, 2021). They collected 489 studies published in English, and largely related to English language learning (432 of the total, i.e. 89%). The studies are converted into a corpus of 2.5 million words and divided into five time periods, in order to gain historical perspective. The timeframe considered goes from 1989 to 2019. While the study counts and study coding (according to the characteristics of the publication, the population, the procedures, and the design adopted) offer insight into the frequency of publication types through time, the corpus analysis on the conclusion sections of the articles allows the authors to look into the future directions for research that were outlined over the years, and how these impacted on subsequent research studies.

As can be seen in Figure 2.3, empirical studies in the initial years were very scarce, and continued to be so for at least 15 years. From 2005, the yearly increase of empirical studies is steadier, with peaks in 2012 (over 30), 2015 (almost 50) and 2017 (about 65). If we divide the 30-year period into three

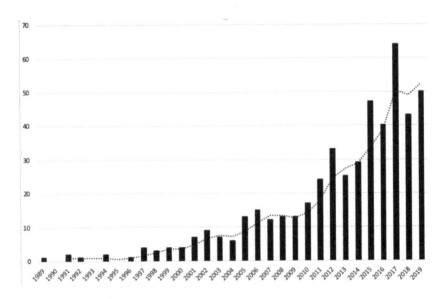

Figure 2.3 DDL for (mainly) English language learning: study counts by publication date (from Boulton & Vyatkina, 2021, p. 72).

decades, we may see that the average number of studies increases very slowly at the beginning (n < 5), moderately in the middle (5 < n < 18), and quite significantly in the end (18 < n < 64). This is in line with what is stated in both the historical outlines we have to date (Boulton, 2017, p. 484; Boulton & Vyatkina, 2021), namely that innovation in teaching tends to start with a few tentative studies by visionaries, followed many years later by ever-more sophisticated studies, which will then be numerous enough so as to allow a 'stock take' of what has been done, and project directions for the future.

As a result, the increase in number of empirical studies eventually lent itself to meta-analyses. Their aim was to gain an overall understanding of DDL effects by combining the quantitative results of individual studies. The first metanalysis to be conducted was that of Mizumoto and Chujo (2015). The context was limited to EFL in Japan, and the meta-analysed studies were only 14, but moderator variables related to learning aims were considered for the first time. The study found that DDL was the most effective at the level of learning vocabulary. Boulton & Cobb (2017) later published a more comprehensive meta-analysis, including 88 unique samples from a total of 64 studies, and broadening the list of moderator variables to 25. They found overall large effect sizes across the various conditions, while identifying the conditions which enhanced the beneficial effects of DDL. One year later, Lee at al. (2018) published another meta-analysis, reproducing all the moderator variables identified in Boulton & Cobb (2017), though restricting the scope to the DDL studies focusing only on vocabulary. They found overall medium effect sizes.

Surveys on textbooks and manuals, for teachers and learners, that more or less explicitly make reference to DDL and corpora have been less frequent over the years. Nevertheless, a survey of this kind is found in Boulton (2010), where a broad analysis of teaching materials is reviewed in relation to those that can identify as DDL textbooks. In many cases, the pedagogical materials are informed by corpus-based analyses, though without putting the learner in direct contact with the exploration of corpus data (e.g., the *Touchstone* and *Viewpoint* series, by Cambridge University Press), while in other cases the materials are closer to DDL, both in relation to how corpus data is presented and to the inductive nature of the associated learning activities (e.g., Sinclair, 2003). Over time, books and resources on how to adopt DDL in the classroom have become more and more practical and openly available online. In terms of how-to guides for teachers and/or learners, one of the early examples is from Tribble and Jones' *Concordances in the classroom. A resource guide for teachers* (Tribble & Jones, 1997), followed by *From Corpus to Classroom: Language use and language teaching* (O'Keeffe et al., 2007) and *Using Corpora in the Language Learning Classroom: Corpus linguistics for teachers* (Bennett, 2010). With *Corpora and Language Education* (Flowerdew, 2012) we are provided with a volume that seeks to bridge the gap between corpus-based research and teaching arenas, through the presentation of a number of case studies.

In terms of textbooks that could be labelled as actual DDL textbooks, in 2009, Boulton claimed that

> to date only two DDL textbooks exist: *Exploring Academic English: A Workbook for Student Essay Writing* (Thurstun & Candlin 1997) and *Concordances in the Classroom* (Tribble & Jones 1997). The fact that both of these are over 10 years old shows the difficulties involved in preparing general purpose 'off the peg' materials, and while they are still widely cited, this tends to be as sources of example activities rather than for use in their own right.
>
> (Boulton, 2009, p. 18)

While other textbooks that might be considered as such are the volumes published in the *Collins COBUILD Concordance Sampler* by Annette Capel (1993), Malcom Goodale (1995, 1996) and Geoff Thompson (1995), in more recent years things seem to have changed. More publications of this kind have appeared, with books aimed at language teachers, language teacher trainers, trainees and students addressing more and more the practicalities of implementing DDL in teaching and learning contexts, which have so often over the years been one of the obstacles preventing the spread of the approach, and its normalisation in teaching practices (Friginal, 2018; Karpenko-Seccombe, 2021; Pérez-Paredes, 2020; Poole, 2018). Online

28 *Data-driven learning*

resources for teachers are also increasingly being developed and made available, as in the case of the abovementioned *Incorporating corpora* project, led by Nina Vyatkina, and the *Corpus for Schools* project, led by Dana Gablasova.

Since the beginning, there has been a tendency to make DDL materials openly available online. Tim Johns' 'kibbitzers' are an example of this, together with others listed in Boulton (2009, p. 18). The unfortunate thing about earlier online resources is that they often fail to be maintained, and eventually become unavailable. The history of DDL is vast, complex, and fascinating. It can follow many more threads than the two we have chosen here (overall publications, with a specific focus on empirical studies, and teaching materials). How to define it, how to study the effects and processes associated with it, and how to spread it are part of the 'perpetual challenge' (Johns, 2002) and 'perpetual enigma' (Boulton, 2011) of DDL. Empirical research is needed to provide proof that DDL works, but in order for it to work there needs to be more guidance for those ultimately implementing it. This marks a close relationship between empirical studies and guiding materials for DDL in practice. In the next section, we look at the history of DDL in Italian learning and teaching contexts, which covers a similar timeframe in length, though, as we shall see, with quite a number of differences.

2.5 DDL in Italian L2 learning and teaching

In tracing the history of DDL in Italian learning and teaching contexts, I sought to collect all publications available on the topic. Publications written in both English and Italian were included, as well as publication types going beyond empirical accounts, as they immediately appeared too few to get a sense of where the field is going, in the specific domain of Italian L2 studies. Each publication was coded according to the following parameters:

(a) Year of publication (from 1993 to 2020);
(b) Language of publication (English/Italian);
(c) Publication type (chapters/research articles/training materials/MA or PhD theses/conference proceedings);
(d) Publication focus (descriptive/empirical/methodological/theoretical/synthesis).

Each publication was given a single label for each category, except for category (d). For this category, we labelled each publication with up to two labels, to take into account possible overlaps between the theoretical, methodological and descriptive foci. We shall start with a quantitative analysis, which will then be complemented with a qualitative dimension. We found a total of 26 publications, the earliest from 1993 and the latest from 2020, thus covering a period of almost 30 years. The number of overall publications,

Data-driven learning 29

including not only empirical studies, is extremely limited in comparison to studies focusing of English. As we shall see, however, beginning to develop an historical perspective on the interest that corpora have certainly attracted among scholars of Italian L2 studies is useful in order to see how the field is changing and where it is going. It is also useful to contextualise and highlight the work that has been done and that continues to gain ground, especially in the more recent years.

As we see in Figure 2.4, single studies on DDL focusing on Italian are quite sparse in the 1993–2008 timeframe: we observe gaps of three (1998–2001), five (1993–1998) and even seven (2002–2009) years where no studies seem to have appeared. Except for 2016, the 2009–2020 timeframe shows some first signs of systematicity: each year, there is at least one study on DDL for Italian, with 2019 reaching a peak of five studies. Overall, the moving average trendline in the graph signals the presence of a steady increase in studies from 2016 to 2020.

In terms of language of publication, though most of the studies are in English (n = 16; 61.5%), a good number of them are in Italian (n = 10; 38.5%). In terms of publication types, research articles are the most frequently found (n = 10; 38.5%), followed by conference proceedings (n = 8; 30.8%), book chapters (n = 6; 23.1%), training materials (n = 1; 3.8%) and MA or PhD theses (n = 1; 3.8%). The overall increase in number over the years has also produced some increased variation in the distribution of publication types: while from 1993 to 2009 the few publications that have appeared are either research articles or conference proceedings, from 2009 onwards we observe the presence of training materials, a PhD thesis and book chapters. In terms of publication focus, papers focusing on the

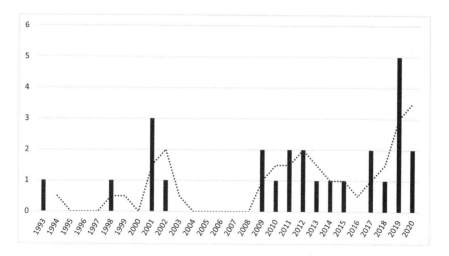

Figure 2.4 DDL for Italian language learning: study counts by publication date.

descriptive dimension are the majority (n = 18; 48.7%), followed by those focused also, though not exclusively, on methodology (n = 9; 24.3%), empirical evaluations (n = 8; 21.6%) and the theoretical underpinnings of the approach (n = 2; 5.4%). No survey or synthesis exist, most likely because the number of studies is still very low.

The increase in numbers in more recent years, which is populated by an increase in conference proceedings, might be biased by the fact that conference proceedings, or teaching materials, are not generally indexed in bibliographical databases and are thus more difficult to find. We did, however, consult the reference manuals for corpus linguistics in the context of Italian studies (Chiari, 2007; Cresti & Panunzi, 2013; Spina, 2001), and found no mention of pedagogical uses of corpora for learning Italian, beyond the references found in our own search.

We now briefly review what lies behind these numbers. A major starting point in the domain of DDL for Italian is certainly the article by Loredana Polezzi, published in 1993 in the journal ReCALL (Polezzi, 1993). As mentioned earlier, Polezzi taught Italian for specific purposes at the University of Warwick (UK) to post-graduate students specialising in Italian Renaissance Studies. All students were beginner-level learners of Italian. Polezzi was thus faced with two stark challenges that characterise DDL even today: how to make corpus data relevant for very specific language learning needs, and how to make corpus data suitable for beginner learners of the language. She created an ad hoc corpus by transcribing the recorded lectures on Renaissance theatre, which had been delivered orally. Students were then invited to explore the corpus to observe and internalise some elementary patterns of the Italian language in that particular context of occurrence, such as the use of impersonal forms. Polezzi names her corpus a 'didactic language corpus', specifying the characteristics it should have in order to meet the learners' needs.

The works by Claire Kennedy and Tiziana Miceli (Kennedy & Miceli, 2001, 2010, 2017), all published in English and in major international CALL journals, are some of the most well-known studies in DDL. The authors created an ad hoc corpus of Italian written texts (Kennedy & Miceli, 2002), in order to provide Italian L2 university students with a suitable corpus-based tool to improve their writing in Italian. As stated in Boulton (2017, p. 490), 'Kennedy & Miceli's characterisation of "pattern hunting" (looking for content or language ideas) vs. "pattern defining" (checking usage) has achieved widespread recognition'. To the best of our knowledge, the first publication on DDL for Italian written in Italian appears in 2001. It is by Manuela Sassi and Maria Luigi Ceccotti, researchers at the Institute of Computational Linguistics in Pisa. They describe the architecture and search criteria of some corpora of Italian, and illustrate how they can be used beneficially for pedagogical purposes (Sassi & Ceccotti, 2001). In the same year, Daniela Zorzi published *The pedagogic use of spoken corpora: Learning discourse markers in Italian* (Zorzi, 2001), within an edited volume referring mostly to learning English. This is perhaps the only contribution to DDL for Italian where corpora of speech, instead of writing, are considered.

Systematic work on the pedagogical uses of corpora has been conducted over the years at the University of Turin, Italy. While Corino & Marello (2009) and Marello (2012) focus on the direct uses of corpora in Italian L2 contexts, other publications from the same authors focus on indirect applications, such as those pertaining to language testing (Marello, 2009), or on other, though very close, domains such as teacher training and CLIL (Corino, 2014a, 2014b, 2019). The publications by Ducati and Leone (2009) and Guidetti et al. (Guidetti et al., 2012) are clearly tailored for language teachers or students training to become language teachers. They show a series of pedagogical activities based on the output of a corpus. Viganò (2011) is one of the very few publications in Italian and on teaching Italian L2 through corpora that provides the background to the approach and really advocates the use of corpora in Italian L2 pedagogy. The case for corpora in Italian L2 teaching is made in Chiari (2011) from a variationist perspective: various corpora of Italian are described in terms of their specific sociolinguistic features, so as to reflect their pedagogical potential in developing teaching materials geared toward observation of variation in language use.

A series of descriptive and methodological works has also been published by Ruska Ivanovska-Naskova (Ivanovska-Naskova, 2014, 2018, 2015). In her works, she describes the use of Italian corpora to raise learners' awareness of specific Italian constructions, but also provides an overview of some of the main resources that can be used to develop DDL activities for the Italian L2 classroom. Lyding et al. (2013) describe how a large web corpus of Italian (i.e. Paisà), which includes automatic text readability tools, can be used to guide learners through the exploration of Italian language features.

Furthermore, in Forti & Spina (2019), we find a reflection on the gap between corpora for linguists and corpora for learners, including an example of how the findings of a particular LCR study can inform the development of a DDL activity, whereas Spina et al. (2020) explores the connections between DDL and usage-based theories, with reference to learning and teaching Italian for academic purposes. Finally, the review on DDL for languages other than English published by Jablonkai et al. (2020) contains perhaps the first attempt, though extremely limited in nature, to trace a comprehensive history of DDL for Italian. A total of 26 studies covering a 27-year timeframe, with an average of less than one study per year, can be seen as the sign of a field that is still developing, despite a continued and renewed interest over the years. As we continue to keep track of the field, we now move to the debates that have characterised DDL throughout its history.

2.6 DDL debates

Debates on DDL may be divided into those regarding DDL directly, namely the criticism that DDL itself has received, and those regarding DDL indirectly, namely those involving the theories on language and language learning that support and inform DDL practices. In this section, we will focus solely on the first kind of criticism, identifying rebuttals for each of the issues raised. The criticism that DDL has attracted over the years derives from both the teaching and the research domains. Various arguments against DDL emerge from surveying the literature reporting on teacher and learner attitudes towards the approach, as well as from researchers in other domains. Some of these are summarised in Boulton & Cobb (2017), others in Braun (2005). All these criticisms reflect a series of limitations that DDL can indeed have, but which can be relatively easily overcome with a number of strategies.

The first of the various arguments is that both students and teachers are reluctant to work with computers, reflecting the fact that using computers, or digital equipment in general, is not normalised within pedagogical practices. The shift from books, notebooks, pens, pencils, and paper to digital devices seems to be perceived as demanding. However, this reluctance can be considerably mitigated by the availability of teacher/learner-friendly corpora, such as justtheword, SkELL, BNClab, FLAX, and others. In addition to this, DDL can be also paper-based, with corpus-based data extracted and printed on paper by the teacher before the lesson, with a variety of options in terms of how these paper-based activities can be designed. Various projects aimed at making teachers and students more comfortable with corpus-based activities, whether computer or paper-based, have developed in the past few years. These include a book for students to autonomously explore corpora (Poole, 2018), a book for teachers and teacher trainers to gain a more comprehensive understanding of corpus linguistics for the specific purposes of pedagogical practices (Friginal, 2018) and another book specifically focused on corpus use to aid academic writing (Karpenko-Seccombe, 2021). While books to facilitate corpus-based teaching and learning had previously been published, these three take stock of the latest developments in terms of online corpora, and contain numerous activities ready for the classroom. Extremely valuable work is underway at Lancaster University, within the 'Corpus for Schools' project,[3] led by Dana Gablasova. The team regularly produces worksheets with corpus-based activities geared towards exploring engaging topics, both in the context of EFL and A-level (school-leaving exam) pedagogy. Other valuable work in making DDL more accessible to teachers is the 'Incorporating corpora' project,[4] led by Nina Vyatkina (Vyatkina, 2020). This project integrates both teacher guides and corpus exploration tools in one single open access platform. The claim that students and teachers are reluctant to work with computers can be certainly restricted to the cases in which both teachers and students are unaware of the resources that are currently available to circumvent such reluctance, or cases in which such resources are not available yet.

A second criticism that is often made of DDL is that working with concordances entails an entirely different way of reading text in comparison to more familiar ways (vertical vs. horizontal reading). However, the fact that reading groups of sentences all together vertically, instead of one by one horizontally, can trigger resistance depends largely on how a DDL activity is developed and presented to the learners. With the plethora of newly published resources just described, a teacher can introduce concordance work very gradually, ensuring that the concordance lines contain level-appropriate linguistic input, and well-linked to the context of a lesson. The novelty of working with groups of sentences, and reading them in an unconventional manner, can spark the learners' curiosity, if presented in a stimulating and enthusiastic way by the teacher. According to a third line of criticism, corpora rarely contain data that is relevant to learner needs. However, this view does not consider the possibility of selecting domain- and genre-specific corpora, so as to suit learner needs. Furthermore, as we will show, ad hoc corpora can be created for the specific needs of the teaching and learning context, and this can be done either by the teacher or by the learners themselves (see for example Polezzi, 1993 for Italian, and more recently Charles, 2019, for English).

A further argument against DDL is the belief that for teachers to work with corpora in the classroom, extensive preliminary training sessions are needed for the learners, and that this is time-consuming. In response to this, the first thing that may be noted is that the potential time-consuming nature of introducing DDL in classroom practices is mitigated by the enormous scope of pedagogically operationalising DDL, in terms of choosing the most appropriate corpora, depending on the linguistic data it contains and how its interface works, and how to present the data. Moreover, most empirical DDL studies that are included in the latest meta-analyses do not envisage preliminary corpus training. The presence of preliminary training is one of the many variables considered in the evaluation of DDL effects, and it was found to be non-significant (Lee at al., 2018). The idea that DDL requires extensive preliminary training, thus being more time-consuming than beneficial, may very well be considered a myth.

Another criticism of DDL is related to whether the linguistic data is actually 'authentic'. In a 1978 paper, Widdowson (1978) states that genuinely produced texts, instead of artificial ones, are not a guarantee for learning. In order for a text to be useful to a learner, the learner will need to 'authenticate' the text, in the sense that they need to establish a relationship with it. This is what Sabine Braun discusses at length some years later: the linguistic information that is contained in corpora can be authenticated through DDL by ensuring that the data is relevant to the learners in terms of difficulty and motivation, thus addressing the learners' specific learning needs (Braun, 2005, pp. 53–55). Furthermore, it is interesting to note that the studies aimed at eliciting learner attitudes towards DDL reveal that learners appreciate the opportunity of working with language that is 'authentic', reflecting language that is 'really' used (Chambers, 2007; Cheng et al., 2003).

A final criticism regarding DDL could be named as the 'cotext vs. context' debate. Again, we find Widdowson claiming that the cotext of a lexical item is rarely sufficient to reconstruct the broader context within which the lexical item is found to occur, and learning is effective only if meaningful (Widdowson, 2003). Once more, Sabine Braun addresses this criticism by holding that

> we do not perceive a communicative situation directly but [...] we construct a context in our mind, drawing on our perceptual abilities, our knowledge about the communicative situation in question, our previous experience with it, our attitudes towards it, our background knowledge as well as textual clues (including co-text) and other factors. If communication is to be successful, a relevant context has to be constructed by the discourse participants.
>
> (Braun, 2005, p. 52)

Braun addresses the 'cotext vs. context' debate by proposing to reconceptualise it in terms of a 'cotext to context' pedagogy. Once more, the DDL studies focusing on learner perceptions of the approach are revealing: learners speak of 'context' when discussing the linguistic information they are provided with through a set of concordance lines, even if they are only ever dealing with 'cotext' (Chambers, 2007, p. 11). Furthermore, we might add that many, though not all, corpora used in DDL do allow access into the full single text of a given concordance line. In those cases where the cotext of concordance lines is insufficient to gain meaning, learners will have an additional option to go beyond concordance lines.

2.7 Chapter summary and conclusions

This chapter provided an overview of the origins, the theoretical underpinnings, and the development through time of DDL. In doing so, it addressed the relationship between language description, corpora and second language teaching, showing how it stimulated and informed the construction of corpora in the early 1960s. It then pinpointed the main features of DDL pedagogy, which started to develop more systematically from the 1980s onwards thanks to work by Tim Johns at the University of Birmingham. Authentic, frequent, and enhanced input, together with a mostly discovery-based and inductive learning 'cotext vs. context' debate identified as the defining traits of DDL pedagogy. The chapter then explored the theories that underpin DDL pedagogy, with specific reference to theories pertaining to language and language learning. Theories of language underpinning DDL converge towards the idea of language as a highly patterned system. Theories of language learning underpinning DDL pedagogy highlight the importance of noticing patterns and inferencing rules and regularities about language.

The history of DDL was first traced with an international perspective, considering studies published in English (and to a large extent referred to English-language learning contexts) and drawing on data collected in Boulton (2017) and Boulton and Vyatkina (2021). The specific domain of DDL for Italian was then described historically, considering studies published in both English and Italian. Although studies on DDL for Italian are quite low in number if compared to studies on DDL for English, they cover just about the same time span and are seeing a steady growth in the last few years.

The chapter ends with a brief review of the main debates that have characterised the development of DDL over the years. Some of the main criticisms are outlined, such as the learners' and teachers' reluctance to work with computers, the assumed problematicity of vertical reading, the issue of authenticity, and the issue concerning the cotext vs. context dichotomy. Each of these debates raised throughout the years are addressed with a number of counterarguments, as to how these apparent limitations of DDL can be dealt with or how they can be look at differently.

History, theory and criticism are fundamental to grasp the nature and evolution of a pedagogical approach such as DDL. All these aspects are particularly crucial when seeking to design an empirical study aimed at investigating the effects of DDL on language learning. As we shall see, theory can inform the formulation of research questions and hypotheses that are relevant not only to the specific domain of DDL, but also fit within the wider dimension of SLA studies. Being aware of how DDL has evolved through time allows us to envision new research pathways that are yet to be explored (e.g., the cognitive dimension of engaging in DDL activities), and new ways to approach old questions (e.g., which conditions favour the beneficial effects of DDL?). In the next chapter, we analyse the research evidence related to the effects of DDL on second language pedagogy, through a range of different perspectives.

Notes

1 See https://lexically.net/TimJohns/Kibbitzer/homepage.htm (last accessed: 22/08/2022).
2 The full list is accessible at the following webpage: https://lexically.net/TimJohns/ (last accessed: 22/08/2022).
3 More information about the project, including a range of student worksheets and teacher notes free to download, can be accessed at the following webpage: http://wp.lancs.ac.uk/corpusforschools/ (last accessed: 22/08/2022).
4 The open access platform related to the project can be accessed at the following webpage: https://corpora.ku.edu/ (last accessed: 22/08/2022).

References

Bax, S. (2003). CALL – past, present and future. *System*, *31*(1), 13–28.
Bazell, C.E., Catford, J.C., Halliday, M.A.K., & Robins, R.H. (Eds.) (1966). *In Memory of J. R. Firth*. Longman's Linguistics Library.
Bennett, G. (2010). *Using Corpora in the Language Learning Classroom: Corpus linguistics for teachers*. University of Michigan Press.
Bernardini, S. (2000). Systematising serendipity: Proposals for concordancing large corpora with language learners. In L. Burnard & T. McEnery (Eds.), *Rethinking Language Pedagogy from a Corpus Perspective* (pp. 225–234). Peter Lang.
Boulton, A. (2009). Data-driven learning: Reasonable fears and rational reassurance. *Indian Journal of Applied Linguistics*, *35*(1), 81–106.
Boulton, A. (2010). Data-driven learning: On paper, in practice. *Corpus Linguistics in Language Teaching* (pp. 17–52). Peter Lang.
Boulton, A. (2011). Data-driven learning: The perpetual enigma. In S. Gozdz-Roszkowski (Ed.), *Explorations across languages and corpora* (pp. 563–580). Peter Lang.
Boulton, A. (2017). Research Timeline. Corpora in language teaching and learning. *Language Teaching*, *50*(4), 483–506.
Boulton, A., & Cobb, T. (2017). Corpus use in language learning: A meta-analysis. *Language Learning*, *67*(2), 348–393.
Boulton, A., & Vyatkina, N. (2021). Thirty years of data-driven learning: Taking stock and charting new directions. *Language Learning and Technology*, *25*(3), 66–89.
Braun, S. (2005). From pedagogically relevant corpora to authentic language learning contents. *ReCALL*, *17*(01), 47–64.
Bybee, J.L. (2006). From Usage to Grammar: The Mind's Response to Repetition. *Language*, *82*(4), 711–733.
Bybee, J.L., & Hopper, P. J. (Eds.). (2001). *Frequency and the emergence of linguistic structure*. Benjamins.
Capel, A. (1993). *Collins COBUILD Concordance Samplers 1: Prepositions*, Collins.
Chambers, A., & Bax, S. (2006). Making CALL work: Towards normalisation. *System*, *34*(4), 465–479.
Chambers, A. (2007). Popularising corpus consultation by language learners and teachers. *Language and Computers*, *61*(1), 3–16.
Chapelle, C. A. (2003). *English language learning and technology: Lectures on applied linguistics in the age of information and communication technology*. Benjamins.
Charles, M. (2014). Getting the corpus habit: EAP students' long-term use of personal corpora. *English for Specific Purposes*, *35*, 30–40.
Charles, M. (2019). Do-it-yourself corpora for LSP: Demystifying the process and illustrating the practice. *Scripta Manent*, *13*, 156–166.
Cheng, W., Warren, M., & Xun-feng, X. (2003). The language learner as language researcher: Putting corpus linguistics on the timetable. *System*, *31*(2), 173–186.
Chiari, I. (2007). *Introduzione alla linguistica computazionale*. Laterza.
Chiari, I. (2011). Teaching language variation using Italian corpora. In N. Kübler (Ed.), *Corpora, Language, Teaching, and Resources: From Theory to Practice* (pp. 301–323). Peter Lang.
Cobb, T. (1999). Applying constructivism: A test for the learner-as-scientist. *Educational Technology Research and Development*, *47*(3), 15–31.

Corino, E. (2014a). Didattica delle lingue corpus-based. *EL.LE – Educazione Linguistica. Language Education*, 3(2), 231–258.
Corino, E. (2014b). Formare insegnanti 2.0. La didattica delle lingue moderne tra libri di testo e nuove tecnologie. *RiCOGNIZIONI*, 1(1), 163–176.
Corino, E. (Ed.). (2019). *Data-driven Learning: La linguistica dei corpora al servizio della didattica delle lingue straniere e del CLIL. Special issue EL.LE – Educazione Linguistica. Language Education*, 8(2), 271–434.
Corino, E., & Marello, C. (2009). Didattica con i corpora di italiano per stranieri. *Italiano LinguaDue*, 1(1), 279–285.
Corino, E., & Onesti, C. (2019). Data-driven learning: A scaffolding methodology for CLIL and LSP teaching and learning. *Frontiers in Education*, 4(7).
Cresti, E., & Panunzi, A. (Eds.). (2013). *Introduzione ai corpora di italiano*. il Mulino.
Ducati, R., & Leone, P. (2009). *Corpora e apprendimento del lessico. Risorse per docenti dai programmi nazionali. Programma Operativo Nazionale 2007–2013 'Competenze per lo Sviluppo' cofinanziato dal Fondo*. Sociale Europeo.
Ellis, N.C. (2002). Frequency effects in language processing. *Studies in Second Language Acquisition*, 24(02), 143–188.
Firth, J.R. (1957). *Papers in linguistics 1934–1951*. Oxford University Press.
Firth, J.R. (1962). A synopsis of linguistic theory, 1930–1955. In *Studies in Linguistic Analysis (Special volume of the Philological Society)*. Blackwell.
Flowerdew, L. (2012). *Corpora and Language Education*. Palgrave Macmillan UK.
Flowerdew, L. (2015). Data-driven learning and language learning theories: Whither the twain will meet. *In multiple affordances of language corpora for data-driven learning* (pp. 15–36). Benjamins.
Forti, L., & Spina, S. (2019). Corpora for Linguists vs. Corpora for Learners: Bridging the Gap in Italian L2 Learning and Teaching. *EL.LE – Educazione Linguistica. Language Education*, 8(2), 349–362.
Frankenberg-Garcia, A. (2012). Integrating corpora with everyday language teaching. In J.E. Thomas & A. Boulton (Eds.), *Input, Process and Product: Developments in Teaching and Language Corpora* (pp. 33–51). Masaryk University Press.
Friginal, E. (2018). *Corpus Linguistics for English Teachers: Tools, Online Resources, and Classroom*. Routledge.
Gabrielatos, C. (2005). Corpora and Language Teaching: Just a fling or wedding bells? *The Electronic Journal for English as a Second Language*, 8(4), 1–32.
Gass, S., Spinner, P., & Behney, J. (Eds.). (2018). *Salience in Second Language Acquisition*. Routledge.
Goldberg, A.E. (1995). *Constructions: A construction grammar approach to argument structure*. University of Chicago Press.
Goldberg, A.E. (2006). *Constructions at work: The nature of generalization in language*. Oxford University Press.
Goodale, M. (1995). *Collins COBUILD Concordance Samplers 2: Phrasal Verbs*, Collins.
Goodale, M. (1996). *Collins COBUILD Concordance Samplers 4: Tenses*, Collins.
Guidetti, M. G., Lenzi, G., & Storchi, S. (2012). Potenzialità e limiti nell'uso dei corpora linguistici per la didattica dell'italiano LS. *Laboratorio Itals. Italiano Come Lingua Straniera. Supplemento Alla Rivista EL.LE – Educazione Linguistica. Language Education*.
Halliday, M.A.K. (1992). Language as system and language as instance: The corpus as a theoretical construct. In J. Svartvik (Ed.), *Directions in corpus*

linguistics: proceedings of the Nobel Symposium 82, Stockholm, 4–8 August 1991. Mouton de Gruyter, 61–78.
Halliday, M.A.K. (1966). Lexis as a linguistic level. In C.E. Bazell, J.C. Catford, M.A.K. Halliday, & R.H. Robins (Eds.), *In Memory of J.R. Firth* (pp. 148–162). Longman's Linguistics Library.
Hoey, M. (1991). *Patterns of lexis in text*. Oxford University Press.
Hoey, M. (2005). *Lexical priming: A new theory of words and language*. Routledge/AHRB.
Hornby, A. S. (1954). *Guide to Patterns and Usage in English*. Oxford University Press.
Hunston, S., & Francis, G. (2000). *Pattern Grammar*. Benjamins.
Ivanovska-Naskova, R. (2014). Il corpus parallelo italiano-macedone come strumento nella didattica dell'Italiano LS. In *Dal manoscritto al web: Canali e modalità di trasmissione dell'italiano. Tecniche, materiali e usi nella storia della lingua. Atti del XII Congresso SILFI Società Internazionale di Linguistica e Filologia Italiana* (pp. 471–479). Franco Cesati.
Ivanovska-Naskova, R. (2018). L'insegnamento della grammatica dell'italiano LS attraverso corpora. *Italica Wratislaviensia*, 9(1), 71–87.
Ivanovska-Naskova, R., & Zaccaro, V. (2015). I corpora e l'insegnamento dell'italiano LS. In V. Zaccaro & R. Ivanovska-Naskova (Eds.). *Incroci. Studi sulla letteratura, la traduzione e la glottodidattica* (pp. 105–123). Università degli Studi di Bari Aldo Moro – Università 'Ss. Cirillo e Metodio' di Skopje.
Jablonkai, W.R., Forti, L., Castelló, M.A., Iguenane, I.S., Schaeffer-Lacroix, E., & Vyatkina, N. (2020). *Data-driven learning for languages other than English: The cases of French, German, Italian, and Spanish* (pp. 132–137). In K.-M. Frederiksen, S. Larsen, L. Bradley, & S. Thouësny (Eds.), *CALL for widening participation: Short papers from EUROCALL 2020*, Research-publishing.net.
Johns, T. (1986). Micro-concord: A language learner's research tool. *System*, 14(2), 151–162.
Johns, T. (1988). Whence and whither classroom concordancing? In T. Bongaerts, P. de Haan, S. Lobbe, & H. Wekker (Eds.), *Computer applications in language learning* (pp. 9–27). Foris.
Johns, T. (1990). From printout to handout: Grammar and vocabulary teaching in the context of Data-driven Learning. *CALL Austria*, 10, 14–34.
Johns, T. (1991). Should you be persuaded – Two examples of data-driven learning materials. *Classroom Concordancing, English Language Research Journal*, 4, 1–13.
Johns, T. (1997). Contexts: E background, development and trialling of a concordance- based CALL program. In A. Wichmann, S. Fligelstone, T. McEnery, & G. Knowles (Eds.), *Teaching and Language Corpora* (pp. 100–115). Addison Wesley Longman.
Johns, T. (2002). Data-driven learning: The perpetual challenge. In B. Kettenmann & G. Marko (Eds.), *Teaching and learning by doing corpus analysis* (pp. 107–117). Rodopi.
Karpenko-Seccombe, T. (2021). *Academic Writing with Corpora: A Resource Book for Data-Driven Learning*. Routledge.
Kennedy, C., & Miceli, T. (2001). An evaluation of intermediate students' approaches to corpus investigation. *Language Learning & Technology*, 5(3), 77–90.
Kennedy, C., & Miceli, T. (2002). The CWIC project: developing and using a corpus for intermediate Italian students, In B. Kettemann & G. Marko (Eds.), *Teaching and Learning by Doing Corpus Analysis* (pp. 183–192). Rodopi.

Kennedy, C., & Miceli, T. (2010). Corpus-assisted creative writing: Introducing intermediate Italian learners to a corpus as a reference resource. *Language Learning & Technology*, *14*(1), 28–44.

Kennedy, C., & Miceli, T. (2017). Cultivating effective corpus use by language learners. *Computer Assisted Language Learning*, *30*(1–2), 91–114.

Larsen-Freeman, D. (1997). Chaos/Complexity Science and Second Language Acquisition. *Applied Linguistics*, *18*(2), 141–165.

Larsen-Freeman, D. (2013). Complexity theory: A new way to think. Revista Brasileira de Linguística *Aplicada*, *13*(2), 369–373.

Larsen-Freeman, D., & Cameron, L. (2009). *Complex systems and applied linguistics*. Oxford University Press.

Laufer, B., & Hulstijn, J. (2001). Incidental vocabulary acquisition in a second language: The construct of task-induced involvement. *Applied Linguistics*, *22*(1), 1–26.

Lee, H., Warschauer, M., & Lee, J. H. (2018). The effects of corpus use on second language vocabulary learning: A multilevel meta-analysis. *Applied Linguistics*, *40*(5), 721–753.

Lyding, V., Borghetti, C., Dittmann, H., Nicolas, L., & Stemle, E. (2013). Open corpus interface for Italian Language Learning. In *Proceedings of ICT for Language Learning, 6th Edition, Florence (Italy)* (pp. 1–6). Libreriauniversitaria. it Edizioni.

Marello, C. (2009). Distrattori tratti da corpora di apprendenti di italiano LS/L2. In E. Corino & C. Marello (Eds.), *VALICO. Studi di linguistica e didattica* (pp. 177–193). Guerra.

Marello, C. (2012). Corpora di apprendenti. Come usarli nella didattica dell'italiano in Svizzera. In *Lingua e letteratura italiana 150 anni dopo l'Unità* (pp. 299–315). Meidenbauer.

McEnery, A., Xiao, R., & Tono, Y. (2006). *Corpus-based language studies: An advanced resource book*. Routledge.

McKay, S. (1980). Teaching the Syntactic, Semantic and Pragmatic Dimensions of Verbs. *TESOL Quarterly*, *14*(1), 17–26.

Meunier, F. (2020). Data-driven learning: From classroom scaffolding to sustainable practices. *EL.LE – Educazione Linguistica. Language Education*, *8*(2), 423–434.

Mizumoto, A., & Chujo, K. (2015). a meta-analysis of data-driven learning approach in the Japanese EFL Classroom. *English Corpus Studies*, *22*, 1–18.

O'Keeffe, A. (2020). Data-driven learning – A call for a broader research gaze. *Language Teaching*, *54*(2), 259–272.

O'Keeffe, A., McCarthy, M., & Carter, R. (2007). *From Corpus to Classroom: Language use and language teaching*. Cambridge University Press.

Ortega, L., & Han, Z.H. (Eds.). (2017). *Complexity theory and language development. In celebration of Diane Larsen-Freeman*. Benjamins.

Papp, S. (2007). Inductive learning and self-correction with the use of learner and reference corpora. In E. Hilgado, L. Quereda, & J. Santana (Eds.), *Corpora in the foreign language classroom* (pp. 207–220). Rodopi.

Pérez-Paredes, P. (2019). A systematic review of the uses and spread of corpora and data-driven learning in CALL research during 2011–2015. *Computer Assisted Language Learning*, *35*(1–2), 36–61.

Pérez-Paredes, P. (2020). *Corpus Linguistics for Education*. Routledge.

Pérez-Paredes, P., Mark, G., & O'Keeffe, A. (2020). *The impact of usage-based approaches on second language learning and teaching.* Cambridge Education Research Reports.

Polezzi, L. (1993). Concordancing and the teaching of ab initio Italian language for specific purposes. *ReCALL, 5*(09), 14–18.

Poole, R. (2018). *A Guide to Using Corpora for English Language Learners.* Edinburgh University Press.

Quirk, R. (1960). Towards a description of English usage. *Transactions of the Philological Society, 59*(1), 40–61.

Sassi, M., & Ceccotti, M.L. (2001). L'utilizzo didattico di corpora: Proposte metodologiche. Didamatica 2001. Informatica per La Didattica.

Schmidt, R.W. (1990). The Role of Consciousness in Second Language Learning. *Applied Linguistics, 11*(2), 129–158.

Schmidt, R.W. (2001). Attention. In P. Robinson (Ed.), *Cognition and second language instruction.* Cambridge University Press.

Schmidt, R.W. (2012). Attention, awareness, and individual differences in language learning. In W.M. Chan (Ed.), *Proceedings of CLaSIC 2010, Singapore, December 2–4* (pp. 721–737). National University of Singapore, Centre for Language Studies.

Sinclair, J.M. 1966. Beginning the study of lexis In C.E. Bazell, J.C. Catford, M.A.K. Halliday, & R.H. Robins (Eds.), *In Memory of J. R. Firth* (pp. 410–30). London: Longman's Linguistics Library.

Sinclair, J.M. (1991). *Corpus, Concordance, Collocation.* Oxford University Press.

Sinclair, J.M. (2003). *Reading Concordances.* Pearson.

Spina, S. (2001). *Fare i conti con le parole: Introduzione alla linguistica dei corpora.* Guerra.

Spina, S., Forti, L., & Grego Bolli, G. (2020). Input, frequenza e modelli usage-based: il Data-driven learning come interfaccia tra teorie acquisizionali e pratica didattica. In S. Rastelli & C. Bagna (Eds.), *Manifesto per l'insegnamento della lingua italiana agli studenti internazionali. Otto commenti.* Pacini editore.

Swain, M. (2006). Languaging, agency and collaboration in advanced second language proficiency. In H. Byrnes (Ed.), *Advanced Language Learning: The Contribution of Halliday and Vygotsky* (pp. 95–108). Bloomsbury Academic.

Taylor, J.R. (2012). *The mental corpus: How language is represented in the mind.* Oxford University Press.

Thompson, G. (1995). *Collins COBUILD Concordance Samplers 3: Reporting,* Collins.

Thorndike, E.L. (1921). *The teacher's word book.* Teachers College, Columbia University.

Thurstun, J., & Candlin, C. (1997). *Exploring academic English: A workbook for student essay writing.* CELTR.

Tomasello (2005). *Constructing a language: A usage-based theory of language acquisition.* Harvard University Press.

Tribble, C. (2015). Teaching and language corpora: Perspectives from a personal journey. In A. Leńko-Szymańska & A. Boulton (Eds.), *Multiple Affordances of Language Corpora for Data-driven Learning* (pp. 37–62). Benjamins.

Tribble, C., & Jones, G. (1997). *Concordances in the classroom. A resource guide for teachers.* Althelstan.

Viganò, P.B. (2011). I corpora e il loro sfruttamento in didattica. *Italiano LinguaDue*, *3*(2), 115–128.

Vyatkina, N. (2020). Corpus-Informed Pedagogy in a Language Course: Design, Implementation, and Evaluation. In M. Kruk & M. Peterson (Eds.), *New Technological Applications for Foreign and Second Language Learning and Teaching*. IGI Global.

Vygotsky, L.S. (1934). *Thought and language, revised and expanded edition*. MIT Press.

Widdowson, H. (1978). *Teaching language as communication*. Oxford University Press.

Widdowson, H. (2003). *Defining issues in English language teaching*. Oxford University Press.

Wood, D., Bruner, J.S., & Ross, G. (1976). The role of tutoring in problem solving. *Journal of Child Psychology and Psychiatry*, *17*(2), 89–100.

Zorzi, D. (2001). The pedagogic use of spoken corpora: Learning discourse markers in Italian. In G. Aston (Ed.), *Learning with Corpora* (pp. 85–107). CLUEB.

3 Delving into the research evidence on data-driven learning effects

After exploring the history of DDL throughout the years in Chapter 2, in this chapter we examine the epistemological foundations of DDL. What do we know about the effects of DDL on language learning? How is this knowledge reflected in the domain of Italian L2 pedagogy? By drawing on the most recently published meta-analyses, research syntheses and surveys, the chapter provides an empirically-grounded description of DDL effects. It does so by looking into what learners are able to gain from DDL activities, in terms of developments in language competence, and into how DDL is perceived by both learners and teachers. In illustrating the empirical evidence available for Italian L2 learning, the chapter underlines the need for more and more varied research, while highlighting the value of the research conducted so far.

3.1 Does DDL work?

As with any relatively novel pedagogical approach, when it comes to DDL, a question such as 'Does DDL work?' seems to be the ultimate question that researchers ask themselves and each other, and in turn are asked when speaking about DDL with language teachers or doubtful researchers from adjacent fields. As we will see, though a general answer might be 'Yes', one should immediately be more specific: 'Yes, but it depends'. The investigation of whether DDL actually works in fostering language gains, and ultimately 'reaching the parts other teaching can't reach' (Boulton, 2008), has led to an increasingly high number of empirical studies over the years. The best way to gain an overall picture regarding the effects of DDL on language learning, especially when the empirical studies start to become numerous, is through meta-analyses. A meta-analysis can be defined as a systematic quantitative synthesis aimed at integrating the quantitative findings of different studies focusing on the effect of one variable over another, also by analysing the possible effects of moderator variables (Cramer & Howitt, 2004, p. 101). Central in meta-analyses is the notion of *effect size*, which is defined as 'the size of the effect (influence) of the independent variable on the dependent variable' (Cramer & Howitt, 2004, p. 102). Effect sizes are usually measured

DOI: 10.4324/9781003137320-3

by Cohen's *d*, that is 'the difference between two means divided by the combined standard deviation' (Cobb & Boulton, 2015, p. 489).

In order to interpret Cohen's *d* values, a set of benchmark threshold values have been identified, for the purposes of research in the behavioural sciences at large, in Cohen (1988). On the basis of these thresholds, a Cohen's *d* of up to 0.2 would indicate a small effect size, a Cohen's *d* between 0.2 and 0.5 would indicate a medium effect size, and a Cohen's *d* of up to 1.0 would indicate a large effect size. These values were however revised to better fit a second language acquisition research context by Oswald & Plonsky (2010) and then later refined in Plonsky & Oswald (2014). According to these authors, the threshold values should be the following: $d = 0.4$, $d = 0.7$ and $d = 1.0$ for small, medium and large effects respectively (Oswald & Plonsky, 2010, p. 99). When studies are based on pre/post-tests or within-group designs, the authors suggest the following thresholds: $d = 0.6$, $d = 1.0$ and $d = 1.4$ for small, medium and large effects respectively (Plonsky & Oswald, 2014, p. 889).

Meta-analyses are thus able to provide us with an overall picture concerning whether DDL has a positive impact on language learning, and they are able to do so in relation to a number of different moderator variables. The positive effects of DDL are likely, in fact, to be dependent on a potentially wide range of moderator variables, reflecting the complexities that are inherent within any language learning experience, but also the various design and methodological aspects characterising a given study. DDL effects are likely to vary based on *what* is being learned through corpus-based activities, on *who* is learning it by engaging in DDL activities, on *how* DDL has been operationalised, that is what kind of corpus-based materials and activities have been proposed to learners, and on *what* kind of context DDL comes to be part of. The effects emerging from empirical studies on DDL may also be influenced by the way the study was designed, by the size of the participant sample, and by the length of the pedagogical intervention. We now review three meta-analyses on DDL: Mizumoto & Chujo (2015), Boulton & Cobb (2017) and Lee et al. (2018).

In the meta-analysis published by Mizumoto and Chujo (2015), the moderator variables considered are related to what is being learned through DDL and the learner sample. As for the first set of variables, the following areas were examined: vocabulary items, grammar items (basic grammar and grammatical categories such as word classes, nouns, adverbs, derivations, inflections) and phrase items (noun phrase and verb phrase structures, as well as TOEIC/Test of English for International Communication-type questions). As for the second kind of variables, proficiency level was considered as measured by the TOEIC Bridge Test. This meta-analysis focused on studies conducted in Japan and referred to an EFL learning context with Japanese learners. It also included studies published in Japanese, alongside those published in English. This is particularly noteworthy, as previous preliminary meta-analyses such as Boulton and Cobb (2015), as well as subsequent ones, consider only studies published in English, for ease of analysis. Mizumoto and Chujo (2015) include 14 studies in their meta-analysis, corresponding to 32 unique samples of participants. What the authors found was that DDL is most effective for learning vocabulary ($d = 2.93$), and then, though at quite a distance, for learning phrasal items ($d = 0.86$) and the various categories of grammatical items ($d = 0.81$). If we interpret these values against the threshold levels provided by Plonsky and Oswald (2014), the language area exhibiting a large effect size in terms of DDL effectiveness is vocabulary. In terms of how DDL effects measure up against changes in proficiency level, the authors found that the effect size was small ($d = 0.40$). In other words, a DDL approach in second language pedagogy appears to be unlikely to determine changes in proficiency level. However, the authors point out in the discussion of this result that in the case of proficiency changes observable through the TOEIC, a total of at least 100 hours of training is considered as the minimum amount to hope to see changes in proficiency level. DDL studies are rarely set in the context of longitudinal study designs, where the longitudinal timespan is significant and able to incorporate 100 hours of training.

The meta-analysis by Boulton and Cobb (2017) completes their preliminary meta-analysis (Cobb & Boulton, 2015) and introduces 25 moderator variables to the overall analysis of DDL effects:

- *publication* (1. publication date; 2. publication type; 3. journal prestige; 4. paper length);
- *study design* (5. experimental group sample size; 6. control type; 7. constitution of groups; 8. instruments; 9. number of statistical tests; 10. number of other instruments; 11. duration);
- *kind of corpus use* (12. interaction; 13. corpus size; 14. corpus type; 15. corpus use);
- *learning context* (16. ecology – i.e. lab/class; 17. kind of institution; 18. learning specialty – i.e. languages/other; 19. learning aims in terms of language domain – i.e. language for general/specific purposes; 20. foreign/second language);
- *learning aims* (21. learning aims in terms of skills – i.e. listening/speaking/reading/writing/translating; 22. learning aims in terms of language aspect – i.e. vocabulary, lexicogrammar, grammar, discourse);
- *learner background* (23. proficiency level; 24. L1; 25. geographical region).

The breadth of moderator variables considered in this meta-analysis certainly provides insight into the complexity of synthesising DDL effects and breaks new ground in doing so. The meta-analysis includes 64 studies, corresponding to 88 unique samples. In terms of statistical analysis, this time unbiased d (d_{unb}) is the measure of choice. Differently from Cohen's d, unbiased d considers the issue of weighting when studies have small sample sizes, which happens to be frequently the case in DDL research (Boulton & Cobb, 2017, p. 13). The full set of effect sizes for each of the moderator variables considered is available in the supplementary materials of the article (i.e. Appendix S7). The results are reported by making a distinction between within- and between-groups designs, and each reported effect size is based on at least ten samples.

Overall, the authors report finding a large effect size in the evaluation of DDL effects on language gains. The average effect size for within-groups, pre/post designs, the d_{unb} was in fact 1.50. For between-groups, control/experimental designs, the d_{unb} was 0.95, which according to the thresholds set by Oswald and Plonsky would classify as a medium effect size. Low effect sizes were found in cases where the sample size exceeded 50 students in control/experimental designs (d_{unb} = 0.34), and when the proficiency level of the students was lower intermediate (d_{unb} = 0.32). The proficiency level exhibiting the largest effect sizes in both kinds of designs considered was intermediate (d_{unb} = 1.72 for within-groups designs and d_{unb} = 1.27 for between-groups designs). In terms of effect sizes related to the different possible learning aims involved, DDL was found to have an overall medium effect size for developing writing skills (d_{unb} = 1.12). Furthermore, large effects were found for the development of vocabulary and lexicogrammar competence (d_{unb} = 1.54 for both), when considering within-groups designs, while medium effect sizes were found for both language aspects in between-groups designs (d_{unb} = 0.68 and d_{unb} = 0.75 respectively). In terms of the kind of interaction with the corpus that the learners engaged in, large effect sizes were found in studies adopting a computer-based, hands-on approach for within-groups designs (d_{unb} = 1.80), and a slightly lower effect size when considering between-groups designs (d_{unb} = 0.93). As for variables related to the learning context, the meta-analysis found large effect sizes in studies set in foreign language learning contexts, based on either within- or between-groups designs (d_{unb} = 1.56 and d_{unb} = 1.03 respectively). Moreover, DDL was found to be particularly effective with Chinese learners of English (d_{unb} = 1.81) and exhibited a medium effect size when classes were formed by learners of different L1 backgrounds (d_{unb} = 1.35). Negligible effects were found in relation to the following areas: learners forming homogeneous participant samples in terms of L1 background when the L1 is different from Chinese; using a mixed computer/paper-based modality when interacting with corpus data; the development of listening, speaking, reading and translating skills; and the development of discourse competence. These negligible findings may also be due to the fact that not enough studies have been conducted with these foci. Overall, the authors of this meta-analysis report that 60% of the moderator variables produced large effect sizes, whereas 24.5% produced medium effect sizes (Boulton & Cobb, 2017, p. 39).

The meta-analysis published by Lee et al. (2018) differs from that by Boulton & Cobb (2017) in at least three ways. First, it focuses only on DDL for the enhancement of L2 vocabulary learning, and in doing so, it considers different levels of vocabulary knowledge (i.e. precise knowledge; in-depth knowledge; productive use ability). Second, it considers only studies with a between-groups design (i.e. with a control group), and distinguishes between post-test and delayed post-test designs. Third, it adopts a more sophisticated statistical technique (i.e. multilevel regression) and computes the presence of statistically significant differences between the various levels of a given moderator variable. This meta-analysis is based on 29 studies, corresponding to 38 unique samples with post-test effects. Overall, Lee et al. (2018) found that DDL exhibits medium effect sizes with regards to designs with both post-tests (d_{unb} = 0.74) and delayed post-tests (d_{unb} = 0.64). When looking at the different dimensions of vocabulary knowledge, in-depth knowledge returned the highest values (d_{unb} = 0.91), as opposed to productive use ability (d_{unb} = 0.55) and precise knowledge (d_{unb} = 0.40). These values slightly decrease in delayed post-test designs. In both cases, the difference between the effect size produced on the development of in-depth vocabulary knowledge, compared with the other dimensions, is statistically significant. In terms of learners' proficiency levels, a large effect size was found for high proficiency levels (d_{unb} = 1.27), followed by intermediate (d_{unb} = 0.69) and low (d_{unb} = 0.40) proficiency levels. Again, these effects decrease when considering the longer temporal dimensions of the studies, as a medium statistically significant difference was found. This, together with the limited data available for the higher proficiency groups, lead the authors of this meta-analysis to cautiously claim that 'corpus use could be more effective for intermediate and high proficiency learners than for low proficiency learners' (Lee et al., 2018, p. 23).

When considering the different ways in which DDL can be pedagogically operationalised, Lee et al. (2018) found that a mixed approach, combining computer- and paper-based modalities, has large effect sizes, both in short-term (d_{unb} = 1.30) and long-term (d_{unb} = 1.11) studies. A comparison of effect sizes between the different levels revealed medium-sized statistically significant differences. Another aspect that this meta-analysis considers is the length of the DDL intervention. When comparing a short (i.e. two hours in total or one session), a medium (i.e. about three to eight sessions) and a long exposure (i.e. ten sessions or more) to the approach, the largest effect sizes are found in relation to long exposures (d_{unb} = 0.90). However, no statistically significant differences were found between the different levels of this variable, possibly, as the authors point out, because of the small sample sizes (Lee et al., 2018, p. 25). In terms of corpus type, in addition to public and local corpora, Lee et al. (2018) add 'pre-selected concordance lines'. This turns out to be a good choice, as the largest effect size that the meta-analysis finds in relation to this aspect is this newly added level (d_{unb} = 0.98). The difference between this level and the other ones was significant. As the authors say, in fact, 'we found that careful selection of concordance lines by teachers or researchers had a large impact on improving L2 vocabulary knowledge' (Lee et al., 2018, p. 25). Finally, one moderator variable that was looked at is whether having received training on corpora has an impact on DDL effects. It was found, with sole reference to the shorter-term studies, that having received training does produce a larger effect (d_{unb} = 0.72) as opposed to not having received any (d_{unb} = 0.58). However, as the difference between these two values is not statistically significant, having received specific training on corpora prior to engaging in DDL activities might be negligible.

The three meta-analyses, synthesised in Table 3.1, highlight a number of avenues and recommendations for future DDL research and future operationalisations of DDL practices. In order to overcome the challenges

Table 3.1 Summary of meta-analyses on DDL

	Mizumoto & Chujo, 2015	Boulton & Cobb, 2017	Lee et al., 2018
Inclusion criteria	- Studies conducted in Japan - English as target language - Studies published in English and in Japanese - All learning aims	- English as target language in most cases - Studies published in English - All learning aims	- English and languages other than English as target language - Studies published in English - Vocabulary only as learning aim
Design	Only within groups (pre/post-test)	Within and between groups (pre/post-test and control/experimental)	Only between groups (control/experimental)
Moderator variables	1. Language learning focus (lemma, category, phrase, proficiency)	1. Publication date, 2. Publication type, 3. Journal prestige, 4. Paper length, 5. EG sample size, 6. Control type, 7. Constitution of groups, 8. Instruments, 9. Statistical tests, 10. Other instruments, 11. Region, 12. Context, 13. L1, 14. Proficiency, 15. Specialty, 16. Institution, 17. Ecology, 18. Duration, 19. Interaction,	1. Publication type, 2. Region, 3. Proficiency, 4. Specialty, 5. Interaction type, 6. Corpus type, 7. L2 vocabulary dimension, 8. Training, 9. Duration.

(continued)

Table 3.1 Cont.

	Mizumoto & Chujo, 2015	Boulton & Cobb, 2017	Lee et al., 2018
		20. Corpus size, 21. Corpus type, 22. Objective, 23. Use, 24. Language skill, 25. Language aspect.	
N. of individual samples	32	88	38 (post-test) 13 (delayed post-test)
Type of measure	Cohen's d	Unbiased d	Multilevel regression Unbiased d
Overall result	$d = 0.90$	$d_{unb} = 1.51$ (within groups, pre/post-test) $d_{unb} = 0.95$ (between groups, control/experimental)	$d_{unb} = 0.74$ (post-tests) $d_{unb} = 0.64$ (delayed post-tests)
Interpretation of results according to Plonsky & Oswald, 2014	Medium effect size	Large effect size (within groups, pre/post-test) Medium effect size (between groups, control/experimental)	Medium effect size (post-tests) Small effect size (delayed post-tests)

that DDL poses, for example, Mizumoto & Chujo (2015) maintain that 'advocates of the DDL approach will need to address these problems and limitations by supplying a complete concrete package, which includes an example of syllabi, teaching plans, sample lessons, materials, teaching manuals, and a user-friendly concordance tool' (Mizumoto & Chujo, 2015, p. 12), thus focusing on the need to make DDL both more teacher- and learner-friendly, so as to extend the contexts in which it may be applied. In concluding that 'DDL works pretty well in almost any context where it has been extensively tried', Boulton & Cobb (2017, p. 386), in fact, point out that there is still a number of contexts for which there is limited or no research evidence for DDL effects. The authors stress the need for better reporting in empirical studies on DDL, so that they are compliant with the needs of meta-analyses, while also calling for more studies on languages other than English, teaching and learning contexts other than academic, and more longitudinal studies in order to gain a more accurate picture concerning delayed effects. Lee et al. (2018) also 'call for the accumulation of more empirical evidence' (Lee et al., 2018, p. 29), while highlighting the value in considering possible interactions between proficiency levels and different dimensions of L2 vocabulary knowledge, and by extension L2 knowledge at large. Next, we look at how learners and teachers engage with DDL in terms of perceived benefits and challenges that may characterise the approach.

3.2 How do learners and teachers respond to DDL?

In order for a teaching and learning approach to work, in terms of being beneficial to learners of a language and to the teachers teaching the language, it is also necessary to look at how it is perceived by learners and teachers, and how learners and teachers react when they are presented with it. While a number of research syntheses in the form of meta-analyses have been published in relation to DDL effects on language gains, as we saw in the previous section, fewer systematic reviews seem to have looked at learner and teacher attitudes. One of these is the paper *Popularising corpus consultation by language learners and teachers*, by Angela Chambers (Chambers, 2007). In this paper, a total of 12 key studies in the domain of DDL are reviewed in relation to the features of DDL that may contribute to its popularisation in language teaching contexts, and to the features of DDL that may still pose obstacles in this respect.

Most of the studies selected by Chambers are specifically focused on learner attitudes towards DDL, which in most, though not all, cases were elicited by means of a questionnaire (Bernardini, 2000, 2002; Chambers, 2005; Chambers & O'Sullivan, 2004; Cheng et al., 2003; Johns, 1997; Kennedy & Miceli, 2001, 2010; Sun, 2003; Yoon & Hirvela, 2004). The author notes not only the low number of studies considered, but also the considerable variety of the studies examined in relation to target languages, size and content of the corpora being used with the learners, and the different ways in which corpora were used with and by learners. The data on learner attitudes elicited in the selected studies is also quite varied in terms of the data elicitation tools adopted. Chambers enlists the following methods: 'accounts of the activities undertaken by the learners accompanied by comments by the author on the students' findings and reactions; comments by the author on the students' findings and reactions; presentations of the results of the students' work with the corpora (in varying degrees of detail); direct accounts of the learners' reactions to and evaluations of the activity, sometimes but not always questionnaire-based; observations by the researcher; trialling; think-aloud protocol' (Chambers, 2007, p. 7). While such a degree of methodological variety certainly poses a challenge to the elaboration of a synthesis, Chambers effectively identifies the positive and the negative attitudes towards DDL that overall the selected papers shed light on.

One aspect of DDL that seems to be appreciated by the learners is related to the perceived authenticity of the language data they interact with, and its relevance for language learning and beyond. In Chambers (2005) we find that

> one student wrote, 'the French used in these articles is authentic, up to date, and relevant'. The word 'real' is also used to describe the corpus, in contrast to the invented examples in course books and grammars, which are described by one student as 'unreal and sometimes stupid'.
>
> (Chambers, 2005, p. 120)

These comments show the learners' sensitivity to the quality of language examples, even when they are shown in a language they are still learning. It also demonstrates their need and their expectation to be able to inform their learning with language that reflects the target language as truthfully as possible, across a range of variational dimensions. Furthermore, Cheng et al. (2003) report that 'students enjoyed learning through corpora because this constitutes systematic study of authentic language', and while referencing Sinclair (1997, p. 31), they also report that students 'agreed that corpora helped to transform the study of language from an environment which has been "evidence scarce" to one which is "evidence abundant"' (Cheng et al., 2003, p. 181). The numerosity of the examples provided by a concordance is, in fact, one aspect of DDL that learners seem to particularly appreciate, and which sets DDL apart from dictionaries.

Examples offered by a concordance are not just deemed abundant in comparison to a dictionary, but also relevant and rich, because they are contextualised. As reported by Yoon & Hirvela (2004, p. 275), a student commented as follows: 'I use a dictionary as the first choice, and if there is ambiguous, and [I want] to know the word in context, then [I] use the corpus as the second resource'. This is a particularly interesting comment, if we consider the terms of the cotext vs. context debate, which we described in section 2.6. While some consider the cotext offered by a concordance as generally insufficient to reconstruct the context it derives from, learners seem to mostly be able to reconstruct such context. More specifically, when focusing on a specific language unit in the form of a word or word combination, learners are able to observe regularities on the basis of the cotexts on the left and on the right of the node word/word combination. When the cotext is not enough to satisfy the need to understand the context of occurrence of the word/word combination, most computer-based corpus exploration tools can enable the learners to retrieve the full text within which the unit occurs. Taken together, authenticity, relevance, and numerosity can be seen as a pathway to extended contextualisation. As put by Silvia Bernardini, students 'rapidly appreciated the relevance of what they had learnt to their current activities and future profession(s)' and they 'offered reflections and insights about their native language that clearly showed they were seeing connections and reflecting on issues that went well beyond those briefly touched upon during our first meeting' (Bernardini, 2002, p. 179). These comments indicate that despite the possibly limited span that the cotext of concordance lines may have – though it can in most cases be expanded – the numerosity and authenticity of the examples are factors that are able to provide learners with sufficient means to perceive a broader context beyond the concordance lines, and even to establish connections between the concordance and other language content derived from elsewhere (e.g., other parts of the lesson, other lessons, linguistic experiences outside the classroom).

Another aspect of DDL that Chambers finds learners reacting overall positively to is the largely inductive, discovery-based process involved in the exploration of corpus data. The presence of the teacher as a guide or demonstrator, accompanying the learners along the way of exploring linguistic data extracted from a corpus, with the view of making learning increasingly more independent, is reported as being highly motivating and empowering. As we read in Bernardini (2002, p. 179), the students 'liked the idea of feeling competent, of having a say in what was happening around them', which may have been something they were not entirely used to. Chambers (2005, p. 120) reports one student commenting as follows: 'I discovered that achieving results from my concordance was a highly motivating and enriching experience. I've never encountered such an experience from a textbook'. These comments are particularly interesting because they show how an inductive, discovery-based and, if needed, adequately scaffolded approach to corpus exploration is conducive to fostering motivation, autonomy and overall positive attitudes towards DDL.

The negative comments reported by students, and synthesised by Chambers, are largely related to the initial difficulty involved in getting familiar with the approach and learning how to use corpus exploration tools. In Cheng et al. (2003), the difficulties described by learners are divided into difficulties related to the corpus exploration activity and difficulties related to the nature of corpus data that were explored (Cheng et al., 2003, p. 182). As for the first category of difficulties, learners lamented that they did not have the 'knowledge and skills in choosing and using corpora and in using computer software like concordancers' and that the available functions of the corpus they used limited the potential gleaning adequate corpus-derived responses concerning the intended area of investigation (Cheng et al., 2003, p. 183). Furthermore, learners found, at times, the corpus data insufficient to enable them to confirm or refute their hypotheses on language use (2003, p. 183). As for the second category of difficulties, learners found it 'too laborious' to obtain and analyse data from a corpus: 'the actual counting of frequencies of occurrence, classifying data into word classes, and working out percentages were tedious tasks to perform' (2003, p. 183). The authors also mention that frequency word lists were 'too overbearing', and that at times learners found it difficult to categorise the examples of a concordance in a meaningful way, that is, in a way that would be useful to their learning process (2003, p. 183). This sense of being overwhelmed by the information provided by a corpus was also found by Yoon & Hirvela (2004), who report that one student who had had limited previous language learning experience 'complained about too many sentences being present on the screen' (Yoon & Hirvela, 2004).

Some students did highlight difficulties related to the truncated nature of the examples found in a corpus (Chambers, 2007, p. 11). Although these comments would tend to be representative of a minority of students (Yoon & Hirvela, 2004; Chambers, 2005), they should still be taken into account as instances of DDL in which the ability to induce a larger context from the cotexts provided in the concordance was not able to be realised. In relation to how DDL might be time-consuming, along with difficult, Yoon & Hirvela (2004) provide an interesting comment by a student:

> Interpretation of the corpus results is difficult. It gives me a headache. Look for all the sentences. I don't know. For dictionary, just put the word, enter, and you find that. Dictionary doesn't give me a headache. Dictionary doesn't take long time. But the problem is dictionary give you a lot of words, but I don't know which one is the right one in the sentence... That is the problem with dictionary. It doesn't take long time, but it gives me another answer. Doesn't give me which one fits in this sentence.
>
> (Yoon & Hirvela, 2004, p. 274)

While expressing annoyance with corpora, and doing so quite vividly (e.g., 'it gives me a headache'), the student compares the use of corpora with the use of dictionaries, and effectively enlists pros and cons of the two resources: corpora give headaches, but also information of the appropriateness of a word within the context of a sentence, while dictionaries do not give headaches, as they provide immediate answers to our questions, but they do not always tell us whether the word fits in a given sentence. In Chambers and O'Sullivan (2004), some of the negative comments by students focused on the fact that a corpus 'doesn't always give you suggestions on how to change a phrase' and that 'there isn't always an occurrence of the word required' (Chambers and O'Sullivan, 2004, p. 169). The latter situation may also depend on the corpus of choice, while the former comment may be linked to the need for mediation with a teacher or with peers. In both of these cases, the issue of training and trainability emerges as crucial, and was one of the moderator variables considered in the meta-analysis by Lee et al. (2018). Overall, as concluded by Chambers (2007), 'while these disadvantages are small in number, they are major obstacles for those who aim to popularise corpus consultation among learners'.

The way in which corpus use is perceived and received in the classroom also concerns the teachers' point of view. While there has been a dearth of evidence regarding this perspective of DDL effects in language learning contexts for quite some time, there are now several studies that shed light on the teachers' take on corpus use in the classroom, in relation to both perceived benefits and perceived challenges. In 2015, Christopher Tribble published the results of a survey aimed at teachers regarding DDL, based on data from 560 respondents from 63 countries (Tribble, 2015). The survey contained a specific section on perceived benefits and challenges of corpora from the teachers' perspectives, where teachers were invited to respond to a number of open-ended questions. Tribble created two corpora: one made of all the responses related to reasons *for* using corpora, and another one made of all responses related to reasons *for not* using corpora. He then extracted four-word clusters from each, in order to view how the most frequent four-word cluster units from each set differed. When considering the reasons *for* using corpora, the words that kept recurring at the top of the list manifested recognition of some of the main benefits in using corpora for language learning: being able to have information on how *language is actually used* (most frequent four-word cluster), thus information that is *relevant for language education* (most frequent four-word cluster, highlighting an aspect different than *authenticity* of corpus data); being able to have *examples of language use* (most frequent four-word cluster, highlighting an aspect different from *authenticity* and *relevance* of corpus data) for a certain form; being able to provide relevant, authentic and quantitatively dense linguistic input *for non native speakers* (most frequent four-word cluster, highlighting an aspect different than *authenticity, relevance* and *numerosity of examples*), who need to enrich the L2 linguistic environment within which their language learning occurs (Tribble, 2015, p. 56). When considering reasons *for not* using corpora, on the other hand, the two main notions emerging relate to the fact that teachers often *do not know how* (most frequent four-word cluster) to use corpora for pedagogical purposes, and even when they have had some exposure to them, that corpus use *can be time consuming* (most frequent four-word cluster, highlighting an aspect different than not knowing how to use corpora in the classroom). These findings seem to reflect Farr (2008)'s results, which were based on a much smaller sample of respondents (n = 25) but were still able to capture a number of key aspects related to positive and negative attitudes towards DDL, which Tribble would later find in his larger study. They are also in line with Mukherjee (2004)'s earlier survey, focused on English language teaching in Germany.

These findings are particularly interesting, as they point out the features of DDL that teachers are most immediately able to perceive, while also stressing the need to expand corpus-informed teacher-training experiences, as well as the development of guides to support teachers in creating DDL activities, materials, corpora and corpus exploration tools that are more suitable to the language classroom (e.g., Vyatkina, 2020). Much can be done in terms of awareness raising when it comes to the benefits of corpus use in the L2 classroom. In a plenary talk given by Ana Frankenberg-Garcia at the 7th Teaching and Language Corpora Conference, a number of task-based activities based on the exploration of corpora and aimed at teachers were shown (Frankenberg-Garcia, 2012). The underlining assumption is that for teachers to be able to guide learners through the discovery of language patterns, they will first need to be themselves guided through this process and through the tools that enable it. Integrating corpora in language teacher training has been shown to have the potential of helping teachers to improve their teaching, while providing researchers with new insight into how the corpus-oriented teacher training course may be improved (Leńko-Szymańska, 2014). Although it has been shown how little effort the integration of corpora in language teacher training course such as CELTA would require (Naismith, 2016), and although new books aimed at teachers are being published (e.g., Friginal, 2018), adding to the list of volumes published previously (see Tribble, 2015, p. 54 for a list of ten books), the way towards normalising DDL practices in the broader language teaching domain seems to still be quite long (Pérez-Paredes, 2019). In conceptualising the notion of bridging the gap between corpus linguistics and the reality of teaching, it has been suggested that this 'could mean an exploration of what already works for English teachers who use corpus methods, and feeding that back into the corpus training that pre-service teachers are provided with' (Kavanagh, 2019).

3.3 Italian L2 and the research evidence on DDL effects

As we saw in 2.5., the empirical data on DDL effects related to the domain of Italian L2 learning and teaching is still quite scarce. It covers a mere 22% of the total (Boulton & Cobb, 2017), and derives from two sources: the studies conducted by Kennedy and Miceli at Griffith University (Kennedy & Miceli, 2001; 2010; 2016), and the studies stemming from my PhD thesis (Forti, 2019), which will be described later in this book. In Kennedy & Miceli (2001), the authors make a series of systematic observations related to how successfully learners manage to extract and interpret linguistic data from a corpus, in the absence of a teacher. The observations were made in relation to the following four steps involved in corpus investigation: '(a) formulating the question; (b) devising a search strategy; (c) observing the examples found and selecting relevant ones; and (d) drawing conclusions' (Kennedy & Miceli, 2001, p. 81). The authors found that corpus consultation by students was often not initiated by a clear question, and that students did not seem to be able to evaluate how specific or generic a question should be. One vivid example of this is shown below:

> We observed this in students' handling of one of the individual set tasks, that of choosing between **Il lunedì scorso** siamo andati all'università and **Lunedì scorso** siamo andati all'università for Last Monday we went to university. The issue is whether the definite article is used with lunedì scorso (last Monday) and the answer is 'no'. Some asked the question 'How does scorso (last) behave?' rather than 'How does lunedì scorso

behave?' This meant dealing with *scorso* in several contexts, some with an article and some without.

(Kennedy & Miceli, 2001, p. 83)

Other issues in the autonomous exploration of corpora that Kennedy and Miceli found were connected to not knowing whether to formulate questions in an open or closed format. After trying out closed-ended questions such as 'Do you say *orario per*', the students reformulated the question as 'So what *do* you use after *orario*?', but did not seem to be able to do so systematically, which led them to some unfruitful corpus searches. Building on these observations, in their 2010 paper Kennedy and Miceli reported on a semester-long apprenticeship in corpus consultation (Kennedy & Miceli, 2010). The apprenticeship was aimed at introducing students to corpora gradually, first by demonstrating their uses 'as an aid to the imagination in writing' (Kennedy & Miceli, 2010, p. 28), and only subsequently as an aid to achieve 'accuracy through specific grammatical problem solving' (Kennedy & Miceli, 2010, p. 28). The authors compare and contrast the uses that students make of a corpus and of a dictionary, examining how effective these uses are, which factors influence their propensity and ability to use these sources, and thus how their designed apprenticeship can be improved (Kennedy & Miceli, 2010, p. 35). Much valuable insight is gathered from the three case studies they conducted, especially in relation to how the three participants involved in the study were able to develop individual 'reference-resource-using styles', although these styles did not always include all the ways in which the authors would have liked students to use the corpus (Kennedy & Miceli, 2010, p. 40).

Kennedy and Miceli's paper published in 2016 further builds on the previously published studies, by evaluating the effectiveness of the apprenticeship in corpus use that the authors design on the basis of their experience (Kennedy & Miceli, 2016). Their aim here is to '*downplay* the learner-as-researcher notion, and instead seek to cultivate in learners a propensity for open-ended searches, and 'observe and borrow chunks' mentality' (Kennedy & Miceli, 2016, p. 3). This time, their study involved a larger group of participants (n = 24), and focused on how the corpus was used and how fruitfully in enhancing the students' writing skills, on what makes a learner an effective corpus user, and in what ways the designed apprenticeship helps learners' development as corpus users for their language learning needs. By analysing data from students' accounts of corpus use, a reflection forum, and individual interviews, the authors report on largely positive outcomes, and conclude that although in many respects their approach is highly context-specific, their conceptualisation of learner-oriented corpus-consultation literacy can have great potential in the development of autonomous language learners, beyond the specific context they investigate.

The empirical work done by Kennedy & Miceli over the years is highly valuable as it informs us on the process of becoming acquainted with a corpus, from a learners' perspective, with emic data from the learners themselves. As far as DDL for Italian is concerned, no empirical evidence seems to be available in relation to teachers' perspectives, which is likely to be due to the approach still being largely unknown to the Italian L2 teaching community, both in and outside of Italy.

3.4 Chapter summary and conclusions

In this chapter we surveyed the research evidence available in relation to DDL effects. Two main perspectives were considered: the perspective related to language competence gains as a result of exposure to and interaction with corpora, and the perspective reflecting learners' and teachers' attitudes and perceptions related to DDL. As for the first perspective, the chapter underscored the value of meta-analyses in providing an overall view of DDL effects, and synthesised the ones that are available to date. While different approaches have been adopted over the years, both in terms of meta-analytic focus and in terms of statistical techniques used, DDL is found to be generally effective for language learning purposes. However, a number of limitations in empirical DDL research emerge, which in turn nurture a series of desiderata: more DDL empirical research is needed, with an increased attention to languages other than English, contexts other than academic, different dimensions of language knowledge and sound reporting practices, in order to favour comparability among studies, especially for meta-analytic purposes. As for the second perspective, we saw how the research evidence sheds light on positive and negative attitudes stemming from the exposure to DDL. While even more research is needed here to nurture our understanding of this perspective, the challenges found by learners and teachers are a precious resource to help us operationalise DDL in a way that overcomes such challenges. As we will see in the next chapter, translating DDL principles into language learning activities is a fascinating domain in which much is still to be explored. Furthermore, corpus exploration tools with language learners in mind are being developed at a faster pace than before. As a result, more empirical research is to be expected where these tools are the main foci of evaluation.

The empirical evidence on DDL effects would certainly benefit from more studies integrating both perspectives. The combination of these two perspectives seems to still be quite rare, with most studies focusing on either one or the other. Integrating both perspectives in single studies, and thus with reference to a single participant cohort, would help provide a more ecological view of DDL effects, with the possibility of examining the relationships between the two perspectives. More data on the longer-term effects of DDL would help us trace the complexities involved in making learners better learners, by fostering self-regulation and autonomy through DDL activities. More data on teachers' views and needs would provide a significant contribution for fostering the co-development of DDL pedagogical practices with a better integration within more general teaching practices. More data on learners' views would be instrumental in bridging the gap between corpora for linguists and corpora for learners (Forti & Spina, 2019), by addressing learner needs from the very construction of corpora and corpus exploration tools. While contributing to the normalisation of DDL in language learning and teaching (Pérez-Paredes, 2019), an increase in these lines of research would certainly provide a new foundation for our understanding of DDL benefits and potential. In the next chapter, we look at how the numerous methodological challenges involved in conducting empirical DDL research may be addressed.

References

Bernardini, S. (2000). Systematising serendipity: Proposals for concordancing large corpora with language learners. In L. Burnard & T. McEnery (Eds.), *Rethinking language pedagogy from a corpus perspective* (pp. 225–234). Peter Lang.

Bernardini, S. (2002). Exploring new directions for discovery learning. In B. Kettemann & G. Marko (Eds.), *Teaching and learning by doing corpus analysis* (pp. 165–182). Rodopi.

Boulton, A., & Cobb, T. (2017). Corpus use in language learning: A meta-analysis. *Language Learning, 67*(2), 348–393.

Chambers, A. (2005). Integrating corpus consultation in language studies. *Language Learning and Technology, 9*(2), 111–125.

Chambers, A. (2007). Popularising corpus consultation by language learners and teachers. *Language and Computers, 61*(1), 3–16.

Chambers, A., & O'Sullivan, Í. (2004). Corpus consultation and advanced learners' writing skills in French. *ReCALL, 16*(01), 158–172.

Cheng, W., Warren, M., & Xun-feng, X. (2003). The language learner as language researcher: Putting corpus linguistics on the timetable. *System, 31*(2), 173–186.

Cobb, T., & Boulton, A. (2015). Classroom applications of corpus analysis. In D. Biber & R. Reppen (Eds.), *The Cambridge handbook of English corpus linguistics* (pp. 478–497). Cambridge University Press.

Cohen, J. (1988). *Statistical power analysis for the behavioral sciences*. Lawrence Erlbaum Associates.

Cramer, D., & Howitt, D. (2004). *The SAGE dictionary of statistics*. SAGE.

Farr, F. (2008). Evaluating the use of corpus-based instruction in a language teacher education context: Perspectives from the users. *Language Awareness, 17*(1), 25–43.

Forti, L. (2019). *Developing phraseological competence in Italian L2: A study on the effects of Data-driven learning*. Unpublished PhD thesis. Università per Stranieri di Perugia.

Forti, L., & Spina, S. (2019). Corpora for linguists vs. corpora for learners: Bridging the gap in Italian L2 Learning and Teaching. *EL.LE – Educazione Linguistica. Language Education, 8*(2), 349–362.

Frankenberg-Garcia, A. (2012). Raising teachers' awareness of corpora. *Language Teaching, 45*(4), 475–489.

Friginal, E. (2018). *Corpus linguistics for English teachers: Tools, online resources, and classroom activities*. Routledge.

Johns, T. (1997). Contexts: E background, development and trialling of a concordance-based CALL program. In A. Wichmann, S. Fligelstone, T. McEnery, & G. Knowles (Eds.), *Teaching and language corpora* (pp. 100–115). Addison Wesley Longman.

Kavanagh, B. (2019). *Using 'what already works' to 'bridge the gap' between corpus research and corpora in schools*. Learner Corpus Research Conference 2019, Warsaw.

Kennedy, C., & Miceli, T. (2001). An evaluation of intermediate students' approaches to corpus investigation. *Language Learning & Technology, 5*(3), 77–90.

Kennedy, C., & Miceli, T. (2010). Corpus-assisted creative writing: Introducing intermediate Italian learners to a corpus as a reference resource. *Language Learning & Technology, 14*(1), 28–44.

Kennedy, C., & Miceli, T. (2016). Cultivating effective corpus use by language learners. *Computer Assisted Language Learning, 30*(1–2), 91–114.

Lee, H., Warschauer, M., & Lee, J.H. (2018). The effects of corpus use on second language vocabulary learning: A multilevel meta-analysis. *Applied Linguistics, 40*(5), 721–753.

Leńko-Szymańska, A. (2014). Is this enough? A qualitative evaluation of the effectiveness of a teacher-training course on the use of corpora in language education. *ReCALL, 26*(02), 260–278.

Mizumoto, A., & Chujo, K. (2015). A meta-analysis of data-driven learning approach in the Japanese EFL Classroom. *English Corpus Studies, 22*, 1–18.

Mukherjee, J. (2004). Bridging the gap between applied corpus linguistics and the reality of English language teaching in Germany. *Language and Computers, 52*(1), 239–250.

Naismith, B. (2016). Integrating corpus tools on intensive CELTA courses. *ELT Journal, 71*(3), 273–283.

Oswald, F.L., & Plonsky, L. (2010). Meta-analysis in second language research: Choices and challenges. *Annual Review of Applied Linguistics, 30*, 85–110.

Pérez-Paredes, P. (2019). A systematic review of the uses and spread of corpora and data-driven learning in CALL research during 2011–2015. *Computer Assisted Language Learning, 35*(1–2), 36–61.

Plonsky, L., & Oswald, F. L. (2014). How big is 'big'? Interpreting effect sizes in L2 research: Effect sizes in L2 research. *Language Learning, 64*(4), 878–912.

Sinclair, J. (1997). Corpus evidence in language description. In A. Wichmann, S. Fligelstone, A. McEnery, & G. Knowles (Eds.), *Teaching and language corpora* (pp. 27–39). Longman.

Sun, Y.-C. (2003). Learning process, strategies and web-based concordancers: A case study. *British Journal of Educational Technology, 34*(5), 601–613.

Tribble, C. (2015). Teaching and language corpora: Perspectives from a personal journey. In A. Leńko-Szymańska & A. Boulton (Eds.), *Multiple affordances of language corpora for data-driven learning* (pp. 37–62). Benjamins.

Vyatkina, N. (2020). Corpora as open educational resources for language teaching. *Foreign Language Annals, 52*(2), 359–370.

Yoon, H., & Hirvela, A. (2004). ESL student attitudes toward corpus use in L2 writing. *Journal of Second Language Writing, 13*(4), 257–283.

4 Methods in researching data-driven learning effects

In this chapter, we outline the basic requirements that a solid empirical research design needs to satisfy when seeking to evaluate the effects of DDL on second/foreign language learning. We also illustrate the variety of options that are available when choosing the variables that one wishes to focus on. The pedagogical operationalisation of the DDL construct, in particular, is presented as key in the definition of the empirical data collection tools. The nature of the activities designed to implement DDL principles will determine the activation of specific learning processes. The collection of empirical data will need to tap into those processes in order to make the evaluation of their effects possible. The chapter also contains some general guidelines for the analysis and interpretation of the collected data.

4.1 The nature of knowledge in researching DDL effects

In 2007, Alex Boulton presented a paper entitled 'But where's the proof? The need for empirical evidence for data-driven learning' at the British Association for Applied Linguistics (BAAL) conference. This interest for investigating the empirical foundation of DDL, to prove that it was not just an approach that corpus linguists enthusiastically supported but a real opportunity for improving language learning and teaching, would lead to the more systematic meta-analysis of empirical studies that we reviewed in the previous chapter (Mizumoto & Chujo, 2015; Boulton & Cobb, 2017; Lee et al., 2018).

The need for empirical evidence is more crucial than ever today. Corpora are still largely unknown to the population of language teachers and DDL is far from being consistently integrated into teacher-training programs. Open educational resources for teachers and/or in-training teachers have been starting to surface on the web in the past couple of years, in the form of websites, open-source books and even Moocs (Crosthwaite, 2020; Le Foll, 2021; Vyatkina, 2020). Books specifically tailored for teachers and learners have also been published of late (Friginal, 2018; Poole, 2018). However, demonstrating that DDL works remains crucial in the process of spreading and normalising the approach within teaching practices. To

DOI: 10.4324/9781003137320-4

conduct empirical studies on DDL effects that can help us proceed in this direction, it is necessary to take a step back and look at what it means to conduct scientific research. How can scientific research help us in gaining insights into DDL effects and effectiveness?

A number of manuals on research methods in the educational and social sciences are good starting points (Dörnyei, 2007; Howitt & Cramer, 2020; Mackey & Gass, 2012; Phakiti et al., 2018; Riazi, 2016b). While referring to these manuals for more in-depth readings, we will now summarise some of the main aspects characterising the scientific method, which will be helpful to the DDL researcher.

One essential question is: what is knowledge? Another essential question is: how do we know what we know? And finally, why do we choose knowledge based on the scientific method as opposed to knowledge deriving from other sources? In relation to the first question:

> Knowledge can refer to both theoretical and practical understanding of a subject, which includes facts, descriptions, information, and skills acquired through experience or learnt through books or other means. In other words, knowledge can be *implicit knowledge* as with practical skills or *explicit knowledge* as with the theoretical understanding of a subject.
>
> (Thomas, 2021, p. 2)

In view of DDL dissemination practices, both kinds of knowledge are key: researchers must have practical skills in relation to how a DDL activity may be constructed, as well as a theoretical understanding of the pedagogical and linguistic underpinnings of the approach. They must also have solid information on how DDL has been implemented in language classrooms and what the state of the art is in relation to its potential benefits. But how do we gain knowledge reflecting the nature of a subject? Christensen (2007) identifies six main sources of knowledge:

1. tenacity
2. intuition
3. authority
4. rationalism
5. empiricism
6. science

Tenacity is defined as 'a method of acquiring knowledge based on superstition or habit' (Christensen, 2007, p. 5). The author adds that 'the more we are exposed to something or the more familiar it becomes, the more we like it' (2007, p. 5). This is a form of knowledge stemming from 'mere exposure', thus deriving from a personal repeated experience. However, the author points at two main shortcomings characterising this kind of knowledge.

First, knowledge acquired through the exposure to certain experiences may be inaccurate. For example, if we think of the proverb 'You can't teach an old dog new tricks', we may believe what it says because we are used to being exposed to situations that confirm this statement, but we may miss out on the cases where elderly people can and do, in fact, learn. Similarly, we may very well feel tenacious about our beliefs regarding DDL, be enthusiastic about corpora, about their descriptive power, and feel that they would be so beneficial in teaching and learning in a vast range of domains. We may have personal exposure to the benefits of DDL, in the context of our personal teaching experience, but this may be inaccurate and hardly generalisable. Second, tenacity does not have a way of correcting beliefs, as those expressed by commonly known sayings, in the face of evidence. Those statements are absolute, thus they do not allow for previsions of the contrary to what they maintain. Interestingly, Christensen points out how tenacity nevertheless plays a role in scientific research, and how the determination of a researcher in the face of initial lack of evidence, may be the very factor leading them towards the development of methods and research tools that will eventually lead to the elicitation of the desired or expected data. DDL researchers may be tenacious about the benefits of DDL, in spite of negative evidence.

The second way of gaining knowledge is through intuition. It is defined as 'an approach to acquiring knowledge that is not based on reasoning or inferring' (Christensen, 2007, p. 6). An example of intuitive knowledge is that of psychics, which are not based on any form of reasoning or inference. The example provided by Christensen is that we may have an intuition about women being better judges of the quality of a relationship in comparison to men. This intuition will not be based on any reasoning or inference, so it will not constitute a form of scientific knowledge. Rather, it may be considered as a cultural stereotype. Nevertheless, it can be useful in guiding us towards devising a scientific study able to investigate this intuition, to establish whether there is any evidence supporting this claim. We may question the interconnection between the ability of evaluating the quality of a relationship and gender. We may even question the binary conceptualisation of gender itself. We may, in other words, devise a study based on our intuition and collect data in search of evidence, which may very well be unsupportive of our intuition. In DDL, we may have the intuition that it might be a beneficial approach beyond what we know about it, in terms of the empirical evidence available, because of its sound theoretical basis. We would still collect the data to see if our intuition is correct.

The third way of gaining knowledge is through authority. This happens when we accept certain pieces of information solely based on where they come from: a 'highly respected source' (Christensen, 2007, p. 7). When a totalitarian state issues a decree declaring something to be illegal (e.g., the use of foreign words during the years of Fascism in Italy), no one will have the right to question what the decree is declaring. Facts imposed by decree will not derive from accurate knowledge, they will just have to be accepted and there will be no way of establishing their inaccuracy. Nevertheless, authority can still be used in science. As Christensen points out, consultation with a person considered as an authority within a given field may help in assessing the testability of an intuition or hypothesis. In fact, large research projects are usually led by authorities, who are assumed to have significant experience and knowledge related to a given research topic. Early career researchers, starting from PhD candidates, will have advisors helping them throughout the various stages of their research endeavours, especially in the development of the design of the study. However, knowledge stemming from authority can still be inaccurate and misleading, thus requiring other sources to be supported and reliable.

A fourth way to attain knowledge on a given topic is via rationalism, which is defined as 'the acquisition of knowledge through reasoning' (Christensen, 2007, p. 7). It maintains that truth can be reached only through a correct reasoning process. Christensen shares an anecdote reflecting an extreme example of knowledge gained through rationalism. It is a story recounted by Francis Bacon. It is about a quarrel over the number of teeth that are present in the mouth of a horse. For 13 days, several disputants engaged in discussion. On the fourteenth day, a proposal was made by a young friar: to look inside the mouth of a horse. This proposal was deemed unacceptable. The disputants agreed that the problem would have needed to be considered as 'an everlasting mystery because of the grievous dearth of historical and theological evidence' (Christensen, 2007, p. 8). Rationalism as reasoning with no connection to reality will inevitably lead to issues in relation to how accurate it might reflect reality itself. DDL 'makes sense', in that it can rationally be argued as being a pedagogical approach that could improve teaching and learning practices. But is it really so? Of course, like in the other cases, rationalism has its place in science. A scientist will use rationalism in formulating hypotheses and developing appropriate methods to test them. However, it would not be able to stand on its own, without an empirical basis.

A fifth way to gain knowledge is, thus, through empiricism. 'The approach says, 'If I have experienced something, then it is valid and true" (Christensen, 2007, p. 7). Christensen provides the example of members of religious groups claiming to have heard satanic messages when playing some music records backwards. Because they claim to have heard such messages, the phenomenon they are talking about is considered as true, valid and irrefutable. However, there are several issues here. First, perception can be affected by other factors. One can, for example, wear a special kind of glasses which make the world look as if it is turned upside down. In this respect, Christensen mentions the experiment carried out by G.M. Stratton and reported in the article 'Vision without inversion of the retinal image', published in the journal *Psychological Review* in 1897. Stratton wore the special glasses for several days. At first, everything looked the opposite as to how Stratton was used to seeing it. After three days, he began to feel less confused and after eight days things no longer looked upside down.

Furthermore, what we perceive is scarcely objective not only because it may change with special glasses, for example, but also because our memory is fallible. Over time, what we remember changes both in terms of which memories we actually retain, and in terms of how we retain them. Memories can, in fact, be lost and/or transformed. Something similar may happen in the language classes in which we are using DDL activities. We may perceive learners to be enthusiastic about the approach, and able to learn much from it. We may very well observe changes in their language competence over time. But are we in a position to make inferences based on what we observe, and generalise what we observe in our daily experience to support a claim about the method (i.e. DDL is an effective way to learn a second language)? The answer is generally 'no', as, although science relies on the observation of phenomena, it does so in the framework of a study designed to collect unbiased data. Our observation of a personal teaching practice will inevitably be unsystematic and biased. It can, at most, be used to generate intuitions which would then need to be tested empirically.

We thus come to the sixth way to gain knowledge: science. In his book *What is this thing called Science?*, philosopher of science Alan Chalmers wrote that

> science is highly esteemed. Apparently it is a widely held belief that there is something special about science and its methods. The naming of some claim or line of reasoning or piece of research 'scientific' is done in a way that is intended to imply some kind of merit or special kind of reliability. But what, if anything, is so special about science?
>
> (Chalmers, 1999, p. xix)

4.2 The nature of scientific knowledge in researching DDL effects

In this section, we outline what characterises scientific knowledge. In particular, we see which steps need to be taken in conducting scientific research leading to scientific knowledge, and which principles these steps need to reflect. These will constitute the foundation upon which we will be able to design studies aimed at investigating DDL effects. The scientific method seeks to investigate the nature of a hypothesis. More specifically, it aims at ascertaining whether the formulated hypothesis is supported by evidence gleaned from observed phenomena. As a result, our starting point will be the identification of a research problem of interest, and the subsequent formulation of a research hypothesis. We can do this in several ways. In our daily teaching practice, we may have observed an increase in lexical variety or in the appropriate use of collocation arising from the writings of learners using online corpora enthusiastically. They may have gotten into the habit of looking up words and how they are used in context, and this may have had an impact on the variety or collocational appropriateness of their produced texts. To step out of the subjectivity of the experience and the uncertainty of the extent to which the observation might be applicable to larger contexts, an empirical study must be conducted. Does the use of corpus tools increase lexical variety or collocational competence in learner production? We may arrive at stating this research problem also by noticing a research gap in the literature. Conducting a thorough literary review is a crucial step in identifying our research problem and generating our working hypothesis. Several guides are available in this respect. A popular one is Booth et al. (2016).

Once a hypothesis is formulated, we can predict what we will observe in the collected data. We might expect DDL to help in the development of problem-solving skills, thanks to activities where learners use a corpus to autonomously correct their own writing. Or we might expect DDL to trigger higher retention rates through frequency effects, thanks to concordance-based activities containing multiple examples related to the same form or combination of forms. If our predictions hold, then we can accept our initial hypothesis. In order for a study to be scientific it needs to be based on a hypothesis that is empirically testable, its methods and procedures need to be transparent so as to make it replicable, and the way it is conducted needs to be objective. These characteristics make scientific knowledge a desirable pathway to investigate DDL effects on language learning. To conduct a scientific study, a research design needs to be developed. This will involve the following basic tasks:

- choosing the learners and the learning context;
- designing the DDL activities;
- collecting empirical data on DDL effects;
- developing the study design;
- coding, analysing and interpreting the data.

The next paragraphs illustrate each one of these steps.

4.3 Choosing the learners and the learning context

Choosing which learners to involve means defining our sample. The sample is the set of individuals or items that we are able to observe through the data we elicit from them. One fundamental aspect of the notion of sampling is its relationship with the notion of population. The population is the set of individuals or items that share certain characteristics, but which may not be observable in its entirety. For example, we may consider the population of all second language learners in the world, at any given point in time. As we would not be able to elicit data from all of them, we select a sample of them. In other words, the sample is a subset of the population. Figure 4.1 shows the general relationship between population and sample.

Methods in researching data-driven learning effects 65

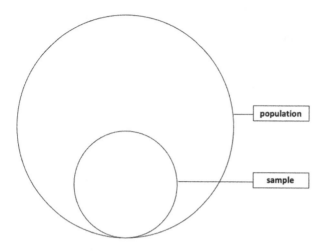

Figure 4.1 Population and sample.

The criteria that we adopt to define our sample influence our ability to generalise our findings. We may decide to define our sample in terms of a number of learner variables, such as L1, proficiency level, learning context, age. Our sample may be formed by L1 French learners of English, with an advanced level of proficiency, studying English literature at the same university and belonging to the same age group, say 18–25 years old. A sample like this may be particularly useful to study L1 influences in the effectiveness of DDL, especially if a second learner group, with a different L1 background, is integrated into the study. In this case, our population will be all L1 French learners learning English. Our hypothesis, constructed on the basis of our sample, will then aim to generalise to the entire population once the collected data is analysed and interpreted. The relationship between sample and population is a very crucial one, as it connects with the representativeness of the sample. Every sample aims to be representative for some variable. For example, our sample of L1 French learners of English might be representative for the population of all L1 French learners in the world, but perhaps not so representative for all learners of English in the world, regardless of their L1. We may also choose a sample of participants with a variety of L1 backgrounds, which may be considered more representative of all learners of English in the world, in comparison to our sample of French learners. In any case, our sample must be defined according to precise criteria and the variables characterising it must be controlled for.

The way in which we select the sample must follow specific criteria, in order for it to be deemed representative. Sampling can be either probability or non-probability sampling. The crucial difference is that in the first case each item of a population has a certain probability of being selected to be part of the sample, while in the second case this does not apply. The advantage of knowing the probability with which an individual or item will be selected consists in being able to calculate the sampling error, namely 'the extent to which a sample drawn from a population differs from the original population' (Thomas, 2021, p. 136). In non-probability sampling, this is not possible, thus leaving the extent to which the sample differs from the population largely unknown.

In Table 4.1, three probability sampling methods are represented visually: *simple random sampling, systematic random sampling* and *stratified random sampling*. In *simple random sampling*, individual sample units are selected randomly, provided that each of them has the same chance of being selected. This method is generally used for small and largely homogeneous populations. In *systematic random sampling*, individual sample units are selected randomly but also systematically. If the required sample size from a population is 50 of 1000, and if the units of a population constitute a finite set and can be listed, the number of intervals is found out by dividing the population by the sample (1000/50 = 20). Then, a unit of the list is selected at random (e.g., the 6th), and every other unit is selected according to the interval (i.e. 26th, 46th, etc.) until the required number of units to make up the sample is reached. Finally, in *stratified random sampling*, individual sample units are selected according to the homogeneous subgroup (or stratum) of the population that they belong to. Subsets of the population are identified according to shared characteristics. Random sampling is then used to draw units from each of these subsets, so that the obtained sample reflects the characteristics of the population. This method is generally used for heterogenous populations.

Table 4.2 shows four non-probabilistic methods: *convenience sampling, judgment sampling, quota sampling,* and *snowball sampling*. In *convenience sampling*, individual sample units are drawn from those that are more easily accessible (e.g., one's own students). This is the simplest form of non-probabilistic sampling. When adopting this method, the risk of bias is quite high and generalisability may be difficult. In *judgment sampling*, individual sample units are selected according to some judgment. For example, the different subsets of a population may be judged differently in terms of representativeness. The research may have solid arguments to support the higher representativeness of a certain population subgroup, thus supporting the choice of selecting individual sample units solely from this subgroup. In *quota sampling*, individual sample units are drawn from the subsets of a population. It is similar to *stratified random sampling*. In this case, however, once the subsets are identified, either convenience or judgment sampling is used to form the sample, instead of random sampling. In *snowball sampling*, individual sample units are selected on the basis of the additional ones found by an initial set of subjects. These subjects will be asked to recruit new participants. This method is used when the desired sample characteristics are difficult to find. It is a specific kind of convenience sampling.

Methods in researching data-driven learning effects 67

Table 4.1 Main types of probability sampling methods

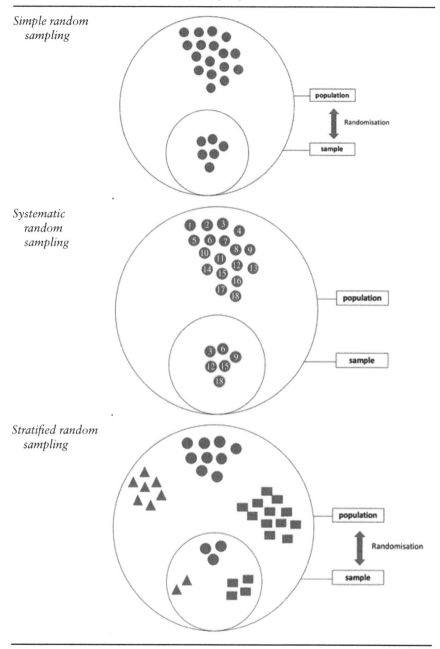

Illustrations created on the basis of definitions provided in Thomas, 2021: 135–139.

68 *Methods in researching data-driven learning effects*

Table 4.2 Main types of non-probability sampling methods

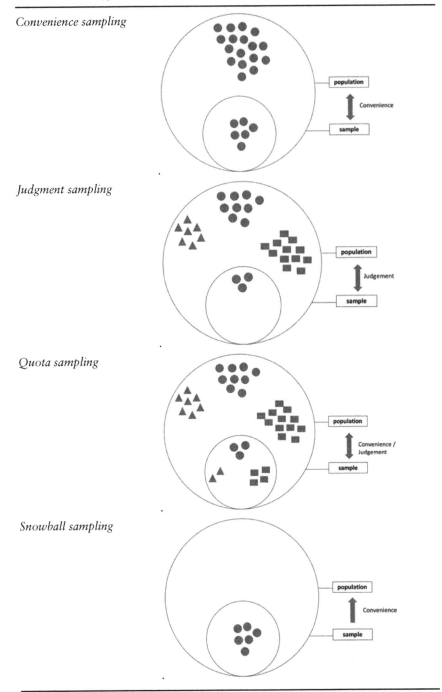

Illustrations created on the basis of definitions provided in Thomas, 2021: 135–139.

In DDL empirical research, participant samples are usually identified on the basis of non-probabilistic sampling techniques. Convenience samples are quite common. Judgment and quota sampling are at times implied in the criteria that are adopted to identify the participant sample. However, a deeper look at the techniques that exist to define a sample of participants which will engage in DDL, and which we will elicit empirical data from, is necessary. This will be especially useful in the interpretation of the results, in light of their generalisability. The learning contexts within which we intervene with our DDL activities may vary according to a wide number of factors. The nature of the learning context is also intimately interconnected with the way in which we decide to operationalise DDL, as we will see in the next section.

4.4 Designing the DDL activities

DDL lends itself to a variety of possible tasks and activity formats. First of all, these need to suit actual learner needs, which may be identified through a literature review or through an ad hoc analysis limited to the participants taking part in a study. Therefore, any DDL study should start with a learner needs analysis, reflecting as closely as possible the needs of the specific learners selected for the study. DDL experiences should then be designed so as to be as integrated as possible with the existing curriculum and existing learning and teaching practices. This is a key element in fostering the normalisation of DDL, beyond the empirical research needs that DDL researchers may have. In other words, paying attention to rigorous research design should not disregard the relevance of the pre-existing learning and teaching context, along with the importance of providing a stimulating experience.

The identification of learning aims stems from both the analysis of the learning and teaching context which one may find oneself in, in combination with a review of the relevant literature. Learning aims may relate to language areas, such as phonology, morphology, lexis, semantics, syntax, pragmatics, which may be conceived in light of specific theoretical frameworks (e.g., lexicogrammar, constructions, etc.). The language areas identified in the recent meta-analyses which we surveyed in Chapter 3 refer to vocabulary, lexicogrammar, grammar and discourse. This sheds light on the opportunity and possibility to expand the scope of DDL research to language areas that have not been explored so far. DDL research may also identify the development of specific skills as learning aims around which an empirical research study may be constructed. So far, meta-analyses on DDL have identified an interest in the following areas: listening, reading, speaking, writing and translating.

Once the learning aims have been identified, it is essential to identify the learning aim properties. The DDL researcher will need to know how the learning aims relate to learning processes. What do we know about the development of knowledge and competence concerning the learning aim we have chosen? How, if at all possible, can DDL help? The answer to the first question requires a literature review and the identification of the main difficulties that a learner may encounter. This level of literature review will go beyond the specific DDL domain, into broader SLA domains. To answer the second question, we need to match what we know about DDL, in terms of pedagogical potential, with what remains to be done to help second language learners in what they struggle with the most. An example of how this can be done is provided in Chapters 6 and 7, in relation to the development of phraseological competence.

We then need to decide which kind of corpus data we need to use for our pedagogical intervention. This is essentially a choice regarding which corpus (or corpora) are able to suit our pedagogical needs and for which purposes. In Chapter 6, an example is provided in relation to how a learner corpus may be used to identify the most problematic areas in the development of phraseological competence, and a native reference corpus is used to develop DDL activities. Two different corpora are, thus, used in relation to a given learning aim, but with different functions and different roles in the development of a DDL experience. The choice of the data and of the corpora is strictly connected to the choice of the learning aims. We need to make sure, in fact, that the corpus (or corpora) that we choose contains instances of our learning aims in a qualitatively and quantitatively relevant measure. If we decide to focus on the development of discourse competence, we need to ensure that our corpus contains enough discourse units.

What needs to then be decided is how the corpus data is presented to the learners. In devising DDL activities for research purposes, it is necessary to pedagogically operationalise DDL so as to identify the specific properties that characterise it, the effects of which we will thus seek to measure. In this volume, we focus on concordance-based DDL, namely activities that qualify as DDL not only because they contain data extracted from corpora, but also because this data is presented by means of numerous examples. This is, of course, not the only possible type of DDL. We may also have a more visual DDL, where corpus-data is visualised graphically either to show frequency or co-occurrence phenomena. The GraphColl function in Lancsbox (Brezina et al., 2020), as well as the visualisation tools in SketchEngine (Kilgarriff et al., 2004, 2014) and AntConc (Anthony, 2020) are all tools which visualise corpus data also without showing concordance lines. What is shown is a combination of quantitative and qualitative data instead. DDL activities may also make use of frequency lists, wordclouds or wordsketches, such as those that are available with SkELL (Baisa & Suchomel, 2014). The different ways in which corpus data may be shown are likely to determine different learning processes. While authenticity of the data remains the common thread of all visualisation modalities, concordance-based DDL will be the one which will be more in line with the possibility of eliciting frequency effects (Ellis, 2002). Interaction with multiple exemplars related to a single word or word combination can lead learners to identify patterns, on the basis of which they can make inferences and formulate generalisations. When presented with a word cloud, for instance, the frequency is visualised already. Learners can still make inferences and formulate generalisations, but they will not be directly exposed to multiple instances of a single word or word combinations. They will be exposed to data shaped differently. When designing an empirical study, care needs to be taken when DDL is pedagogically operationalised. This is an important step, as we need to know what the measured effects actually relate to in terms of pedagogical intervention. What is it exactly that is producing a certain effect on language learning?

A final step in devising DDL activities relates to how we intend to let learners interact with the data. The meta-analyses on DDL have identified three main interaction modalities: paper-based, computer-based and mixed modality. In the first case, data extracted from the corpus is printed on paper and given to the learners in the form of a learning activity. Examples of paper-based activities can be found in Tim Johns' work (Johns, 1991) and John Sinclair's *Reading concordances* (Sinclair, 2003). The advantages of paper-based DDL are numerous. Teachers are able to select concordance lines in advance, thus ensuring their relevance and appropriateness in relation to a given learning aim and/or learning context. Selecting concordance lines in advance also has the advantage of manipulating the way they are presented. This can, for instance, allow teachers to develop concordance-based matching activities or concordance-based gap-fill activities, and develop a series of activities along a cline of increasing difficulty and/or increasing learner autonomy in interacting with the corpus data. This can also allow teachers to make sure that the corpus data is level-appropriate, by omitting complex subordinate clauses, for example, and/or specialised language. Furthermore, in-presence group work among students sitting around a table is facilitated.

Finally, teachers can easily reuse the materials multiple times. Paper-based DDL may also involve disadvantages or present possible issues. When interacting with corpus data via prepared paper-based materials, learners' autonomy in the exploration of a corpus may be more restricted in comparison to the freer corpus exploration activities that are typical of a computer-based approach. Access to corpus data directly, via a computer and software interface, certainly allows the learners to have greater freedom in the use of a corpus. Learners may turn to a corpus whenever they have a doubt that a dictionary is unable to solve. Very specific needs can be addressed, even without the mediation of a teacher. However, computer-based DDL requires one of at least two conditions: (1) that the learners are able to access a corpus that is suitable for their learning needs, namely that was created for learners and with the specific aim of guaranteeing accessibility for learners; (2) that in case the learners do not have such a corpus, they are familiar with the querying strategies and data interpretation modalities that characterise corpora that were not built to be used primarily by learners.[1]

The boundaries between paper-based and computer-based DDL seem to blur when considering online resources such as those on the *Incorporating Corpora* website[2] or the *CROW – Corpus & Repository of Writing* one.[3] These are two excellent examples of how what have for long been known as paper-based activities are transferred online. The computer is not the medium to access the corpus, but it becomes the medium to access corpus-based activities. The blur is only apparent because of the involvement of the computer. The function of computers changes according to how corpus data is accessed by learners and, in particular, according to whether and how it is mediated by a teacher. This may lead us to invent new labels for these two modalities. We may move, in fact, from the paper-based/computer-based (or 'hands-on'/'hands-off', or even 'hard' and 'soft' DDL) dichotomy to a 'mediated'/'unmediated' dichotomy. Online, mediated corpus-based activities have the undoubted advantage of providing guided activities in a remote learning setting, which may be carried out individually or collectively in groups online.

Mixed DDL refers to an integrated use of both paper-based and computer-based DDL, i.e. a mix of mediated and unmediated corpus-based activities. The main advantage that lies in this approach is that learners can be introduced to corpus-based activities gradually. This can be important when the aim is to help learners get into the habit of noticing patterns in their input, or rather in the 'condensed' (Gabrielatos, 2005, p. 8) input, that a set of concordance lines is able to provide. More controlled, teacher-mediated, paper-based activities may be developed to introduce learners to pattern-hunting activities. The acquired skills may thus be strengthened and then transferred to the online corpus. More time may be needed to notice any results. Longer-lasting effects may be produced as a result of approaching data exploration in different modalities and through different perspectives.

4.5 Collecting empirical data on DDL effects

To collect empirical data that is able to inform us on the effects that DDL has on language learning, a key step lies in the choice and development of data collection tools. First and foremost, we need to know about our participant sample. Background questionnaires are usually a good tool in this respect. The information we gather about the different variables of our participants is crucial in establishing homogeneity in our sample. Typical data that is elicited by means of background questionnaires is:

- Name and surname
- Age
- Motivation for learning the language

- Time spent studying the language in home country
- Time spent studying the language in country where the language is spoken as national language

Background questionnaires normally come with consent forms which inform learners about their involvement in a research project and about how the data we collect will be used. Although we may already have information about their proficiency level (e.g., through a placement test), we may need or wish to have them sit a test that is specifically linked to our research topic (e.g., a phraseological competence test). These kinds of data are necessary as they will then need to be analysed in connection with data informing us on DDL effects more specifically. An excellent survey of empirical data types and data coding techniques can be found in Mackey and Gass (Mackey & Gass, 2012). In general, we can identify etic and emic data collection tools. The etic/emic dichotomy derives from the field of cultural anthropology, according to which

> an emic representation of the ideas or actions of the members of a culture is drawn from the views of its own participants; an etic one is drawn from outside. For example, the external observer may regard certain phenomena as symptoms of a disease – this is an etic judgment. But the cultural group in question may recognise other symptoms as characteristic of a particular illness that is not recognised elsewhere – this would be called an emic explanation.
>
> (Morris, 2012, p. 80)

The boundaries between these two perspectives are debated (Headland et al., 1990). Nevertheless, applied linguistics manuals devoted to research methods refer to this dichotomy as a way to reach a more effective and well-rounded understanding of a certain research problem (Riazi, 2017).

Etic data collection tools which may be used in investigating DDL effects are:

1. proficiency level tests;
2. competence tests (matched with learning aims involved in DDL intervention);
3. production data;
4. audio recording of search strategies;
5. key-logging and screen recording data;
6. eye-tracking;
7. neuroimaging;
8. think-aloud protocols;
9. stimulated recall.

Each one of these etic data collection tools is able to inform us about whether a DDL approach has had a beneficial effect in terms of improvements in proficiency level, specific areas of language competence (e.g., collocation knowledge, reading and comprehension skills, etc.), quality of writing or speaking. Each one of these dimensions may be investigated by means of specifically designed or chosen tools. As for proficiency level, we may use standardised and validated tests. If we wish to investigate specific areas of language competence, we will need to devise or select a test targeting our specific target. On the other hand, if we seek to investigate how DDL may affect leaner production, we may use a variety of techniques. For example, we could analyse language production via learner corpus research methods and/or CAF (complexity, accuracy, fluency) measures.

Etic data collection tools also include tools that are able to inform us about the processes involved in DDL. Audio recording of search strategies allows us to capture the individual or collective reasoning behind working with a corpus or through a corpus-based activity. Key-logging and screen-recording are particularly suited to the analysis of computer-based DDL. They, respectively, capture the activity on a keyboard and the corresponding activity on the screen of a computer. Eye-tracking and neuroimaging are at the frontiers of DDL research as they do not seem to have been employed as data collection tools so far (McKinley & Rose, 2020, p. 370). They pertain to the fields of psycho- and neuro-linguistics, and capture eye movements and brain activity respectively. With think-aloud protocols we are able to tap into the thinking processes of learners interacting with the corpus data in order to solve a certain language problem and glean information from the corpus (McKinley & Rose, 2020, p. 302). While think-aloud takes place in real-time, namely while the DDL is unfolding, stimulated recall elicits information from the learner(s) in relation to the unfolding of the DDL activity, after the activity is finished. This recall process is usually based on the provision of a stimulus given to the learner(s), which may be a video or audio-recording of the activity (McKinley & Rose, 2020, p. 312). The analysis of processes and effects in DDL research certainly holds great potential for the future, as new methods will gradually be sought.

As previously mentioned, emic data relate to the subjective perspective. Tools to elicit emic data include:

1. Questionnaires
2. Open-ended interviews
3. Semi-structured interviews
4. Focus groups

Questionnaires are perhaps the most common emic data collection tool used in DDL research. As previously reviewed, Angela Chambers (2007) published a survey of questionnaires centring on DDL effects in relation to student attitudes, synthesising the findings of the various studies collected, while emphasising the sheer variety characterising them in terms of design and focus. In an attempt to standardise the collection of emic data in DDL research, Mizumoto et al. (2016) developed a scale to measure learners' perceptions of DDL. The introduction of this scale has the enormous advantage of facilitating the comparison between different kinds of emic studies. However, as DDL interventions may have multiple forms, and since the collection of emic data would need to inevitably reflect the features of such interventions, the development of ad hoc questionnaires could still be a necessity for many DDL studies. A good manual to refer to is the one by Dörnyei (2010). Questionnaires may contain closed-ended items (e.g., likert-scale items) and open-ended items (e.g., open-ended questions). In each case, special care needs to be taken in order for the items to be developed reliably. In open-ended interviews, learners are asked questions, which are mostly predetermined by the interviewer. In semi-structured interviews, questions are only partly predetermined, while most of them will not be planned in advance. In focus groups, a group of learners who have engaged in DDL activities share their views on the approach and interact with respect to their shared experiences (McKinley & Rose, 2020, p. 290).

Thanks to Boulton and Vyatkina's (2021) survey of 489 DDL studies, we learn that DDL studies usually collect data using more than one instrument. Questionnaires are the most widely used instruments (53%), followed by interviews (21%) or group discussions (8%), for what concerns the emic perspective (Boulton & Vyatkina, p. 74). As for the etic perspective, the authors note that data collection instruments focused on the processes involved in DDL (e.g., key-logging and screen recording) are being used with increasing frequency over the years. This seems to point to the fact that the research questions involved in DDL research are evolving through time and that more attention is being devoted to *how* DDL unfolds in the language learning process.

4.6 Developing the study design

Learning occurs over time. As a result, to observe any measurable effects related to a certain pedagogical intervention, empirical designs planned to capture change over time are recommended. As noted in Boulton & Vyatkina (2021, p. 75), empirical DDL studies have increasingly called for more longer-term designs. This has been motivated by the fact that DDL effects may not be observable over the short time span which characterises most studies conducted so far. While pointing out the difficulty in establishing treatment duration due to the different reporting practices, Boulton and Vyatkina quantify the exposure to DDL in terms of a mean value of '13 hours, 9 sessions, 8 weeks, or slightly over 1 semester for the longer ones' (2021, p. 75).

In terms of study design and data collection planning, DDL studies have generally opted for either a pre-/post-test design or for a pre-/post-/delayed-post test design. In the former, the chosen or developed data collection instrument (see previous paragraph) is used before the beginning of the pedagogical treatment (i.e. the exposure to DDL materials and/or activities) and then after the exposure and interaction with corpus data has taken place. In the latter, a third step is added: the data elicitation tool is used also after some time has passed after the end of the exposure to the DDL treatment. The latter method is recommended to capture any longer-term effects related to DDL. In the supplementary materials provided in Boulton and Cobb's (2017) comprehensive meta-analysis of empirical DDL studies, we have interesting information related to how DDL studies have been designed in relation to the definition of the data collection plan. More specifically, over a total of 64 studies, only nine elicited post-delayed empirical data on DDL effects (i.e. 14%). If we look at the length of the delay, we see that the range spans from a minimum of 10 days to a maximum of 10 weeks. If we merge the data related to the overall time span of empirical DDL studies with that concerning the numerosity of data collection points, as well as their proximity to the DDL treatment, we see how much needs to be done in seeking to analyse how DDL may affect language learning through time. In other words, more longitudinal designs are needed in order to reflect the long-term processes involved in language learning.

The way in which exposure to DDL may be organised can concern either a between-groups or a within-groups setting. In the first case, different groups of participants are measured in relation to different DDL modalities or in relation to whether they were or were not exposed to a DDL treatment. Between-group designs would usually have a control (or comparison[4]) group, whenever the researcher intends to observe whether the presence of DDL principles in learning and teaching is able to make a difference in terms of developing language competence and language skills. In between-groups designs, the groups of participants will need to share the same set of characteristics, including a statistically significant homogeneity in starting conditions. In order to avoid any biases in assigning a group to a certain condition, assignment is conducted randomly. Randomisation is a key trait of experimental designs. If true randomisation is not possible (i.e. when there are intact classes involved, with students already placed in each one of them), randomisation based on the pre-determined groups of participants (i.e. classes) is possible. In this case, we speak of pseudo-randomisation or quasi-randomisation. If no randomisation is involved in assigning the participants to one of the study conditions, the study will be a nonexperimental study. Examples of DDL studies based on a between-groups design are Frankenberg-Garcia (2012, 2014), Daskalovska (2015) and Supatranont (2005). Within-groups designs, on the other hand, are based on the collection of data from a single group of participants. These may be exposed to a single DDL treatment, to multiple types of DDL treatments, or to a combination of multiple types of DDL treatments and no DDL treatment. Examples of DDL studies based on a within-groups design are Horst & Cobb (2001), Cotos (2014) and Yang et al. (2016). In Boulton

& Vyatkina's (2021) survey, 177 studies include a control group over the total of 489 reviewed (about 36%).

One decisive aspect of study design in DDL research concerns the control of confounding variables. If our aim is to discover how DDL produces an effect on language learning, we will be interested in assessing the effect of an independent variable (i.e. the variable that we manipulate, that is not affected by other variables, e.g., DDL treatment) on a dependent variable (i.e. the variable that is affected by the independent variable, whose changes we seek to measure, e.g., the development of language competence over time). As explained in Riazi (2016b, p. 51), we need to make sure that a certain observed effect is caused solely by the independent variable (i.e. DDL treatment and the specific ways in which it was operationalised). In order to be able to do so, we need to neutralise the presence of what are known as confounding variables. These variables may relate to both the independent and the dependent variables. To this end, a number of controlling techniques need to be adopted.

As far as an empirical study design seeking to investigate DDL effects goes, some of the main variables that we might wish to control for include:

- learning aims effects;
- task effects;
- participant effects;
- researcher effects.

In the first case, the unit of observation on the basis of which the data collection is conducted must closely reflect the research question. If we wish to analyse DDL effects related to improvements in the development of phraseological competence, as will be shown in this volume, we need to elicit data concerning phraseological competence only. Furthermore, the tasks of the DDL activities that we will have developed need to centre on phraseological units. If the design includes a control group, the activities that this group will be exposed to need to be explicitly described. A group of students enrolled in an institutional language course will be exposed to some form of formal instruction. How is this kind of instruction structured with regards to the DDL treatment? Are phraseological units (or any other learning aims) addressed at all? If so, how are they addressed? Control groups in between-subjects designs are generally conceived as groups characterised by an absence of the independent variable (i.e. DDL treatment). If we consider these groups as comparison groups, that is groups that do receive some form of instruction, we can control for the kind of instruction that is received. This allows us to neutralise confounding variables that might be present in the control (or comparison) groups (e.g., the uneven presence of instruction related to our learning aims). Participant effects should be controlled for at the level of sampling, which is why this phase of the research is particularly crucial. Researcher effects in an empirical DDL study might be neutralised in two ways: the researcher might be either the instructor in all participant groups or pass this role onto a language teacher. In any case, in order to avoid researcher/teacher effects, all groups should be characterised by the same features in terms of who is administering the activity. This way, teaching differences related to either teaching style, student rapport or other factors are minimised, and the way in which the independent variable was operationalised (e.g., concordance-based activities vs. non-concordance-based activities) more clearly observable.

While there are numerous types of data that may be elicited to investigate DDL effects, studies mixing different kinds of data are highly recommended, as argued in Riazi (2016a, 2017). Merging the quantitative with the qualitative, and the etic with the emic dimension, helps in gaining a more well-rounded picture of the investigated phenomenon. In Vyatkina & Boulton (2021)'s review, nine categories of data types are listed:

- questionnaires;
- interviews;
- productions;
- tests;
- journals, diaries, reports, think-aloud, stimulated recall;
- tracking;
- discussions, focus group interviews;
- observation;
- other.

If we consider the emic vs. etic distinction, we can determine how many of the 489 studies have collected data related to both dimensions and how many consider one dimension only. Overall, we see that most studies have adopted a combined approach, integrating both the emic and the etic dimensions (206 studies, 43% of the total), followed by studies with only etic data (148 studies, 30% of the total) and studies with only emic data (129 studies, 27% of the total).

4.7 Coding, analysing, and interpreting the data

In order to be analysed, the data that we collect must be coded. Coding is defined as 'the process of categorising the raw data, usually into descriptive categories' (Howitt & Cramer, 2020, p. 347). Three coding procedures are normally identified: pre-coding, researcher-imposed coding and coding which emerges from the data. Pre-coding refers to data that originates as coded because it is elicited by means of a research instrument designed for that purpose. For example, if we develop a phraseological competence test to measure DDL effects, we might have different test item types (i.e. multiple choice, matching, gap-fill, etc.) and each of these items will refer to a specific phraseological unit. The accuracy data we will collect with such instruments will then already refer to the different kinds of phraseological units and test item types we have used.

If we have collected written production texts and seek to measure DDL effects, we will have to opt for a researcher-imposed coding. In other words, we need to develop a coding scheme with which we will annotate the phenomena we are interested in. This will be the basis to measure DDL effects. We might be interested in how DDL affects accuracy, so we might decide to annotate errors, or we might be interested to see how semantic transparency of phraseological units develops over time when being exposed to DDL. In both cases, we will need to develop a coding scheme. As applying a coding scheme to raw data will involve margins of subjectivity, annotator training sessions are usually conducted and, most importantly, a calculation of coder reliability through inter-annotator agreement rates is normally performed. In the cases where coders disagree significantly, post-annotation consensus building sessions may be held.

In order for coding to be effective, it must be valid and reliable. Validity attains to 'how appropriately and precisely an operationalisation matches a construct's theoretical definition', in other words 'the degree to which the coding categories and procedures allow for accurate and meaningful interpretations to be made about the construct in question' (Révész, 2012, p. 204). Coding must then be reliable, in the sense that data must be categorised consistently. With pre-coded data, uniformity is ensured by the adoption of a single data collection instrument; with researcher-imposed coding, consistency is measured thought the annotation agreement calculations we mentioned earlier. The last kind of coding identified by Howitt and Cramer is coding which emerges from the data. This kind of coding is typical of qualitative data, which may or may not lend itself to quantification. It focuses on common themes or trends which may emerge from the collected data. Various types of validity and reliability are further described in Howitt & Cramer (2020).

Once our data is coded, we are ready to analyse it. The first approach to the statistical analysis of collected data is descriptive statistics. Basic information related to measures of central tendency (i.e. mean, median, etc.) are useful to gain a first view into the data. Descriptive statistics, however, relate to our specific sample and does not allow us to make any inferences and/or generalisations related to the overall population that our sample is drawn from. With descriptive statistics alone, we have no way of knowing how significant our findings are and we are in no position to make predictions in relation to the probability of observing a certain phenomenon on sample that we have not collected. This is why the use of inferential statistics is becoming more and more widespread in DDL research. Mixed-effects modelling, in particular, is gaining widespread recognition as a solid approach to data analysis (Linck & Cunnings, 2015).

A number of useful manuals are available to the DDL researcher starting out in the statistics field. Part IV of the volume *The Routledge handbook of research methods in applied linguistics* (McKinley & Rose, 2020) is a good place to begin. It contains chapters on statistical software programs (arguing for the use of R as opposed to SPSS), descriptive and inferential statistics, as well as statistical modelling and pointers on how to conduct qualitative content analysis and text analyses.

Visualisations are of great help in making sense of the analysed data, particularly as a stepping stone towards the interpretation of the findings. Manuals on visualisations in R are numerous. A good starting point is Levshina (2015) as well as Gries (2013). Both volumes go over some of the basics in statistics, paving the way towards analysing data in R successfully and meaningfully, also by means of visualisations.

Once the data is collected, coded and analysed, we must interpret it. Why did we get certain results? Were they results that we expected? Are they in line with the current literature on the topic? How can the findings be explained in relation to the study design? These are all key questions that a DDL researcher will want to address while interpreting the findings of their analysis. However, as the authors of *The craft of research* (Booth et al., 2016) maintain, the most significant question of all is, 'So what?'. Why are the research questions addressed in the DDL study that a researcher is conducting relevant to the broader audience of language learners, and language teaching practitioners? Why would they be interested? How can the findings of a particular DDL study benefit the language learning community? Are there benefits that extend beyond the language learning community? We will see how these questions may be addressed and answered in Chapters 6, 7 and 8.

4.8 Chapter summary and conclusions

This chapter outlined the various methodological steps involved in setting up and conducting a DDL empirical study. It opened with a reflection on how we gain knowledge, which traits distinguish different forms of knowledge and why scientific knowledge is so central to our understanding of the world in general and language learning phenomena in particular. As the principles underlying the scientific method need to inform any DDL research, we set out by illustrating how a group of participants can be identified and selected to take part in our study. More specifically, different sampling techniques were described, and the most common ones used in DDL research pointed out. A specific section was devoted to how DDL activities can be designed. To this end, the several approaches used so far in corpus-informed teaching were summarised in relation to the need to pedagogically operationalise the DDL construct. This is needed in order to know what it is that we are measuring in terms of the pedagogy and of the effects it will have on learning. While outlining the various kinds of data that can be extracted from a corpus, and which may inform the development of DDL materials and/or activities, a specific focus is placed on concordance-based DDL.

The different tools available to collect data related to DDL effects are also presented. In outlining the various possible ways of designing a DDL study, particular emphasis was placed on the need for more longitudinal designs. This is mainly because learning inevitably occurs over time. However, the information gathered from the surveys and meta-analyses on DDL (Boulton & Cobb, 2017; Boulton & Vyatkina, 2021) indicates a scarcity of long-term studies on DDL effects. The average time span of DDL studies is, in fact, eight weeks (Boulton & Vyatkina, 2021, p. 75). A final section of the chapter is dedicated to the coding, analysis and interpretation of the collected data.

While restating the need to not only have more longitudinal but also studies which mix different perspectives and, thus, different kinds of data, in this chapter we saw how this can be done methodologically. The range of competencies needed to build a DDL study is certainly wide: skills in pedagogical material design, research design, statistics, data coding and handling, language testing, all merge when designing a DDL study. It is a truly interdisciplinary endeavour, where methods and skills from different disciplines unite. Before launching into the illustration of a DDL study focused on the development of phraseological competence in Italian L2, the next chapter will survey the range of corpus resources that are available to conduct a DDL study focused on Italian.

Notes

1 On the distinction between corpora for linguists and corpora for learners and its implications, see Forti & Spina (2019).
2 https://corpora.ku.edu/ (last accessed: 22/08/2022).
3 https://writecrow.org/ (last accessed: 22/08/2022).
4 'In educational research, usually the term comparison groups is used instead of experimental and control groups. The reason is that educational researchers usually compare different groups receiving different treatments. Whereas in medical and psychological experiments it may be possible to use a placebo (no treatment) in control groups, in educational experiments, the researchers study the difference in the results of two or more treatments. As such, it is perhaps better to use comparison groups instead of experimental and control groups in educational experimental designs'. (Riazi, 2016b, p. 60). See Boers et al. (2020) for a discussion on study design in language education research and meta-analyses involving control/comparison groups.

References

Anthony, L. (2020). AntConc (Version 3.5.9) [Computer Software]. Waseda University. Available from www.laurenceanthony.net/software.
Baisa, V., & Suchomel, V. (2014). SkELL: Web interface for English language learning. *Eighth Workshop on Recent Advances in Slavonic Natural Language Processing*, 63–70.

Boers, F., Bryfonski, L., Faez, F., & McKay, T. (2020). A call for cautious interpretation of meta-analytic reviews. *Studies in Second Language Acquisition, 43*(1), 2–24.

Booth, W.C., Colomb, G.G., Williams, J.H., Bizup, J., & Fitzgerald, W.T. (2016). *The craft of research*. University of Chicago Press.

Boulton, A., & Cobb, T. (2017). Corpus use in language learning: A meta-analysis. *Language Learning, 67*(2), 348–393.

Boulton, A., & Vyatkina, N. (2021). Thirty years of data-driven learning: Taking stock and charting new directions. *Language Learning and Technology, 25*(3), 66–89.

Brezina, V., Weill Tessier, P., & McEnery, A. (2020). #LancsBox v. 5.x. [Software]. Available at: Http://corpora.lancs.ac.uk/lancsbox.

Chalmers, A. (1999). *What is this thing called science?* University of Queensland Press.

Chambers, A. (2007). Popularising corpus consultation by language learners and teachers. *Language and Computers, 61*(1), 3–16.

Christensen, L. (2007). *Experimental methodology*. Pearson.

Cotos, E. (2014). Enhancing writing pedagogy with learner corpus data. *ReCALL, 26*(02), 202–224.

Crosthwaite, P. (2020). Taking DDL online: Designing, implementing and evaluating a SPOC on data-driven learning for tertiary L2 writing. *Australian Review of Applied Linguistics, 43*(2), 169–195.

Daskalovska, N. (2015). Corpus-based versus traditional learning of collocations. *Computer Assisted Language Learning, 28*(2), 130–144.

Dörnyei, Z. (2007). *Research methods in applied linguistics*. Oxford University Press.

Dörnyei, Z., with Tatsuya Taguchi. (2010). *questionnaires in second language research. Construction, administration, and processing.* (2nd ed.). Routledge.

Ellis, N.C. (2002). Frequency effects in language processing. *Studies in Second Language Acquisition, 24*(02), 143–188.

Forti, L., & Spina, S. (2019). Corpora for linguists vs. corpora for learners: Bridging the gap in Italian L2 learning and teaching, *EL.LE. – Educazione Linguistica. Language Education, 8*(2), Venezia: Ca' Foscari Digital Publishing, 349–362.

Frankenberg-Garcia, A. (2012). Integrating corpora with everyday language teaching. In J.E. Thomas & A. Boulton (Eds.), *Input, Process and Product: Developments in Teaching and Language Corpora* (pp. 33–51). Masaryk University Press.

Frankenberg-Garcia, A. (2014). The use of corpus examples for language comprehension and production. *ReCALL, 26*(02), 128–146.

Friginal, E. (2018). *Corpus Linguistics for English Teachers: Tools, Online Resources, and Classroom*. Routledge.

Gabrielatos, C. (2005). Corpora and language teaching: Just a fling or wedding bells? The Electronic Journal for English as a Second *Language, 8*(4), 1–32.

Gries, S.T. (2013). *Statistics for linguistics with R: A practical introduction* (2nd ed.). De Gruyter Mouton.

Headland, T.N., Pike, K.L., & Harris, M. (Eds.). (1990). *Emics and Etics. The Insider/Outsider Debate*. SAGE Publications.

Horst, M., & Cobb, T. (2001). Growing academic vocabulary with a collaborative on-line data-base. In B. Morrison, D. Gardner, K. Keobke, & M. Spratt (Eds.), *ELT perspectives on IT and multimedia: Selected papers from the ITMELT Conference 2001* (pp. 189–225). Hong Kong Polytechnic University.

Howitt, D., & Cramer, D. (2020). *Research methods in psychology* (6th ed.). Pearson Education Limited.

Johns, T. (1991). Should you be persuaded – Two examples of data-driven learning materials. Classroom Concordancing. *English Language Research Journal* 4, 1–13.

Kilgarriff, A., Baisa, V., Bušta, J., Jakubíček, M., Kovář, V., Michelfeit, J., Rychlý, P., & Suchomel, V. (2014). *The sketch engine: Ten years on. 1*, 7–36.

Kilgarriff, A., Rychlý, P., Smrž, P., & Tugwell, D. (2004). The sketch engine. *Proceedings of the 11th EURALEX International Congress*, 105–116.

Le Foll, E. (2021). *Creating corpus-informed materials for the English as a foreign language classroom. A step-by-step guide for (trainee) teachers using online resources* (3rd ed.). Open Educational Resource. https://elenlefoll.pressbooks.com. CC-BY-NC 4.0.

Lee, H., Warschauer, M., & Lee, J.H. (2018). the effects of corpus use on second language vocabulary learning: A multilevel meta-analysis. *Applied Linguistics*, 40(5), 721–753.

Levshina, N. (2015). *How to do linguistics with R. data exploration and statistical analysis*. Benjamins.

Linck, J.A., & Cunnings, I. (2015). The utility and application of mixed-effects models in second language research: Mixed-effects models. *Language Learning*, 65(S1), 185–207.

Mackey, A., & Gass, S.M. (Eds.). (2012). *Research methods in second language acquisition: A practical guide* (1st ed). Wiley-Blackwell.

McKinley, J., & Rose, H. (Eds.). (2020). *The Routledge handbook of research methods in applied linguistics* (1st ed.). Routledge.

Mizumoto, A., & Chujo, K. (2015). A meta-analysis of data-driven learning approach in the Japanese EFL classroom. *English Corpus Studies*, 22, 1–18.

Mizumoto, A., Chujo, K., & Yokota, K. (2016). Development of a scale to measure learners' perceived preferences and benefits of data-driven learning. *ReCALL*, 28(02), 227–246.

Morris, M. (2012). *Concise dictionary of social and cultural anthropology* (1st ed). Wiley-Blackwell.

Phakiti, A., De Costa, P., Plonsky, L., & Starfield, S. (Eds.). (2018). *The Palgrave handbook of applied linguistics research methodology*. Palgrave Macmillan UK.

Poole, R. (2018). *A guide to using corpora for English language learners*. Edinburgh University Press.

Révész, A. (2012). Coding second language data validly and reliably. In A. Mackey & S. Gass (Eds.), *Research methods in second language acquisition. A practical guide* (pp. 203–221). Wiley-Blackwell.

Riazi, A.M. (2016a). Innovative mixed-methods research (IMMR): Moving beyond design technicalities to epistemological and methodological realisation. *Applied Linguistics*, 37(1), 33–49.

Riazi, A.M. (2016b). *The Routledge encyclopedia of research methods in applied linguistics: Quantitative, qualitative and mixed-methods research*. Routledge.

Riazi, A.M. (2017). *Mixed methods research in language teaching and learning*. Equinox.

Sinclair, J.M. (2003). *Reading concordances*. Pearson.

Supatranont, K. (2005). *A comparison of the effects of the concordance-based and the conventional teaching methods on engineering students' English vocabulary learning*. Unpublished PhD Thesis. Chulalongkorn University, Thailand.

Thomas, C.G. (2021). *Research methodology and scientific writing (2nd edition)*. Springer.

Vyatkina, N. (2020). Corpora as open educational resources for language teaching. *Foreign Language Annals, 52*(2), 359–370.

Yang, J.-S. (2016). The effectiveness of study-abroad on second language learning: A meta-analysis. *Canadian Modern Language Review, 72*(1), 66–94.

5 Italian L2
Corpus resources and language learning research

This chapter traces a brief history of Italian corpus linguistics, situating it within the broader context of Italian L2 research and practice. It shows how the interest towards the applications of corpus linguistics in second language teaching and learning has a long tradition in Italian L2 studies. This interest has, however, remained rather underdeveloped over the years, both because of the intermittent interest manifested by Italian scholars and teachers in the subject, and because of the scarcity of Italian language corpora suitable for pedagogical purposes. However, the last few years have seen some rapid changes in this respect. To demonstrate this, the chapter provides an updated account of the resources available today to inform pedagogical practices with corpus data. Corpora of L1 and L2 Italian, along with software tools for building and managing self-compiled corpora, are described in relation to their main functionalities and pedagogical affordances.

5.1 A brief history of Italian corpus linguistics

The history of Italian corpus linguistics is deeply intertwined with the history of corpus linguistics at large and yet this is not what we would normally read in the most popular manuals of corpus linguistics. Traditionally, in fact, the history of corpus linguistics has coincided with a history of English corpus linguistics (Kennedy, 1998; McEnery & Wilson, 2001). We learn about the *Brown corpus of American written English*, the very first corpus being built according to the contemporary notion of corpus in the early 1960s, leading to the development of all subsequent corpora. We read about how the need to improve English language learning and teaching materials was part of the initial impulse to compile larger and more adequate corpora to serve this purpose. The *Survey of English Usage* is a clear example in this respect (Quirk, 1960). We also learn about how the discipline of *corpus linguistics* unfolded through the shaping of its foundational terminology and also about its relationship with generativism. If we, however, broaden the horizon and look into the history of what makes a corpus function electronically, namely its computational basis, we will discover another fascinating side of the history of corpora and corpus linguistics.

In the 1940s, Father Roberto Busa was a young Jesuit priest based in Gallarate (Milan, Italy). He wanted to study the notion of 'presence' in St. Thomas Aquinas' writings. To do this, he set out to index the complete works of St. Thomas Aquinas and study the uses of 'in'. As content words related to the notion of presence, such as *praesens* or *praesentia*, were 'peripheral' (Busa, 1980, p. 83), Father Busa thought that he could study the way in which the function word 'in' affected the contexts in which it occurred with other content words. He wanted to have a rigorously comprehensive view of the way that St. Thomas Aquinas used language to illustrate one of the main tenets of his philosophical work. To do this, he needed to index all the words used in all the writings produced by Aquinas, so he started to compile hand-written cards. Each card contained a single form, the phrases in which the form occurred and the lemma it belonged to. Each card was then sorted according to its position with respect to the other forms in the texts. Father Busa soon reached 10,000 hard-written cards. In order to complete this work and cover all of St. Thomas Aquinas' writings, however, he would have needed to arrive at 10,000,000 cards. He was not going to be able to reach this goal by continuing with the hand-written card system. It was just not feasible. He realised that he needed mechanical help. So he ventured out into the United States, visiting several universities before arriving at the IBM headquarters in New York. This is where he met Thomas J. Watson, head and founder of IBM. Father Busa proposed what was termed as 'a daring project to produce an index to the complete writings of St. Thomas Aquinas' (Winter, 1999, p. 4). It was 1949, and this is how Father Busa recounts the meeting:

> I knew, the day I was to meet Thomas J. Watson, Sr., that he had on his desk a report which said IBM machines could never do what I wanted. I had seen in the waiting room a small poster imprinted with the words: 'The difficult we do right away; the impossible takes a little longer'. (IBM always loved slogans.) I took it in with me into Mr. Watson's office. Sitting down in front of him and sensing the tremendous power of his mind, I was inspired to say: 'It is not right to say "no" before you have tried'. I took out the poster and showed him his own slogan. He agreed that IBM would cooperate ... 'provided that you do not change IBM into International Busa Machines'. I had already informed him that, because my superiors had given me time, encouragement, their blessings and much holy water, but unfortunately no money, I could recompense IBM in any way except financially. That was providential!
>
> (Busa, 1980, p. 84)

The work conducted by Father Busa at IBM culminated many years later in the publication of the *Index Thomisticum Online*[1] (2005), thanks to a collaboration between Fundación Tomás de Aquino, IBM, CAEL

(*Computerizzazione delle Analisi Ermeneutiche Lessicologiche*[2]) and the University of Navarra. The figure of Father Roberta Busa and his work are recognised internationally in a number of forms. In 1988, the Association for Literary and Linguistic Computing (ALLC)[3] and the Association for Computers in the Humanities (ACH) created the Busa Award. The award is given yearly to people who have distinguished themselves in the field of computational linguistics. More specifically, as we read on the dedicated webpage: 'The Busa award is given to recognise outstanding lifetime achievements in the application of information and communications technologies to humanistic research'.[4] A Facebook group has also been created, gathering almost 500 scholars and enthusiasts from all around the world who remember the history and the value of Father Busa's work and commitment.[5] Moreover, Father Busa's legacy survives to this day through the *CNR – Istituto di Linguistica Computazionale di Pisa*, which was founded in 1980 by one of his students, Antonio Zampolli.[6]

The history of corpus linguistics in Italy certainly received a boost from Tullio De Mauro. His entry 'Statistica linguistica' (i.e., Statistical linguistics), published in 1961 with the *Enciclopedia Italiana*,[7] placed an emphasis on the importance of quantification in the study of language. Statistical linguistics is defined as

> l'applicazione del metodo statistico all'esame dei fatti linguistici: le unità costitutive di una lingua (fonemi, parole, ecc.), soprattutto considerate sotto il profilo della frequenza con cui appaiono nei testi, costituiscono un tipico insieme di fenomeni di massa e sono perciò suscettibili di indagini statistiche per rilevare le frequenze medie del loro distribuirsi nel discorso e, nel tempo, le eventuali trasformazioni di tali frequenze.[8]
> (De Mauro, 1961, p. 820)

This view would have a great influence from then on in the introduction of fundamental laws related to the quantification of language phenomena, such as Zipf's law and its various elaborations, in Italian linguistics, which had until then been dominated by the historical-comparative approach.

The first large-scale project aimed at developing a corpus-based account of Italian language frequency phenomena was the *Lessico di Frequenza* (LIF), launched in 1972 by the *Centro Nazionale di Calcolo elettronico* in Pisa, in collaboration with IBM-Italia (Bortolini et al., 1972). This frequency list was based on a 500,000-word corpus, which generated statistical data on a list of 5,000 lemmas. Great care was taken in creating a balanced corpus. The corpus was in fact formed by five balanced sections each containing one of the following text types: theatre, novels, films, newspapers, school coursebooks. The corpus is, unfortunately, no longer available. This corpus-based wordlist was primarily conceived as a lexicographic tool, which would then inform much of De Mauro's work on different quantitative and qualitative aspects of Italian language usage (cfr. De Mauro, 1980, 1995).

88 Corpus resources and language learning research

The history of corpus linguistics in Italy can also be traced through the introductory manuals published over the years for the Italian audience. In 1997, Stefania Spina published the volume *Parole in rete. Guida ai siti internet sul linguaggio* (Spina, 1997). This book was published as part of a series directed by Raffaele Simone entitled '*Biblioteca di italiano e oltre*'. At a time when computers and the internet were still little known in Italy and in the world, Stefania Spina was one of the very few scholars in Italy who were gaining familiarity with their potential quite rapidly. With an attentive view to how the developments of the web and of computers were unfolding all around the world, her book introduced the Italian community of scholars who were active in the field of linguistics to how the internet was changing the way in which language studies were being conducted. In this sense, her book was truly pioneering. The aim of the book was twofold: to inform and to guide. The book contains an inventory of online linguistics-related resources, which are divided into information resources and tools for language studies. Each resource is reviewed critically.

However, to consider Spina's work as a mere selection, classification, and analysis of the wealth of online language resources available at the time would be highly reductive. What the book achieves goes well beyond these aspects in that (1) it demonstrates, through the systematic inventory, how the way in which linguistics research was changing and would continue to change in the years to come, with respect to the impact that the computer and the web were having and (2) it projected the community of Italian scholars towards an international setting, where numerous ways of taking advantage of the latest technological advances in computer sciences were already being explored. As declared in the premise of the book, the overarching aim of this work is to collect 'un certo numero di risorse chiave, non solo per la consistenza scientifica delle informazioni riportate, ma anche per il loro valore di modello di ciò che la rete può offrire del modo in cui ciascuno può contribuire al suo sviluppo con le proprie competenze'[9] (Spina, 1997, p. XVII).

As far as we know, the first manual of corpus linguistics in Italy was published by Stefania Spina in 2001 and was entitled *Fare i conti con le parole*[10] (Spina, 2001). The novelty of this manual resides not only in the fact that for the first time the Italian audience of students and scholars would be able to read about corpus linguistics in Italian, but also in how the book fostered a new way of thinking about language and language analysis, through a corpus lens. This is particularly evident in passages such as the following one:

> l'elaboratore, più che come esecutore veloce di operazioni consuete, è utilizzato come generatore di problemi nuovi; l'accento viene posto non tanto sulle capacità fisiche (memoria, rapidità) quanto su quelle logiche. L'analisi informatizzata di dati linguistici non è il completamento di

un metodo tradizionale, ma la sua completa rifondazione, la globale rivisitazione di strategie di ricerca consolidate alla luce di strategie di ricerca nuove.[11]

(Spina, 2001, pp. 12–13)

In later years, Spina would highlight how there is still a 'historical prejudice against data' in the domain of Italian humanities research, which still tends to be influenced by Benedetto Croce's historicising approach (Spina, 2017). While Spina would underline the theoretically revolutionary nature of corpus-based inquiry, along with the need to see it as complementary to the other approaches explored thus far, Francesco Sabatini, well-known linguist and former president of the *Accademia della Crusca*, would underscore a certain continuity in the adoption of a corpus-minded framework in approaching linguistic analysis, especially when pertaining to lexicographic goals. The history of Italian lexicography is, in fact, based on the collection of corpora, which would be analysed in view of realising lexicographic entries. Notwithstanding the developments in the field of computer science, Sabatini views the tradition of historical Italian linguistics as largely coinciding with that of Italian corpus linguistics. As quoted also in Barbera (2013, p. 13), Sabatini maintains that

il fare preciso ricorso ad un corpus di testi è una costante nell'intera nostra tradizione grammaticografica e lessicografica e, in termini ancora più ampi, nella storia delle dispute linguistiche fin dall'epoca di Dante. Una costante che trova la sua ragion d'essere in una condizione particolare, solitamente considerata penalizzante, della nostra lingua: la sua nascita attraverso l'opera di scrittori e la sua lunga permanenza in vita attraverso l'uso scritto, e quindi grazie al continuo sostegno dato da un canone di autori.[12]

(Sabatini, 2007, p. xiii)

Following Spina, a number of other introductory manuals were published over the years. In 2007, Isabella Chiari published *Introduzione alla linguistica computazionale*, a clear and to-the-point introduction to the basics of computational and corpus linguistics (Chiari, 2007). Lenci et al. (2005) are the authors of a successful introduction to computational linguistics intitled *Testo e computer*, which has now reached several reprints. One of the most recently published volumes is *Introduzione ai corpora dell'italiano*, by Emanuela Cresti and Alessandro Panunzi (Cresti & Panunzi, 2013). This is the first volume explicitly focused on corpus linguistics in Italy and with reference to the Italian language. Today, corpus linguistics modules are active in several Italian universities. Furthermore, academic courses more broadly devoted to the digital humanities tend to incorporate more and more teaching related to corpus linguistics.

5.2 Italian corpus linguistics in the Italian L2 landscape

Advances in computer science in general, and in computational and corpus linguistics in particular, have intersected with the tradition of Italian language learning studies on a number of occasions but in an arguably still very limited way. This is evident when consulting what is, to the best of our knowledge, the main bibliographical resource available for Italian language learning studies: the *BELI – Bibliografia dell'Educazione Linguistica in Italia*,[13] curated by Paolo E. Balboni, leading scholar in Italian L2 research, based at Università Ca' Foscari Venezia. The bibliography collects language education studies conducted in Italy pertaining to Italian and other languages, whether modern or classical. The bibliography begins with studies published in 1960 and extends to 2020. It is divided into three parts: part 1 deals with publications from 1960 to 1999; part 2 covers publications from 2000 to 2010; part 3 includes publications from 2011 to 2020. If we search the repertoire with the keywords 'corpus', 'corpora', 'data', 'dati', 'concordance', concordances', concordanza', 'concordanze', 'DDL', including studies concerning not only Italian L2 but also other languages, we are able to obtain an overall picture of how these notions have evolved in the context of Italian L2 studies over the years.

Before we illustrate the findings, a few words on the method that we followed are in order. The analysis of the bibliographical repertoire considers the keywords that are present only in the title of single studies, with the exclusion of edited volumes (e.g., Rossini Favretti, 2000), which are treated separately. Furthermore, titles containing more than one keyword (e.g., Gavioli, 1998) are counted twice in Table 5.1, but only once in Figure 5.1, when categorising the studies according to their typology. Studies published in multiple volumes (e.g., Amato, 1974 & Amato, 1978) are counted only once. Non-pertinent occurrences (e.g., Balboni, 1983) were excluded. 'Dati' and 'data' are considered only when they occur with specific reference to corpora, and are excluded when they refer more generally to language learning data (e.g., Colombo & Marello, 2014). Occurrences of keywords in studies that are not pertinent with our aims are included in Table 5.1 but excluded in Figure 5.1 (e.g., Cesiri et al. 2015).

Table 5.1 contains a synthesis of the data. As can be seen, over the 40-year interval between 1960 and 1999, only 11 times do we have occurrences of keywords that might be associated with corpora and language learning. This number increases dramatically in the 2000–2010 interval (n = 57) and continues to do so in the subsequent (n = 71). We can also notice a strong concentration of occurrences for the words 'corpus' and 'corpora' from the year 2000 onwards ('corpus' = 59 occurrences; 'corpora' = 51 occurrences), though in some cases, as will be shown in Figure 5.1, the occurrence may refer to generically termed collections of texts, rather than corpora in a stricter sense. No occurrences emerge in any of the year intervals considered in relation to the following keywords: *concordance, concordances, concordanza, concordanze*.

Corpus resources and language learning research 91

Table 5.1 Occurrences of corpus-related keywords in BELI over time

	1960–1999	2000–2010	2011–2020
corpus	3	25	34
corpora	2	29	22
data	2	0	11
dati	2	1	2
concordance	0	0	0
concordances	0	0	0
concordanza	0	0	0
concordanze	2	1	0
DDL	0	1	2
TOTAL	11	57	71

Figure 5.1 shows the distribution of study types over the three temporal intervals present in BELI. The study types are identified in terms of the following eight categories:

1. GEN, keywords used as generic terms or with reference to fields other than language learning (e.g., corpus as syllabus *or* corpora for uses in translation);
2. ICL, brief introductions to corpus linguistics;
3. DLC, descriptions of learner corpora (including methodological issues);
4. CALL, corpora used to analyse learner language;
5. CLL, corpora used to learn a language;
6. CALL+CLL, corpora used to analyse learner language + corpora used to learn a language;
7. CAPM, corpora used to analyse pedagogical materials;
8. CAPLL, corpus applications (language testing, translation, etc.).

As can be seen, the most prominent type of study is related to the uses of corpora to learn a language, with six studies published between 1960 and 1999, 27 studies between 2000 and 2010 and then 36 between 2011 and 2020. This testifies to a continued interest in the field of Italian educational linguistics at large in how corpora can have beneficial effects on language learning. The second-largest category is that of CALL, that is corpora used to analyse learner language. In this case, we have one study in the first timeframe, and 13 studies in the subsequent two timeframes. All the other categories are present in much smaller numbers. Descriptions of learner corpora are present with five studies in both the second- and third-time interval. As for studies pertaining to the combination of corpora used to analyse learner language with that of corpora used directly by the learners to learn a language, we find five studies in the 2009–2010 interval, and then three in the

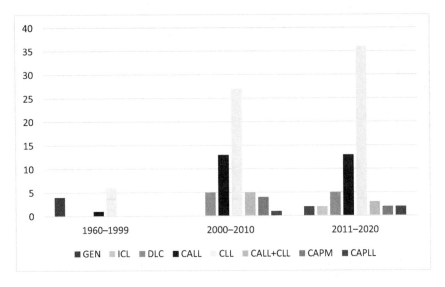

Figure 5.1 Temporal distribution of corpus-related publication types in BELI.

subsequent one. Furthermore, the generic uses of the searched keywords are concentrated in the first temporal interval (1960–1999), while they appear to be absent in the second (2000–2010) and then resurface, though to a lesser extent, in the third time interval (2011–2020). Brief introductions to the field of corpus linguistics, in relation to second language acquisition, are published only in the most recent time interval, though introductory manuals had already been published in previous years (Spina, 2001; Lenci et al., 2005). Applications in translation studies and language testing are also present in the most recent years, though in limited numbers, together with studies exploring the characteristics of coursebooks via corpus-based techniques. Along with the single studies represented in Figure 5.1, several edited volumes (Rossini Favretti, 2000; Taylor Torsello et al., 2001; Aston, 2001; Hédiard, 2007; Martelli & Pulcini, 2008; Andorno & Rastelli, 2009; Maiello & Pellegrino, 2012; Corino & Onesti, 2017), together with one special journal issue (Corino, 2019), have appeared in Italy over the years, thus helping to spread the principles and practices and corpus linguistics in the field of educational linguistics.

However, not all the studies pertaining to the Italian domain of educational linguistics are found in the BELI repertoire. Some notable absences include the studies conducted by Kennedy and Miceli (2001, 2010, 2016) on DDL for Italian. This is due to the fact that the BELI repertoire covers studies related to educational linguistics research conducted by scholars who are active in Italy, or who have been active in Italy for some years. In order to have a comprehensive view of the relationship between corpus linguistics and educational linguistics related to the Italian language, a number of different sources will need to be consulted.

5.3 Developing data-driven learning practices for Italian: resources and affordances

What resources are available to teachers and researchers wishing to use Italian corpora for pedagogical purposes, and for DDL activities in particular? In this section, we will review the main corpora of Italian L1 and L2 that have been built so far. They will be presented in chronological order (i.e. considering as a temporal reference the first available publication describing the resource) and through the lens of their main features.

5.3.1 Italian L1 corpora

L1 corpora play a crucial role in the development of DDL activities. For example, they are able to model the target language with reference to specific word patterns and to patterns of variation in the meaning of word patterns. This section reviews the main existing Italian L1 corpora with reference to their main characteristics, but also in relation to their adaptability for pedagogical purposes. To this end, while keeping in mind a sort of continuum which may be identified in distinguishing 'corpora for linguists vs. corpora for learners' (Forti & Spina, 2019), where corpora may fall more or less into one of these two categories, the Italian L1 corpora listed in Table 5.2 are categorised in terms of their degree of pedagogical adaptability. We, therefore, find corpora of the following kinds:

- *Limited adaptability*, referring to corpora which were developed primarily for descriptive purposes, and having in mind linguists as main users; this implies a potentially considerable need of adaptation of the data on the teacher's part. Data will need to be gleaned by the teacher and then passed on to the learners. When corpora have limited pedagogical adaptability, direct/hands on use of corpora by the learners may, in fact, be challenging (e.g., LIP).
- *Some adaptability*, referring to the cases where corpora have been developed for descriptive purposes but also bearing learners in mind. While not necessarily having a fully learner/teacher-friendly interface, these corpora include some resources specifically designed for learners and teachers of second languages (e.g., Paisà, Merlin).
- *Full adaptability*, referring to the cases when the corpus and its interface have been developed with second language learners in mind primarily. As a result, both the data contained in the corpus and the way in which the corpus may be explored are suitable for learner and language teachers and do not require any technical knowledge (e.g., SkELL).

94 Corpus resources and language learning research

Table 5.2 Main corpora of L1 Italian (in chronological order of publication)

	Size (tokens)	Language mode	Text type(s)	Architecture	Adaptability for pedagogical purposes	Year of publication	Accessibility
LIP	ca. 500,000	Spoken	(a) face-to-face conversations; (b) phone conversations; (c) interviews/exams/debates; (d) monologues; (e) TV and radio programs.	Cross-sectional	Limited (assumed)	1993	Freely accessible online.
COLFIS	ca. 3,800,000	Written	(a) newspapers; (b) magazines; (c) books.	Cross-sectional	Limited (assumed)	1995	Freely accessible online.
CORIS/CODIS	ca. 150,000,000	Written	(a) fiction: (b) newspapers; (c) academic; (d) legal; (e) other.	Dynamic	Limited (assumed)	2000	Freely accessible online.
LA REPUBBLICA	ca. 380,000,000	Written	Newspaper texts	Diachronic	Limited	2004	Accessible via noSketchEngine.
VINCA	ca. 168,000	Written	Elicited descriptions	Cross-sectional	Some	2004	Freely accessible online.
C-ORAL-ROM (Italian section)	ca. 300,000	Spoken	Spontaneous speech	Cross-sectional	Limited (assumed)	2005	Accessible on DVD.

CLIPS	ca. 1,000,000	Spoken	(a) radio programmes; (b) elicited speech; (c) read-aloud speech; (d) phone speech	Cross-sectional	Limited	2007	Free online access to raw files.
CORDIC	ca. 1,000,000	Half written, half spoken	Written section: (a) arts; (b) bureaucracy; (c) creative; (d) economics; (e) press. Spoken section: (a) spontaneous; (b) non-spontaneous.	Cross-sectional	Limited	2013	Accessible via noSketchEngine.
ITTENTEN20	ca. 12,000,000,000	Written	Web texts	Dynamic	Limited	2013	Accessible via SketchEngine.
PAISÀ	ca. 250,000,000	Written	Web texts	Cross-sectional	Some	2014	Freely accessible online.
PEC	ca. 26,000,000	Written and spoken	literature, non-fiction, press, academic, school texts, administrative texts and web texts for the written component, and TV, film and spontaneous speech for the spoken component.	Cross-sectional	Limited	2014	Freely accessible online.

(*continued*)

Table 5.2 Cont.

	Size (tokens)	Language mode	Text type(s)	Architecture	Adaptability for pedagogical purposes	Year of publication	Accessibility
SKELL-IT	ca. 320,000,000	Written	Web texts	Cross-sectional	Full	2018 (date of first availability; no publications specifically targeting the Italian version of SkeLL)	Freely accessible online.
KIParla	ca. 1,213,600	Spoken	KIP module: lectures, exams, student-teacher meetings, semi-structured interviews, free conversation. ParlaTO module: interviews.	Cross-sectional	Limited	2019	Freely accessible online.

The *Lessico di frequenza dell'italiano parlato* (LIP)[14] (Voghera et al., 2014) is a cross-sectional spoken corpus of L1 Italian and may be searched via the VoLIP interface. It includes about 500,000 tokens and was built to include diaphasic, diamesic and diatopic dimensions of variations. As for the first two dimensions, the corpus is divided into the following sections: (a) face-to-face conversations; (b) phone conversations; (c) interviews/exams/debates; d) monologues; (e) TV and radio programs. As for the diatopic dimension, the recordings were collected in the following four Italian cities: Milan, Rome, Naples and Florence. The corpus was published in 1993 and may be searched online according to its metadata or on the basis of lexical and/or morpho-syntactic features. In each case, the audio transcription is associated with the audio file. Unfortunately, at the time of writing this book, the webpage for accessing and searching the LIP seems to not be working. For this reason, although we can assume that the pedagogical adaptability of the corpus is limited since it was not built primarily for didactic purposes, we have no way of verifying this with a direct observation of the resource. The *Corpus e Lessico di Frequenza dell'Italiano Scritto* (CoLFIS)[15] (Laudanna et al., 1995) is a corpus of written L1 Italian comprising about 3,800,000 tokens. It is divided into three sections: (a) newspapers; (b) magazines; (c) books. Unfortunately, the webpage dedicated for online access to the corpus was not functioning at the time of writing,[16] so its limited pedagogical adaptability is only assumed. The *Corpus di Italiano Scritto – Corpus dinamico di italiano scritto* (CORIS/CODIS)[17] (Rossini Favretti, 2000) is a corpus which seeks to be representative of Italian L1 writing not only cross-sectionally but also dynamically through time. It has an in-built monitor corpus, in fact, and has now reached a total of 150,000,000 tokens and is free to access online. At the time of writing, the site is not accessible.[18] It contains various types of texts: (a) fiction; (b) newspapers; (c) academic prose; (d) legal prose; (e) other. Its pedagogically adaptability is, however, quite limited as the interface to explore the corpus requires specific query language. While the corpus was evidently built for researchers in the first instance, it may very well be used by teachers indirectly, when searching for specific language data pertaining to specific timeframes.

The *La Repubblica* corpus (Baroni et al., 2004)[19] is a large corpus of newspaper texts collected over a timespan of 15 years (1985–2000). It comprises about 380,000,000 tokens and is accessible via the noSketch Engine platform. Its pedagogical adaptability is limited in the sense that it contains texts belonging to a single genre. However, it may be useful in the context of Italian for specific purposes courses (e.g., course of journalism, open to both L1 and L2 speakers of Italian). The *Varietà di Italiano di Nativi Corpus Appaiato* (VINCA)[20] corpus was built to be a corpus of L1 texts comparable with the learner corpus VALICO (Corino et al., 2017). It contains about 168,000 tokens of elicited descriptions. It is freely accessible online. Its pedagogical adaptability is somewhat higher than in the case of other corpora. It not only requires no registration to be accessed, but the search interface is simple enough to be used by learners and teachers and, most importantly, it is provided with an easy function that allows to export the concordance lines in a word document format. The *Integrated Reference Corpora for Spoken Romance Languages* (C-ORAL-ROM)[21] (Cresti & Moneglia, 2005) is a cross-sectional spoken corpus of L1 Italian, containing about 300,000 tokens of spontaneous speech. The transcribed texts are aligned with the corresponding audio and the texts are balanced in terms of diaphasic features. Unfortunately, the corpus appeared to be inaccessible at the time of writing this book, so we can only assume its limited pedagogical adaptability. The *Corpora e Lessici dell'Italiano Parlato e Scritto* (CLIPS) is a cross-sectional spoken corpus of L1 Italian. It contains about 1,000,000 tokens and was developed to study variation in spoken Italian in relation to diatopic and diaphasic dimensions. As for diatopy, it includes spoken data collected in 15 Italian cities. As for diaphasy, it includes the following spoken text types: (a) radio programs; (b) elicited speech; (c) read-aloud speech; (d) phone speech. The raw files of the corpus are freely accessible online, via registration. This corpus has limited pedagogical adaptability, not only because it was built primarily for descriptive purposes and to be used by linguists, but most of all because it is not available online via a dedicated software interface, but only as downloadable raw files. The CORDIC corpora (Cresti & Panunzi, 2013) comprise a written and spoken section. In total, they reach about 1,000,000 tokens. The texts are divided into (a) arts; (b) bureaucracy; (c) creative; (d) economics; (e) press for the written section, and into (a) spontaneous; (b) non-spontaneous texts for the spoken part. They are accessible via the noSketch Engine platform.

The *ItTenTen20* corpus[22] (Jakubíče et al., 2013) is a web corpus consisting of about 12 billion tokens. It has a dynamic nature, in the sense that new additions are made regularly. It is freely searchable via the SketchEngine platform. Its pedagogical adaptability is limited as its development was not primarily targeted at language learners. However, the visualisations can prove particularly useful to the teacher and materials developer. The Paisà corpus (Lyding et al., 2014)[23] is a web corpus consisting of about 250,000,000 tokens. It is freely accessible online. It features a filtering function which allows to select only easier sentences on the basis of three criteria: (a) the length (only sentences comprising between five and 25 words are considered); (b) the readability index for Italian known as Gulpease (Lucisano & Piemontese, 1988); (c) the number of words belonging to the basic vocabulary of Italian (De Mauro, 1980): only sentences containing fewer than eight words not present in the basic vocabulary of Italian are considered. This filtering function makes Paisà useful for teachers wishing to extract level-appropriate examples from the corpus. It is probably less suitable for direct access by learners, as some technical language is present in the user interface. The *Perugia corpus* (PEC)[24] (Spina, 2014) is a reference corpus of L1 Italian. It contains approximately 26,000,000 tokens covering the following ten textual genres: literature, non-fiction, press, academic, school texts, administrative texts and web texts for the written component, and TV, film and spontaneous speech for the spoken component. Its pedagogical adaptability is limited as it is a corpus primarily built for linguists. However, its easy-to-use web interface makes it an ideal resource for preparing paper-based, hands-off DDL activities. The Italian version of SkELL (*SketchEngine for Language Learning*) (Baisa & Suchomel, 2014)[25] is, as far as we know, the most learner- and teacher-friendly corpus exploration tool that is available to date. It is based on a 320,000,000-word web corpus, which can be explored through a specially devised algorithm that selects 40 good examples for language learners. Though it does not contain graded texts, its content is assumed to be suitable for most proficiency levels. Finally, the KIParla corpus (Mauri et al., 2019; Cerruti & Ballarè, 2021; Goria & Mauri, 2018)[26] is a spoken corpus of L1 Italian, comprising 1,000,000 tokens. It contains two separate modules: the KIP module, with spoken data collected in Bologna, and the ParlaTO module, with spoken data collected in Turin. It is annotated with a range of metadata pertaining to diatopic and diastratic variables, as well as spoken interaction types. It is also text-to-speech aligned. Its pedagogical adaptability is limited in terms of hands-on use by second language learners, but, as in other cases, it can serve as a basis to develop paper-based activities, with pre-selected data.

The main features characterising the corpora we just described are summarised in Table 5.2. Throughout the years, the development of Italian L1 corpora has intensified. While most of the L1 Italian corpora today are not immediately suitable for pedagogical purposes, they nevertheless represent invaluable resources for teachers wishing to inform their pedagogical activities with qualitatively and quantitatively relevant linguistic data. At this stage, the Italian version of SkELL represents the most learner-friendly resource for hands-on DDL.

5.3.2 Italian L2 corpora

Learner corpora have multiple affordances in developing DDL activities. They can assist in identifying challenging areas for the learners, thus informing the development of the curriculum. They can also be used in activities with the learners to stimulate their metalinguistic awareness and foster the discovery of patterns in a contrastive modality, by comparing L1 and L2 texts. One of the most recent overviews of Italian learner corpora was presented at the LCR conference in 2017 by Stefania Spina in the context of her keynote address (Spina, 2017). The overview focused on the main Italian learner corpora built until then and freely available on the web. Spina recognises the pioneering value of the Pavia Project (Chini, 2016; Giacalone Ramat, 2003), one of the very first attempts to build an empirical database containing L2 Italian spoken production data. The project launched in the late 1980s and continued to produce studies well into the 2000s.

The empirical data collected within the Pavia Project involved 20 L2 Italian learners, comprised between four to 20 audio recordings for each learner and covered a timeframe of one month to four years. Thanks to this database, it was possible to describe Italian interlanguage at different levels of proficiency, mainly in relation to morphology (nominal and verbal), syntax and text. The methodology used in the studies contained in Giacalone Ramat (2003) was based on a functionalist approach, with specific reference to the form-to-function approach (VanPatten et al., 2020, pp. 40–62). The studies centred around the Pavia Project acknowledged the value of empirical data in the development of pedagogical practices. Subsequent collections of L2 Italian data would benefit from this experience and apply the methodological procedures which, in the meantime, were being developed within corpus linguistics at large worldwide. Unfortunately, at the time of writing, the url dedicated to this database was inactive.[27]

In 2009, Massimo Palermo published the ADIL2 corpus (Palermo, 2009). The corpus was published by means of a DVD attached to a guidebook. The corpus contains 1168 texts produced by 1126 learners, and reaches a total of 432,606 tokens. It is divided into three sections: cross-sectional written texts (42%), cross-sectional oral texts (20%) and longitudinal oral texts (38%). The proficiency levels present in the corpus range from elementary to advanced, with a slight over-representation of the elementary level. It is currently the only major Italian learner corpus unavailable online. Subsequent Italian learner corpora were, in fact, published online. One instance of this is the case of *Lessico dell'italiano parlato da stranieri* (LIPS) (Gallina, 2015).[28] The corpus is partly longitudinal and contains about 2,000 oral texts, produced by learners and examiners, reaching a total of about 700,000 tokens. The proficiency levels represented in the corpus range from A1 to C2 and the learners' L1s are unspecified, as only data on their nationality is available. The corpus was developed by the University for Foreigners of Siena and was completed in 2019.

The KOLIPSI, developed at Eurac Research in Bolzano (Italy), is a corpus of written texts, half of which collected in the school year 2007/2008, while the remainder in the school year 2014/2015. It contains a total of ca. 4,000 texts, produced by ca. 2,000 students, totalling ca. 800,000 tokens (Glaznieks et al., in preparation). Another major effort in the development of Italian leaner corpora is *Varietà Apprendimento Lingua Italiana Corpus Online* (VALICO) (Corino et al., 2017).[29] VALICO is a cross-sectional corpus comprising 2,502 texts produced by the same number of learners, reaching a total of about 380,000 tokens. The learners have different proficiency levels and different L1s. The corpus was developed in 2003 and published online in 2009 by the University of Turin. Another corpus of learner Italian is the *CORpus del Italiano de los Españoles* (CORITE)[30] (Bailini & Frigerio, 2018), a partly longitudinal, partly pseudo-longitudinal corpus containing 385 written texts. The texts were produced at various datapoints by 90 learners, with proficiency levels ranging between A1 and

B1. The corpus contains a total of 103,147 tokens and was published by Università Cattolica del S. Cuore di Milano in 2018.

The last few years have seen a steady increase in the development of Italian learner corpora also thanks to the University for Foreigners of Perugia. The *Corpus of Chinese Learners of Italian* (COLI)[31] is a pseudo-longitudinal corpus of written and spoken texts, produced by 30 Chinese L1 learners, totalling 82,300 tokens. The corpus is balanced in terms of proficiency levels of the learners (i.e. B1, B2, C1) and was published online in 2009. The *Corpus di Apprendenti di Italiano L2* (CAIL2) (Bratankova, 2015) is a cross-sectional corpus of 400 written texts, produced by the same number of learners, reaching a total of about 237,000 tokens. The learners belong to an intermediate-advanced proficiency level and have a range of different L1s. The corpus was built in the context of Leontyna Bratankova's PhD thesis, supervised by Stefania Spina, and was published in 2015 by the University for Foreigners of Perugia. The *Longitudinal Corpus of Chinese Learners of Italian* (LOCCLI) is a longitudinal corpus comprising 350 written texts, produced by 175 Chinese L1 learners, reaching a total of about 97,000 tokens. The texts were collected at two datapoints separated by a six-month time interval. The corpus was published in 2015 by the University for Foreigners of Perugia (Spina & Siyanova-Chanturia, 2018). The most recent learner corpus developed at the University for Foreigners of Perugia is the CELI corpus (Spina et al., 2022). The corpus is pseudo-longitudinal and contains 3,041 texts written at four different proficiency levels: B1, B2, C1 and C2. The texts were produced in the context of the Italian language certification exams CELI.[32] This provides a robust attribution of the texts to a specific proficiency level. The corpus has a total of about 600,000 tokens and the distribution of the texts with respect to the four proficiency levels is balanced. The nationalities represented in the corpus are various. The most represented ones are Greek, Spanish, Romanian, Swiss and Albanian. The corpus was published in 2022.

Other Italian learner corpora are included in larger multilingual corpora. This is so in the case of two corpora developed at the EURAC research centre in Bolzano (Italy): MERLIN and LEONIDE. The Italian section of the *Multilingual Platform for the European Reference Levels: interlanguage exploration in context* (MERLIN)[33] (Abel et al., 2014; Wisniewski et al., 2013) is a pseudo-longitudinal corpus composed by 803 written texts, produced by the same number of learners, reaching a total of about 107,000 tokens. The learners belong to proficiency levels between A1 and B1 and have different L1 backgrounds. The corpus was published online in 2014. The Italian section of *The Longitudinal LEarner COrpus iN Italiano, Deutsch, English* (LEONIDE)[34] is a longitudinal corpus of about 2,500 written texts produced by 163 bilingual (Italian and German) high school students, reaching a total of about 93,000 tokens. The data collection covered a three-year time span (2015–2018). The corpus was published in 2020 (Glaznieks et al., 2022). In terms of adaptability for pedagogical purposes, as can be seen in Table 5.3 most learner corpora of Italian are

102 *Corpus resources and language learning research*

Table 5.3 Main corpora of L2 Italian (in chronological order of publication)

	\multicolumn{3}{c	}{Learner-related features}	Adaptability for pedagogical purposes	\multicolumn{4}{c	}{Design-related features}		
	N.	L1	Proficiency level		Size (tokens)	Language mode	Architecture	Year of publication	Accessibility
Pavia Project	20	Various (n=11)	Various/ unspecified (post-elementary)	Limited	ca. 600,000	Spoken	Part cross-sectional, part longitudinal	2001	On CD, upon request.
ADIL2	1,126	Various (n=25)	Elementary to Advanced	Limited	ca. 433,000	Written & spoken	Part cross-sectional, part longitudinal	2009	On DVD, purchasable online.
VALICO	2,502	Various (n=10)	Intermediate	Limited	ca. 380,000	Written	Cross-sectional	2009	Freely accessible online.
COLI	30	Chinese	B1 to C1	Limited	ca. 82,000	Written & spoken	Pseudo-longitudinal	2009	Freely accessible online.
MERLIN (Italian section)	803	Various (n=11); unspecified.	A1 to B1	Some		Written	Pseudo-longitudinal	2013	Freely accessible online and downloadable.
CAIL2	400	Various (n=33)	Intermediate/ advanced	Limited	ca. 237,000	Written	Cross-sectional	2015	Freely accessible online.
LIPS	700	Unspecified (indication of nationality only)	A1 to C2	Limited	ca. 700,000	Spoken	Longitudinal	2015	Free online access to raw files.

Corpus resources and language learning research 103

KOLIPSI	2,000	German/ multilingual	Unspecified (lower secondary school)	Limited	ca. 800,000	Written	Pseudo-longitudinal	2015	Freely accessible online.
CORITE	90	Spanish	A1 to B1	Limited	ca. 103,000	Written	Part longitudinal, part pseudo-longitudinal	2018	Freely accessible online.
LOCCLI	175	Chinese	A2 and B1	Limited	ca. 97,000	Written	Longitudinal	2018	Freely accessible online.
LEONIDE (Italian section)	162	German/ multilingual	Unspecified (lower secondary school)	Limited	ca. 93,000	Written	Longitudinal	2020	Freely accessible online and downloadable.
CELI	3,041	Unspecified (indication of nationality only)	B1 to C2	Limited	ca. 600,000	Written	Pseudo-longitudinal	2022	Freely accessible online.

characterised by limited adaptability, as they have been built primarily to investigate features of learner language. Nevertheless, they represent a rich reservoir to create pedagogical activities tailored for learners.

Numerous Italian learner corpora have been developed in the context of PhD theses and small-scale research studies. These corpora, however, have not been published and are thus not accessible to the professional community. While not describing them in detail here for these reasons, we would still like to acknowledge their value and importance in pushing Italian L2 empirical research forward over the years.

5.3.3 DIY corpora

One little-explored option in the development of DDL activities for Italian L2 learning and teaching is the use of DIY corpora. This practice has been extensively discussed in the context of ESL/EFL teaching, with special reference to EAP contexts (Charles, 2012, 2014, 2019). Interestingly, the very first publication on DDL for Italian appearing in a major international CALL journal described the development of DDL activities based on a specialised corpus that was built from the recordings of the teachers' lectures on Italian renaissance theatre (Polezzi, 1993). The main advantage in building your own corpus is that it can be built in a way that reflects very closely the needs of the learners. In this sense, we can qualify the term 'needs' with respect to the proficiency level they belong to, as well as to their motivation for learning the language. Similarly to the context described in Polezzi's study, we may be teaching in classes of students preparing to sit an entrance exam to the Conservatorium of Music or the Academy of Fine Arts. A good number of Chinese L1 learners of Italian, enrolled in Italian language courses at Italian universities, are in fact interested in studying these disciplines. In these cases, teachers and/or researchers may build collections of texts that are relevant to a specific discipline or area of interest. The corpus may be built by the single teacher, for use in a particular language course, or it may be built by the students themselves. Language learners who are particularly keen on learning the terminology pertaining to a specific discipline, because they will go on to study that discipline in a language that is different from their L1, may create their own collection of texts, based on academic interests, and then use it regularly for their needs (e.g., when having to write an essay).

Once the collection is compiled, all a teacher and/or researcher will need to do is use a software program able to automatically extract some qualitative and quantitative information from the corpus. One of the most popular tools is AntConc (Anthony, 2020). It is a freely downloadable corpus exploration tool which allows the extraction of concordances, wordlists and n-grams. It also allows the visualisation of the distribution of a given form. It may be used directly by the students, especially if they are university students, or by the teacher wishing to develop re-usable DDL activities. Another freely downloadable option is Lancsbox (Brezina et al., 2020). With this software it is possible to not only generate concordance lines for inductive pattern-hunting activities, but also use the function named GraphColl. Thanks to this function, it is possible to visualise collocation networks and observe the different kinds of association relationships between words. GraphColl has been used successfully in an EFL context (Liu, 2021). Another option is Voyant Tools,[35] which easily allows the user to paste a text and generate concordance lines and word lists, along with a number of different kinds of colourful visualisations, including collocation graphs, word clouds, relative frequencies of a word related to the different segments of a document, and so on.

5.4 Chapter summary and conclusions

How have Italian scholars contributed to the history of corpus and computational linguistics at large, and how can we situate corpus-informed studies in the context of Italian educational linguistics? These are the main questions addressed in the chapter. By scoping what is one the largest bibliographical repertoires available to the field, namely the BELI – *Bibliografia dell'Educazione Linguistica in Italia*, curated by Paolo E. Balboni, we illustrated how corpora have been present in the studies on Italian for a long time, though in a fragmented manner and with little connection to the practicalities of Italian L2 teaching and learning. Recent years have seen not only an increase in interest regarding this specific domain of corpus-based applications, but also an increase in empirical studies seeking to evaluate the effects of DDL in Italian L2 context. A certain degree of mismatch between the BELI and the literature published in international settings regarding DDL for Italian was found.

The chapter also reviewed the main corpora that are available today for developing DDL activities in the context of Italian teaching and learning. The main Italian L1 and Italian L2 corpora were described with reference to their main features, and in relation to their pedagogical affordances and degree of adaptability to didactic aims. The possibility of creating one's own corpus for fostering the teaching and learning of Italian L2 was also mentioned, with reference to some of the main tools that are freely available to serve this purpose. Overall, most corpus resources built so far for Italian have not been built with the learners in mind. Nevertheless, the variety of ways in which they were designed certainly makes them all precious resources to inform pedagogical practices with authentically pertinent and quantitatively relevant linguistic data.

Next, we look at how these resources can be exploited pedagogically for Italian L2 learning purposes and how the effects of their use can be evaluated empirically. We will consider the perspective pertaining to language gains, as well as the perception of learners involved in using corpus-based materials.

Notes

1 www.corpusthomisticum.org/it/index.age (last accessed: 22/08/2022).
2 English: 'computerisation of hermeneutic and lexicological analyses'.
3 As of 2012, the association is known as *European Association for Digital Humanities* and constitutes a chapter of the *Alliance of Digital Humanities Organizations* (ADHO). Its webpage can be reached with the following URL: https://eadh.org/ (last accessed: 22/08/2022).
4 https://eadh.org/awards/adho-roberto-busa-award (last accessed: 22/08/2022).
5 www.facebook.com/groups/33757027044 (last accessed: 22/08/2022).
6 www.ilc.cnr.it/it/content/storia (last accessed: 22/08/2022).
7 www.treccani.it/enciclopedia/statistica-linguistica_%28Enciclopedia-Italiana%29/ (last accessed: 22/08/2022).
8 'the application of the statistical method to the analysis of linguistic facts: the components of a language (phonemes, morphemes, etc.), considered in particular through the lens of the frequency with which they appear in texts, constitute a typical set of mass phenomena and therefore lend themselves to statistical investigations to determine the average frequencies of their distribution in discourse and, over time, the possible transformation of such frequencies' (my translation).
9 'a certain number of key resources, not only for the scientific value of the information they contain, but also for their value in representing a model of what the web is able to offer and of how each one of us may contribute to its development with their specific competencies' (my translation).
10 In Italian, *fare i conti con…* is an idiom, meaning 'to deal with…[something]', but has also a literal meaning referring to 'counting [something]'. In this case, the title's literal and idiomatic meaning refers to 'counting/dealing with words'.
11 'the machine is used not merely as a fast executor of habitual operations, but also and more prominently as a generator of new problems; the emphasis is not so much on the physical abilities (memory, velocity), but rather on the logical ones. The computer-based analysis of linguistic data is not the completion of a traditional method, but its complete refoundation, the global review of consolidated research strategies, in light of new research strategies' (my translation).
12 'using a corpus of texts is a constant in our entire grammaticographic and lexicographic tradition and, in even more general terms, in the history of linguistic disputes since the time of Dante. A constant which finds its *raison d'être* in a particular situation related to our language, usually considered as penalising: the fact that it was born through the writings of authors and that it long survived solely via the written medium, so thanks to the continued support given by a canon of authors' (my translation).
13 'Bibliography of Language Education in Italy' (my translation). The repertoire is freely accessible at the following url: www.unive.it/pag/16976/ (last accessed: 22/08/2022).
14 https://parlaritaliano.studiumdipsum.it/index.php/it/volip (last accessed: 22/08/2022).
15 www.istc.cnr.it/en/grouppage/colfis (last accessed: 22/08/2022).
16 www.ge.ilc.cnr.it/strumenti.php (last attempted access: 22/08/2022).
17 http://corpora.dslo.unibo.it/coris_eng.html (last attempted access: 22/08/2022).
18 http://corpora.dslo.unibo.it/TCORIS/ (last attempted access: 22/08/2022).

19 https://docs.sslmit.unibo.it/doku.php?id=corpora:repubblica (last accessed: 22/08/2022).
20 www.valico.org/vinca.html (last accessed: 22/08/2022).
21 http://lablita.dit.unifi.it/coralrom (last attempted access: 22/08/2022).
22 www.sketchengine.eu/ (last accessed: 22/08/2022).
23 www.corpusitaliano.it/it/index.html (last accessed: 22/08/2022).
24 www.unistrapg.it/cqpwebnew/ (last accessed: 22/08/2022).
25 https://skell.sketchengine.eu/#home?lang=it (last accessed: 22/08/2022).
26 http://kiparla.it/il-corpus/#design (last accessed: 22/08/2022).
27 https://web.unipv.it/wwwling (last attempted access: 22/08/2022).
28 www.parlaritaliano.it/index.php/it/corpora-di-parlato/653-corpus-lips (last accessed: 22/08/2022).
29 www.valico.org/valico.html (last accessed: 22/08/2022).
30 https://corespiycorite.altervista.org/presentazione/(last accessed: 22/08/2022).
31 www.unistrapg.it/cqpwebnew/ (this webpage hosts all the L1 and L2 corpora developed at the University for Foreigners of Perugia, namely: CIP, PEC, CAIL2, COLI, LOCCLI, CELI) (last accessed: 22/08/2022).
32 The CELI exams are one of the most well-known exams to certify Italian language proficiency. More information about the exams and the exam centre may be found at the following link: www.cvcl.it/home-cvcl (last accessed: 22/08/2022).
33 https://merlin-platform.eu/index.php (last accessed: 22/08/2022).
34 www.porta.eurac.edu/lci/leonide/ (last accessed: 22/08/2022).
35 https://voyant-tools.org/ (last accessed: 22/08/2022).

References

Abel, A., Wisniewski, K., Nicolas, L., Boyd, A., Hana, J., & Meurers, D. (2014). A trilingual learner corpus illustrating European reference levels. Ricognizioni – Rivista Di Lingue, Letterature e Cultura *Moderne*, 2(1), 111–126.

Amato, A. (1974). Verso una metodologia per l'unificazione di due corpus linguistici per la costruzione di una batteria di tests di profitto per la lingua inglese. In A. Amato (Ed.), *Il Testing nella didattica linguistica, in numero monografico di Rassegna italiana di linguistica applicata*, nn. 1–2.

Amato, A. (1978). Verso una metodologia per l'unificazione di due corpus linguistici per la costruzione di una batteria di tests di profitto per la lingua inglese. In R. Titone (Ed.), *Didattica delle lingue straniere in Italia 1957–1977*. Oxford Institutes.

Andorno, C., & Rastelli, S. (Eds.) (2009). *Corpora di Italiano L2: Tecnologie, metodi, spunti teorici*. Guerra.

Anthony, L. (2020). *AntConc (Version 3.5.9) [Computer Software]*. Tokyo, Japan: Waseda University. Available from www.laurenceanthony.net/software.

Aston, G. (Ed.), (2001). *Learning with corpora*, CLUEB.

Bailini, S., & Frigerio, A. (2018). CORESPI e CORITE, due nuovi strumenti per l'analisi dell'interlingua di lingue affini. *CHIMERA: Romance Corpora and Linguistic Studies*, 5(2), 313–319.

Baisa, V., & Suchomel, V. (2014). SkELL: Web interface for English language learning. *Eighth Workshop on Recent Advances in Slavonic Natural Language Processing*, 63–70.

Balboni, P.E. (1983). Proposte per una didattica dell'ascolto in lingua straniera. In *Scuola e didattica*, nn. 8, 10, 14.

Barbera, M. (2013). *Linguistica dei corpora e linguistica dei corpora italiana: Un'introduzione.* Qu.A.S.A.R.

Baroni, M., Bernardini, S., Comastri, F., Piccioni, L., Volpi, A., Aston, G., & Mazzoleni, M. (2004). Introducing the 'la Repubblica' corpus: A large, annotated, TEI(XML)-compliant corpus of newspaper Italian. *Proceedings of LREC 2004.*

Bortolini, U., Tagliavini, C., & Zampolli, A. (1972). *Lessico di frequenza della lingua italiana contemporanea.* Garzanti.

Bratankova, L. (2015). *Le collocazioni Verbo + Nome in apprendenti di italiano L2.* Unpublished PhD thesis. Università per Stranieri di Perugia.

Brezina, V., Weill Tessier, P., & McEnery, A. (2020). *#LancsBox v. 5.x. [Software].* Available at: http://corpora.lancs.ac.uk/lancsbox.

Busa, R. (1980). The annals of humanities computing: The Index Thomisticus. *Computers and the Humanities, 14*, 83–90.

Cerruti, M., & Ballarè, S. (2021), 'ParlaTO: corpus del parlato di Torino'. *Bollettino dell'Atlante Linguistico Italiano (BALI), 44*(2020), 171–196.

Cesiri, D., Colaici, L., & Cesiri, A. (2015), The 'euro crisis' in The Economist, Der Spiegel and Il Sole 24 ore: a contrastive and corpus-based study. *Rassegna Italiana di Linguistica Applicata*, RILA, 155–175.

Charles, M. (2012). 'Proper vocabulary and juicy collocations': EAP students evaluate do-it-yourself corpus-building. English for Specific *Purposes, 31*(2), 93–102.

Charles, M. (2014). Getting the corpus habit: EAP students' long-term use of personal corpora. *English for Specific Purposes, 35*, 30–40.

Charles, M. (2019). Do-it-yourself corpora for LSP: Demystifying the process and illustrating the practice. *Scripta Manent, 13*, 156–166.

Chiari, I. (2007). *Introduzione alla linguistica computazionale.* Laterza.

Chini, M. (2016). Elementi utili per una didattica dell'italiano L2 alla luce della ricerca acquisizionale. *Italiano LinguaDue, 8*(2), 1–18.

Colombo, S., & Marello, C. (2014). Paesaggi dinamici. Dagli atlanti linguistici alla georeferenziazione di dati linguistici in rete. In E. Cugno, L. Mantovani, M. Rivoira, & M.S. Speccia (Eds). *Studi linguistici in onore di Lorenzo Massobrio* (pp. 231–247). Istituto dell'Atlante linguistico Italiano.

Corino, E. (Ed.) (2019). Data-driven Learning: la linguistica dei corpora al servizio della didattica delle lingue straniere e del CLIL. Special issue of *EL.LE – Educazione Linguistica. Language Education, 8*(2). Ca' Foscari edizioni.

Corino, E., Colombo, S., & Marello, C. (2017). *Italiano di stranieri: I corpora VALICO e VINCA.* Guerra.

Cresti, E., & Moneglia, M. (Eds.). (2005). *C-ORAL-ROM. Integrated Reference Corpora for Spoken Romance Languages.* Benjamins.

Cresti, E., & Panunzi, A. (Eds.). (2013). *Introduzione ai corpora di italiano.* il Mulino.

De Mauro, T. (1961). Statistica linguistica. In *Enciclopedia Italiana: Vol. II* (pp. 820–821). Istituto dell'Enciclopedia Italiana.

De Mauro, T. (1980). *Guida all'uso delle parole.* Laterza.

De Mauro, T. (1995). Quantità-qualità: Un binomio indispensabile per comprendere il linguaggio. In S. Bolasco & R. Cipriani (Eds.), *Ricerca qualitativa e computer. Teorie, metodi e applicazioni* (pp. 21–30). Franco Angeli.

Forti, L., & Spina, S. (2019). Corpora for Linguists vs. Corpora for Learners: Bridging the Gap in Italian L2 Learning and Teaching. *EL.LE – Educazione Linguistica. Language Education*, 8(2), 349–362.
Gallina, F. (2015). *Le parole degli stranieri. Il Lessico Italiano Parlato da Stranieri*. Guerra.
Gavioli, L. (1998). Corpora, concordanze e autonomia dello studente. In Accietto, T. & Zorzi, D. (Eds.), *Nuove tecnologie e didattica delle lingue*. CLUEB.
Giacalone Ramat, A. (Eds.), (2003). *Verso l'italiano. Percorsi e strategie di acquisizione*. Carocci.
Glaznieks A., Frey, J.-C., Nicolas, L, Abel, A., & Vettori, C. (in preparation). The Kolipsi Corpus Family. A collection of Italian and German L2 learner texts from secondary school pupils.
Glaznieks, A., Frey, J.-C., Stopfner, M., Zanasi, L., & Nicolas, L. (2022). LEONIDE: A longitudinal trilingual corpus of young learners of Italian, German and English, *International Journal of Learner Corpus Research*, 8(1), 97–120.
Goria, E., & Mauri, C. (2018) Il corpus KIParla: una nuova risorsa per lo studio dell'italiano parlato. In Masini, F. & Tamburini, F. (Eds.), *CLUB Working Papers in Linguistics*, Volume 2 (pp. 96–116). Alma Mater Studiorum Università di Bologna.
Hédiard, M. (Ed.) (2007). *La linguistica dei corpora: strumenti e applicazioni*. Pubblicazioni dell'Università di Cassino.
Jakubíče, M., Kilgarriff, A., Kovár, V., Rychlý, P., & Suchomel, V. (2013). The Ten Ten Corpus Family. *7th International Corpus Linguistics Conference CL* (pp. 125–127). Lancaster University.
Kennedy, C., & Miceli, T. (2001). An evaluation of intermediate students' approaches to corpus investigation. *Language Learning & Technology*, 5(3), 77–90.
Kennedy, C., & Miceli, T. (2010). Corpus-assisted creative writing: Introducing intermediate Italian learners to a corpus as a reference resource. *Language Learning & Technology*, 14(1), 28–44.
Kennedy, C., & Miceli, T. (2016). Cultivating effective corpus use by language learners. *Computer Assisted Language Learning*, 30(1–2), 91–114.
Kennedy, G. (1998). *An introduction to corpus linguistics*. Longman.
Laudanna, A., Thornton, A.M., Brown, G., Burani, C., & Marconi, L. (1995). Un corpus dell'italiano scritto contemporaneo dalla parte del ricevente. In S. Bolasco, L. Lebart, & A. Salem (Eds.), *III Giornate internazionali di Analisi Statistica dei Dati Testuali. Volume I* (pp. 103–109). Cisu.
Lenci, A., Montemagni, S., & Pirelli, V. (2005). *Testo e computer. Elementi di linguistica computazionale*. Carocci.
Liu, T. (2021). Data-driven learning: Using #LancsBox in academic collocation learning. In P. Perez-Paredes & G. Mark (Eds.), *Beyond Concordance Lines. Corpora in Language Education* (pp. 177–206). Benjamins.
Lucisano, P., & Piemontese, M.E. (1988). GULPEASE: una formula per la predizione della difficoltà dei testi in lingua italiana. *Scuola e Città*, *XXXIX*(3), 110–124.
Lyding, V., Stemle, E., Borghetti, C., Brunello, M., Castagnoli, S., Dell'Orletta, F., Dittmann, H., Lenci, A., & Pirelli, V. (2014). The PAISA corpus of italian web texts. *Proceedings of the 9th Web as Corpus Workshop (WaC-9)*, 36–43.
Maiello, G., & Pellegrino, R. (Eds.) (2012). *Database, corpora, insegnamenti linguistici*. Schena.

Martelli, A., & Pulcini, V. (Eds.) (2008). *Investigating English with corpora. Studies in Honour of Maria Teresa Prat*, Polimetrica.

Mauri, C., Ballarè, S. Goria, E., Cerruti, M. & Suriano, F. (2019). KIParla corpus: A new resource for spoken Italian. In R. Bernardi, R. Navigli & G. Semeraro (Eds.), *Proceedings of the 6th Italian Conference on Computational Linguistics CLiC-it, CEUR Workshop Proceedings*.

McEnery, A., & Wilson, A. (2001). *Corpus Linguistics. An Introduction* (2nd ed.). Edinburgh University Press.

Palermo, M. (Ed.). (2009). *Percorsi e strategie di apprendimento dell'italiano lingua seconda: Sondaggi su Adil2*. Guerra.

Polezzi, L. (1993). Concordancing and the teaching of ab initio Italian language for specific purposes. *ReCALL, 5*(09), 14–18.

Quirk, R. (1960). Towards a description of English usage. *Transactions of the Philological Society, 59*(1), 40–61.

Rossini Favretti, R. (2000). Progettazione e costruzione di un corpus di italiano scritto: CORIS/CODIS. In R. Rossini Favretti (Ed.), *Linguistica e informatica. Multimedialità, corpora e percorsi di apprendimento* (pp. 39–56). Bulzoni.

Sabatini, F. (2007). Storia della lingua italiana e grandi corpora. Un capitolo di storia della linguistica. In M. Barbera, E. Corino & C. Onesti (Eds.), *Corpora e linguistica in rete* (pp. xiii–xvj). Guerra.

Spina, S. (1997). *Parole in rete. Guida ai siti internet sul linguaggio*. La Nuova Italia.

Spina, S. (2001). *Fare i conti con le parole: Introduzione alla linguistica dei corpora*. Guerra.

Spina, S. (2014). Il Perugia Corpus: Una risorsa di riferimento per l'italiano. Composizione, annotazione e valutazione. *Proceedings of the First Italian Conference on Computational Linguistics CLiC-It 2014 & the Fourth International Workshop EVALITA 2014, 1*, 354–359.

Spina, S. (2017). Learner Corpus Research and the acquisition of Italian as a second language: The case of the Longitudinal Corpus of Chinese Learners of Italian (LoCCLI) *[Keynote presentation]*. Learner Corpus Research Conference, Eurac Research.

Spina, S., Fioravanti, I., Forti, L., Santucci, V., Scerra, A., Zanda, F. (2022), Il corpus CELI: una nuova risorsa per studiare l'acquisizione dell'italiano L2, *Italiano LinguaDue, 14*(1), 116–138.

Spina, S., & Siyanova-Chanturia, A. (2018). *The longitudinal corpus of Chinese learners of Italian (LOCCLI). Poster presented at the 13th Teaching and Language Corpora conference*.

Taylor Torsello, C., Brunetti, G., & Penello, N. (Eds.). (2001). *Corpora linguistici per la ricerca, traduzione e apprendimento linguistico*. Studi linguistici applicati, Unipress.

VanPatten, B., Keating, G. D., & Wulff, S. (2020). *Theories in Second Language Acquisition*. (3rd ed.). Routledge.

Voghera, M., Iacobini, C., Savy, R., Cutugno, F., De Rosa, A., & Alfano, I. (2014). VoLIP: A searchable corpus of spoken Italian. In J. Emonds & M. Janebová (Eds.), *Language use and linguistic structure: Proceedings of the Olomouc Linguistics Colloquium 2013* (1st ed.). Palacký University Press.

Winter, T.N. (1999). Roberto Busa, S.J., and the invention of the machine-generated concordance. *The Classical Bulletin*, 75(1), 3–20.

Wisniewski, K., Schöne, K., Nicolas, L., Vettori, C., Boyd, A., Meurers, D., Abel, A., & Hana, J. (2013). *MERLIN: An online trilingual learner corpus empirically grounding the European Reference Levels in authentic learner data*. ICT for Language Learning 2013, Conference Proceedings. Florence, Italy. 1–5.

6 Language gains and learner attitudes in data-driven learning
Study design

It is now time to explore how an empirical study on DDL effects may be designed in relation to the development of Italian L2 competence. We will consider both the etic dimension, pertaining to language gains, and the emic dimension, pertaining to learner attitudes. In particular, we will focus on the development of phraseological competence, phraseology being widely recognised as a key component in the development of overall language proficiency in a second/foreign language. We will see how data collection instruments can be constructed in order to suit the specific learning aims that a pedagogical intervention addresses. The chapter will also show how it is possible to take into account various properties that specifically pertain to the chosen learning aims, and how these can be analysed through mixed-effects modelling. Finally, the design of a student questionnaire aimed at eliciting learner attitudes towards different aspects of DDL and phraseology learning will be illustrated.

6.1 Phraseology: a central component in the development of second language proficiency

As highlighted in Chapter 4, one key decision that needs to be made when developing an empirical study on DDL effects is that of defining the learning aim one chooses to focus on. In our case, the chosen focus is on phraseology, and more specifically, on the development of phraseological competence in relation to DDL. In this section, we define what phraseology is, why it is important in second language proficiency development, and what it is that we know about it in terms of scientific evidence.

6.1.1 What is phraseology?

According to Sinclair (1991), the way in which meaning arises from text can be explained on the basis of two main principles: the open-choice principle and the idiom principle. As for the former, 'this is a way of seeing language text as the result of a very large number of choices. At each point where a unit is completed (a word or a phrase or a clause), a large range of choice

DOI: 10.4324/9781003137320-6

opens up and the only restraint is grammaticalness' (Sinclair, 1991, p. 109). As for the latter, the reference is to the fact that 'a language user has available to him or her a large number of semi-preconstructed phrases that constitute single choices, even though they might appear to be analysable into segments' (Sinclair, 1991, p. 110).

The term *phraseology* refers both to the set of 'semi-preconstructed phrases' mentioned by Sinclair, and to the area of linguistics which studies them. There is quite a bit of terminological variation when it comes to identifying the linguistic units of interest as well as the field. *Phraseology* can be interchangeably used with *formulaic language*, for example, and *phraseological units* may also be defined as *formulaic units, formulaic sequences, multiword units, multiword expressions*, and so on. Wray finds 57 different terms used in the literature to refer to this phenomenon (Wray, 2002, p. 9). Expressions such as *fare una passeggiata* ('to go for a walk'), *pioggia torrenziale* ('heavy rain') and *essere al verde* ('to be broke'/'to have no money') are all characterised by at least two words which tend to co-occur in order to produce a certain meaning.

Various working definitions of phraseological units have been proposed, each highlighting specific aspects of the phenomenon. Table 6.1 contains some of the definitions proposed along with the key aspects being emphasised. In Manning & Schütze's (1999, p. 157) definition, the two aspects emerging are the frequency and the unpredictability of the phraseological units. While some words tend to co-occur a lot and, at times, with a high degree of exclusivity (e.g., we say *take a train* and we would not typically say *to

Table 6.1 Working definitions of *pharseological unit*

Definition	Source	Key aspects
'If two words occur together a lot, then that is evidence that they have a special function that is not simply explained as the function that results from their combination'	Manning & Schütze, 1999, p. 157.	Frequency Unpredictability
'A sequence, continuous or discontinuous, of words or other elements, which is, or appears to be, prefabricated: that is, stored and retrieved whole from memory at the time of use, rather than being subject to generation or analysis by the language grammar'	Wray, 2002, p. 9.	Prefabrication Holism
'Complex lexemes that have idiosyncratic interpretations that cross word boundaries'	Sag, Baldwin, Bond, Copestake, & Flickinger, 2002, p. 2	Idiosyncraticity Complexity

seize a train, although *seize* can sometimes be an effective substitute for of *take*), we are not able to predict the fact that they will co-occur on the basis of their individual meanings. In Wray's definition, the prefabricated and holistic nature of phraseological units is emphasised. Since word combinations are considered as predetermined multiword units, they need to be retrieved whole from memory, rather than being built up word by word. In Sag et al.'s (2002, p. 2) definition, the complexity that is inherent in the way certain words tend to combine is the aspect that is most central, along with the idiosyncrasy of the process. Unpredictability, again, seems to return as a key notion together with complexity, which can be linked to the concept of linguistic complexity at large, quite useful in the theoretical and operational understanding of phraseological units.

The notion of linguistic complexity rests on the philosophical definition provided by Rescher (1998, p. 1), which is integrated in linguistics by Bulté and Housen as follows:

(1) the number and the nature of the discrete components that the entity consists of, and
(2) the number and the nature of the relationships between the constituent components.

(Bulté & Housen, 2012, p. 22)

To sum up, we can define phraseological units as lexical units which are frequent in language use, formed by a co-occurrence of items which is largely unpredictable, and is thus prefabricated, retrieved as whole from memory, and with an internal structure that is complex. But why are phraseological units important when studying language? First, phraseological units are highly pervasive in language use. According to an analysis conducted by Bengt Altenberg on the London-Lund Corpus, the total amount of 'string of words occurring more than once in identical form' (Altenberg, 1998, p. 101) was more than 80% of the total utterances contained in the corpus. Erman and Warren (2000) extracted all the combinations 'of at least two words favored by native speakers in preference to an alternative combination which could have been equivalent had there been no conventionalization' (Erman & Warren, 2000, p. 31) from the Lancaster-Oslo-Bergen Corpus, for the written part, and from the London-Lund Corpus, for the spoken part. They found that phraseological units amount to 52.3% in written texts and to 58.6% in spoken texts. A review of the sources stating the pervasiveness, and thus the importance, of phraseology in languages in general may be found in Masini (2009). Second, word meaning is accessible largely by means of its lexical co-occurrences. As Firth famously maintained, 'you shall know a word by the company it keeps' (Firth, 1957), with reference to his *contextual theory of meaning*. As a result, we will be able to disambiguate homonyms on the basis of the context they occur in (e.g., Italian *calcio* can correspond to the English *calcium/soccer/kick* depending on context), and more specifically we will be able to identify the meaning of a word on the basis of the other words it co-occurs with (e.g., *commit a crime, commit oneself, commit to memory)* (Henriksen, 2013, p. 34). Phraseological units play a key role in second language learning, for reasons that we will outline in the following sections.

6.1.2 The role of phraseology in second language learning

As seen above, pervasiveness and meaningfulness are two key reasons that make phraseology a key component in the development of second language competence. However, there are other reasons pertaining more closely to the specific processes involved in second language learning. Phraseology is important because learners rely on phraseological units when in the process of building up their language competence. This has emerged in a number of studies (Boers & Webb, 2018; Webb, 2019). Phraseological units become 'islands of reliability' (Hasselgren, 1994; Wood, 2020) for the learners, in that they represent units of lexis and meaning which are acquired and no longer need attention when being used. This produces a twofold effect: on the one hand, learners can rely on these units without paying too much attention to them so that their attention can be directed toward novel words or word combinations. On the other hand, the fact that they have internalised a certain set of phraseological units allows them to be more fluent in their language use. The relationship between the formation of 'islands of reliability' and fluency leads us to the second reason why phraseology is particularly important in second language acquisition: the opportunity to develop a more target-like language usage. Learning phraseological units allows learners to express themselves more closely to what would be expected by L1 speakers both in relation to the lexical choices made in selecting co-occurring words, and in the frequency with which certain combinations will be used (Columbus, 2010; Ellis, 2002; Ellis et al., 2015; Meunier & Granger, 2008; Wray, 2002).

Phraseology is important to the second language learner also because it is the key to acquire sensitivity towards *semantic prosody* phenomena (Hunston, 2002; Sinclair, 1991; Tognini Bonelli, 2001). Combinations such as *set in* are generally associated with a negative connotation (e.g., *bad weather is setting in*). Knowledge of the semantic features that characterise some phraseological units will increase not only the fluency but also the adequacy of the learner's language use. Another reason that makes phraseology particularly crucial in the development of second language competence relates to the fact that phraseological competence has been identified as a factor that contributes significantly in the measurement of linguistic proficiency as a whole, as demonstrated by an analysis based on standardised language tests (Paquot, 2018). Although phraseology is seen as central in the development of second language competence, the research evidence related to how it is acquired sheds light on the number and the kinds of challenges that learners encounter. The fact that it constitutes a challenge even at advanced levels of proficiency (Bestgen & Granger, 2014; Nesselhauf, 2005) contributes to make it particularly worthy of attention.

6.1.3 What we know about phraseological competence development in second language learning

This section reviews the research evidence available on L2 phraseological competence development in relation to two main aspects: variables related to the specific phraseological units being learned and variables concerning the way in which they are treated pedagogically within the classroom. The section concludes with a brief review of the state of the art pertaining to studies related to Italian L2.

6.1.3.1 The international perspective

Analyses conducted on longitudinal corpora shed light on a number of interesting, non-linear phenomena concerning L2 phraseological development. First, learners in the initial phases of the learning process seem to use a restricted range of highly frequent combinations (Durrant & Schmitt, 2009; Fan, 2009; Hasselgren, 1994), which is in line with the aforementioned 'collocational teddy bear effect'. Furthermore, following the initial phases of learning, such use seems to stabilise and variation starts to develop (Groom, 2009). When comparing the longitudinal development of phraseological competence to other areas of language, there seems to be a lag of the former with respect to the latter (Biskup, 1992; Farghal & Obiedat, 1995; Groom, 2009; Laufer & Waldman, 2011). One other aspect that has been noted in longitudinal studies is that even in highly homogeneous learner groups, the way in which phraseological competence develops is highly varied (Li & Schmitt, 2010).

One aspect that psycholinguistic studies have focused on is whether phraseological units are processed holistically or not. In reference to the *dual-route model* of language processing (Van Lancker Sidtis, 2012), Wray (2008) hypothesises that holistic retrieval of phraseological units is characteristic of L1 speakers, but not necessarily of L2 speakers, who tend to retrieve phraseological units by analysing each individual component they are made of. As a consequence of this hypothesis, processing of phraseological units in L1 speakers is assumed to be faster than in L2 speakers thanks to the fact that the units are retrieved from the mental lexicon as single units. Studies have led to conflicting evidence in relation to this hypothesis. The third study contained in Siyanova & Schmitt (2007), for example, confirms that in the case of noun-adjective collocations, there is a slower processing found in L2 speakers as opposed to L1 speakers. However, when considering verb + noun collocations, Gyllstad & Wolter (2016) find no significant difference in processing cost when comparing L1 and L2 speakers.

Another property of collocations which has recently been looked at in psycholinguistic studies is adjacency. More specifically, Vilkaitė (2016) and Vilkaitė & Schmitt (2019) look at possible differences between adjacent and non-adjacent collocations, comparing L1 and L2 speakers. They find that both categories of collocations produce a processing advantage in comparison to non-phraseological units, although such advantage is reduced in the case of L2 speakers when presented with non-adjacent collocations. Furthermore, psycholinguistics has examined the extent to which specific kinds of input enhancement applied to phraseological units can benefit learning. Choi (2017), for example, investigates the effect of typographically enhanced collocations on learners' processing, finding that this specific type of pedagogical treatment has a beneficial effect. The study supports the findings of previous ones investigating the same aspect (Sonbul & Schmitt, 2013; Szudarski & Carter, 2016). Wolter & Gyllstad (2013) is an interesting study combining different collocation properties, in that it investigates the intersection between frequency and congruency in collocations. The authors find that frequent collocations are processed faster than their infrequent counterparts, regardless of whether they are or are not congruent with the L1 of the learners.

We now turn to cross-sectional studies and look at which themes emerge more frequently. One theme is related to semantic transparency. Phraseological units can be characterised by a higher or lower degree of semantic transparency (Howarth, 1996, 1998). How does this affect the learning of phraseological units? According to the psycholinguistic study conducted by Gyllstad & Wolter (2016), combinations exhibiting a certain degree of semantic opacity lead to a processing cost in both L1 and L2 speakers. According to Licui et al. (2019), they seem to require more learning effort as opposed to fully transparent units. These findings could explain why, even at advanced levels of proficiency, phraseological units which are not fully transparent on the semantic level still attract errors. A number of learner corpus research studies focus explicitly on delexicalised verb constructions (Altenberg & Granger, 2001; Nesselhauf, 2005; Wang, 2016) in order to see how this property affects language production.

Another theme is related to L1 influence. Several studies have concluded that this variable may be involved in the production of phraseological errors (Bahns, 1993; Granger, 1998; Nesselhauf, 2003; Wang, 2016), especially when the empirical data has been collected in FL contexts (Yamashita & Jiang, 2010). In Gilquin (2007) and Parkinson (2015) the focus is on L1-L2 congruency. Congruency refers to the property related to whether a combination in the L2 has a corresponding form, on the basis of the lexical selections it is characterised by, in his or her native language. For example, the Italian *prendere il treno* is congruent with the English *to take a train*, because the verb selected by the noun has the same literal meaning in both languages, whereas the Italian *fare una fotografia* is incongruent with the English *to take a photo*, because the literal meaning of the verb selected by the two languages differs. The authors find that this specific relationship seems to influence the overuse of phraseological units in L2 productions. Various psycholinguistic studies have also examined the effect of this relationship, reaching mixed conclusions, though mostly confirming the possible influence of L1-L2 congruence on the learning of L2 phraseological units (Wolter & Gyllstad, 2011, 2013; Wolter & Yamashita, 2015, 2018; Yamashita & Jiang, 2010). As for frequency, when comparing various collocation corpus-based measures in a total of 19 studies, Durrant (2014) finds that frequency is able to predict learning of collocations across different proficiency levels, more than other quantitative measures.

Another area of investigation lies in the dimension of knowledge considered, and how it can have an impact on phraseological competence development. More specifically, studies have analysed how the receptive-productive distinction can play a role. As explained by Paul Nation, 'Receptive knowledge is the kind of knowledge needed for listening and reading. At its most basic, it involves being able to recall a meaning when meeting a word form. Productive knowledge is the kind of knowledge needed for speaking and writing. At its most basic it involves being able to recall a word form in order to express a meaning' (Nation, 2020, p. 16). Studies such as Jaèn (2009) and Koya (2005), specifically centred on the evaluation of the receptive and production knowledge of collocations in second language learners, have found that the former is likely to develop earlier than the latter, which is in line with more general SLA research evidence.

As for the way in which collocations may be treated pedagogically, some research has examined the so-called 'frequency-of-encounters' effect, with reference to a pedagogical treatment which is able to increase the frequency with which a learner will encounter a certain word combination within an activity, or across several activities and/or lessons. It is an effect that is deemed to have a certain likelihood of emerging when, for example, recycling activities are planned and proposed to the learners, thus potentially fostering better retention rates. Some studies have found the approach to be beneficial (Durrant & Schmitt, 2010; Webb et al., 2013) while others have concluded that different, more significant factors tend to be at play in determining higher retention rates (Pellicer-Sánchez, 2017).

In terms of activity types that can help learners to improve their phraseological competence, matching-type activities have received considerable attention. More specifically, the problematic nature of this activity type in relation to the possibility of creating erroneous matches has been addressed and discussed (Boers et al., 2014, 2017). This has been interpreted as a potentially negative factor in developing phraseological competence, since the learner may tend to transfer the erroneously formed combination to other contexts. Finally, the possible differences pertaining to teaching context, corresponding to either a foreign language (FL) or second language (SL) setting, have been analysed with specific reference to congruency. Yamashita & Jiang (2010) have in fact found that

L1 influence may be more prominent in a FL setting rather than in a SL one. Our understanding of the research evidence available to date has also been considerably enriched by three research syntheses, Henriksen (2013), Durrant (2014), and Boers & Webb (2018).

6.1.3.2 The view from studies on L1 and L2 Italian

Research on phraseology in Italian has seen work from a number of prominent scholars (De Mauro & Voghera, 1996; Elia et al., 1985; Ježek, 2016; Masini, 2009, 2012; Simone & Masini, 2007; Vietri et al., 1985; Voghera, 1994, 2004; Zaninello & Nissim, 2010). A growing interest in Italian phraseology is demonstrated by the publication of dictionaries of collocations or word combinations, such as Urzì (2009), Tiberii (2012) and Lo Cascio (2013). The focus of these studies has, however, been mainly on Italian L1 and the interest in phraseology with specific reference to Italian L2 is still quite limited. Spina (2015) focuses on academic L2 phraseology in a computer-mediated-communication (CMC) university context. It finds that highly frequent collocations are overused, a finding that is in line with the aforementioned studies referring to the same phenomenon. The unpublished PhD thesis by Leontyna Bratankova (2015) compares highly frequent and strongly associated verb + noun (object) collocations in a corpus of Italian written texts, the CAIL2. She finds that the most prominent collocations are the ones with the higher frequency scores. Moreover, the study detects the presence of a U-shaped learning curve, when analysing the texts pseudo-longitudinally on the basis of the different proficiency levels represented in the corpus. In Siyanova-Chanturia (2015) noun + adjective collocations produced in writing by 36 Chinese L1 learners of Italian are examined over a time span of five months. The study reveals a significant increase in the use of these combinations over time, thus suggesting that a more target-like use of collocations is possible even when considering a relatively short time span such as five months. Another longitudinal study on L1 Chinese learners' written productions was conducted by Spina (2019). This time, the time span is six months, and two categories of combinations are considered: noun + adjective and adjective + noun combinations. The study finds that after six months errors decrease for adjective + noun combinations, while they significantly increase for noun + adjective combinations. As for learner-oriented lexicography, the only project which to the best of our knowledge is currently underway is the DICI – A, a learner dictionary of Italian collocations (Spina, 2010, 2016), which is based on criteria that are informed both by corpus-based analyses and by learner needs at different proficiency levels. Despite the scarcity of studies on L1 and L2 Italian that specifically focus on phraseology, we can see how several different trails of innovation are present. This is particularly true if we look at the attention devoted to longitudinal analyses, which is recently gaining ground.

6.2 Rationale, research questions, and hypotheses of the study

The centrality of phraseology in the development of second language competence, as demonstrated in the previous section, lends itself to a study on DDL effects with the intention of establishing whether DDL can actually make a difference in all the areas of phraseology which pose a challenge for second language learners. Since phraseology incorporates a wide range of phraseological unit types, our focus in the present study will be on verb + noun (object) combinations. This choice is motivated by a number of factors. First, verb + noun (object) combinations were found to be the most frequent kinds of combinations in an Italian L1 reference corpus, closely followed by noun + preposition + noun (Spina, 2014). As a result, they are highly likely to be quite frequent also in a learner's language input. Second, they tend to be more structurally flexible than other kinds of combinations, since they may be separated by insertions (e.g., *take a picture, take a quick picture, take the most unusual picture you can think of*), and thus present themselves in either an adjacent or non-adjacent condition (Vilkaitė, 2016; Vilkaitė & Schmitt, 2019), and this feature may affect processing as well as learning, especially concerning the insertion/omission/choice of determiners, for instance. Third, as seen in the previous section, the partial or total lack of semantic transparency that may characterise verb + noun (object) combinations has been seen as a possible challenge for the effective learning of these kinds of phraseological units. Misuse of verb + noun (object) combinations has been examined in several studies (Altenberg & Granger, 2001; Nesselhauf, 2003; Chan & Liou, 2005; Wang, 2016).

In sum, verb + noun (object) combinations constitute a key component in the development of phraseological competence because (a) they are likely to be highly frequent in the learner's input, and (b) they are some of the most problematic areas in the development of phraseological competence, as a result of the structural and semantic properties they are characterised by. To investigate the effect that DDL activities may have on the development of phraseological competence in Italian L2, and on the basis of what we know about the several kinds of variables potentially influencing L2 phraseological competence development, we formulate the following research questions:

1. How does phraseological competence develop over time when comparing a DDL approach with a non-DDL approach?
2. How does a DDL/non-DDL approach influence the development of phraseological competence over time, with respect to certain specific properties of the learning aims (i.e. semantic transparency and L1-L2 congruency)?
3. How does a DDL/non-DDL approach influence the development of phraseological competence over time, with respect to different dimensions of phraseological knowledge (i.e. definitional vs. transferable)?
4. What are the learners' overall attitudes towards DDL activities?

The first research question seeks to explore the learning patterns related to the development of phraseological competence in Italian L2, with specific reference to possible differences between DDL and non-DDL activities. In other words, it seeks to establish whether DDL can reach 'the parts other teaching can't reach' (Boulton, 2008), whether, with respect to certain aspects of phraseological units which pose a challenge for second language learners, DDL is able to make a difference. According to the meta-analyses we reviewed in Chapter 2, DDL is generally more effective than other approaches, for certain learning aims. As we will see shortly, the study adopts the concordance-based version of DDL, based on the exposure to numerous examples of language usage containing the same node, along with the typographical enhancement of the node itself. These aspects lead us to hypothesise that DDL activities could actually be more effective, overall, in the development of phraseological competence when compared to non-DDL activities, where there is no exposure to multiple examples containing the same phraseological unit, nor input enhancement of any kind. The meta-analyses we have at our disposal indicate that effectiveness in DDL tends to be harder to detect in between-groups designs, as each approach is used with a single group, thus requiring a longer timeframe to be able to elicit any observable effects (Boulton & Cobb, 2017; Lee et al., 2018). Another challenge in the elicitation of positive learning effects due to the DDL approach resides in whether or how the corpus data is adapted to learners' needs and proficiency. The meta-analyses and reviews on DDL tend to underline the scarcity of longitudinal designs. This study wishes to increase our understanding of the longitudinal dimension pertaining to DDL effects by including four data collection points. This way, the study goes beyond the pre-/post-/delayed post-test designs that are commonly found in the literature. With the last data collection point being a delayed post-test collection post, retention rates are measured on the basis of more than two further data collection points.

The second research question looks more deeply into which properties of the learning aims may have an influence in determining the effect of DDL on the development of Italian L2 phraseological competence. The properties which are looked at include semantic transparency and L1-L2 congruency. These were seen as crucial when reviewing studies regarding the development of phraseological competence in an L2. Combinations containing a verb that is not fully transparent at the semantic level tend to be challenging for learners. Does this mean that exposure to multiple examples containing the same combination could help learners with this particular type of combination? Combinations that are congruent with a learner's L1 seem to be more easily learned. Does this mean that the learning of incongruent ones would be easier in a DDL setting, thanks to the repeated exposure to a certain category of combinations?

In the third research question another seemingly neglected area in DDL research is addressed, namely the dimension of knowledge of the considered phraseological unit. As mentioned above, receptive knowledge appears to be more easily attained both in the development of phraseological competence and in language proficiency as a whole. In our study, we can expect this to be the case also, with definitional knowledge exhibiting better accuracy levels than transferable knowledge overall. However, the exposure to multiple authentic examples extracted from corpora can make certain word combinations more memorable and transferable to novel contexts. Can we expect transferable knowledge to exhibit better accuracy in the experimental condition?

The fourth research question aims to examine the attitudes that students have towards the DDL approach. How do they perceive a phraseology-oriented series of language lessons, founded on concordance-based activities? Previous literature claims that learner attitudes towards DDL tend to be mostly positive, as learners perceive the usefulness of being exposed to authentic language data, as opposed to artificial instances of language which may be found in coursebooks, and the novelty of having a high number of examples at their disposal for a single word or combinations of words. Learners also appreciate the collaborative and largely inductive nature of the approach. Negative attitudes relate to the initial difficulties that may be encountered in getting familiar with corpus tools and reading concordances: Difficulties with the nature of the language data are also reported.

6.3 Method

6.3.1 Study design

The study is based on a controlled between-groups pseudo-experimental longitudinal design. Eight intact classes of Chinese L1 learners of Italian were randomly assigned to either the DDL or non-DDL condition. Each class consisted of approximately 15 students. All classes were taught a one-hour lesson per week, for eight weeks, by the same instructor (i.e. the researcher). Phraseological competence data was elicited by means of a dedicated test at four points in time and at four-week intervals: before the beginning of the lessons, four weeks into the lessons, eight weeks into the lessons and finally four weeks after the end of the lessons. Table 6.2 summarises the design and the data collection plan.

The variables held constant in the study were those related to the participants (L1, age group, language learning program), pedagogical treatment (teacher, learning aims, lesson planning principles, duration of the lesson, homework), data collection (phraseological competence test, time of administration of the test).

6.3.2 Population and participant sample

The study is based on the population of L1 Chinese students enrolled in the Marco Polo and Turandot governments programmes in Italy. These are

Gains and learner attitudes in DDL 123

Table 6.2 Study design

Data collection point	Week	Experimental groups	Control groups
Phraseological competence test 1	0	Getting to know each other activities Background questionnaire	
	1	DDL activities	non-DDL activities
	2	DDL activities	non-DDL activities
	3	DDL activities	non-DDL activities
Phraseological competence test 2	4	DDL activities	non-DDL activities
	5	DDL activities	non-DDL activities
	6	DDL activities	non-DDL activities
	7	DDL activities	non-DDL activities
Phraseological competence test 3	8	DDL activities	non-DDL activities
	9	No activities	
	10	No activities	
	11	No activities	
Phraseological competence test 4	12	No activities	

foundational one-year language courses aimed at providing prospective Chinese university students with the necessary language skills and competencies in Italian to enroll in university degrees in Italy. The Marco Polo program involves Chinese students wishing to enroll in scientific/technical academic degrees (e.g., Engineering, Chemistry, Physics, etc.), whereas the Turandot program attracts the students seeking to enroll in humanities and art-related programs (e.g., Conservatorium of Music, Academy of Fine Arts, etc.). The sample for the present study was drawn from the set of pre-intermediate Chinese students enrolled in the Marco Polo and Turandot courses at the University for Foreigners of Perugia in the academic year 2016/2017. In order to identify a sample from this population, care was taken to select a sample that would be at the same time large enough to account for possible variation among the learners involved in the study, as well as balanced so that it could be divided into two groups. These groups would then need to be homogenous and reflect and be characterised by the same starting conditions. The sampling of the learners followed judgment sampling criteria (see Chapter 4), and is illustrated in Figure 6.1.

Each intact class was randomly assigned to either the experimental or the control condition. Since it was not possible to randomise at the level of each participant, but only at the level of intact classes, the study is pseudo-experimental. The phraseological competence test administered before the beginning of the lessons was used to establish the initial lack of differences between the two groups. To this end, an independent two-sample t-test was performed, which returned a p-value of 0.4, indicating the presence of a statistically significant difference between the groups. The experimental group, in fact, exhibits a significantly higher number of correct answers. In order to gain more balance

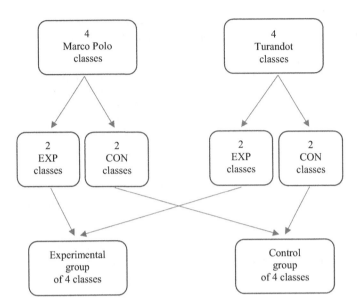

Figure 6.1 Judgment sampling conducted for the study.

between the two groups, the highest score from the experimental group was removed and a second t-test was performed. This time, the t-test returned a p-value of 0.6, attesting a lack of statistically significant differences between the two groups. The characteristics of the final sample of participants, including number, gender, age, months learning Italian before coming to Italy, knowledge of English as a foreign language are summarised in Table 6.3.

6.3.3 Operationalising the DDL construct

6.3.3.1 Identification of learning aims

We now turn to the pedagogical operationalisation of the DDL construct, through the development of the learning materials which were presented to the participants. First, corpus data was used both to identify the learning aims, common to both groups of classes, and to develop the learning activities. In both cases, the data are derived from the L2 Italian corpus LOCCLI (*Longitudinal Corpus of Chinese Learners of Italian*) (Spina & Siyanova-Chanturia, 2018) and the L1 Italian reference corpus PEC (Perugia corpus) (Spina, 2014).

As for the identification of the learning aims, needs-driven and target-driven criteria were followed. The former relates to actual learner needs, as reflected by an examination of a pertinent learner corpus, while the latter related to the most prominent combinations found in a reference corpus of Italian. In the first case,

Table 6.3 Summary statistics of participant sample

	Experimental	*Control*
N.	61	62
Gender (F/M)	38 /23	47/15
Age (range/ mean / median / SD)	18–26 / 21.01 / 2.33	18–27 / 21.43 / 2.50
Months learning Italian before coming to Italy (range / mean / median / SD)	0–12 / 3.72 / 3 / 2.75	0–24 / 4.29 / 3 / 3.93
English as an FL (0 / B / I / A)	0 / 34 / 24 / 3	0 / 35 / 23 / 4

Note: 0 = no English; B = beginner; I = intermediate; A = advanced

all verb + noun (object) combinations were extracted from the LOCCLI, and all combinations containing an error, involving either the verb, the determiner, the noun or the whole combination, were identified. Only some of them would be included in the sets that would then form the basis for lesson planning. A set of eight combinations per week was deemed as a feasible number of combinations to concentrate each single lesson on. The total number of combinations, bearing in mind that the lessons would last for eight weeks, would then be 64. In view of adopting the two sets of criteria in a balanced manner, 32 combinations from those extracted from the LOCCLI were selected, based on the number of errors. These 32 combinations were then grouped into eight themes, each corresponding to the weekly topic of a given lesson. The themes reflected the most common ones that can be found in communicatively-oriented second language learning coursebooks. The themes were: a *una festa* ('at a party'), *il fine settimana* ('at the weekend'), *la mia giornata tipica* ('my typical day'), *la mia casa* ('my house'), *i miei hobby* (my hobbies), *le mie ultime vacanze* ('my most recent holidays'), *un'amicizia* ('a friendship'), *progetti per il futuro* ('plans for the future'). Then, the missing spots for each set of weekly combinations were filled by selecting combinations from the PEC, through the DICI-A (Spina, 2010), which is based on the PEC. The combinations were selected according to their frequency and dispersion values, their thematic relevance to the previously identified topics and the presence of a delexicalised verb. The final list of combination sets, on the basis of which both the experimental and the control lessons were constructed, can be seen in Table 6.4.

6.3.3.2 Development of learning materials

The DDL materials were designed as paper-based activities for two main reasons. First, at the time of conducting this study, there were no corpora of Italian specifically built for second language learners (Forti & Spina, 2019). The second reason, which derives from the first, is that the learners

Table 6.4 Learning aims of the study: Weekly sets of verb + noun (object) combinations

Themes	Combinations
a una festa ('at a party')	1. *fare amicizia* ('to make friends') 2. *fare un sorriso* ('to smile') 3. *avere [numero] anni* ('to be [number] years old') 4. *studiare [materia]* ('to study [subject]') 5. *amare [attività]* ('to love [activity]') 6. *organizzare una festa* ('to organise a party') 7. *fare gli auguri* ('to wish the best') 8. *fare un regalo* ('to give a present')
il fine settimana ('at the weekend')	1. *fare una passeggiata* ('to go for a walk') 2. *prendere il sole* ('to sunbathe') 3. *fare una gita* ('to go on a trip') 4. *prendere aria* ('to get fresh air') 5. *avere fretta* ('to be in a hurry') 6. *pulire casa* ('to clean the house') 7. *spendere soldi* ('to spend money') 8. *fare la spesa* ('to go grocery shopping')
la mia giornata tipica ('my typical day')	1. *prendere l'autobus* ('to take the bus') 2. *fare colazione* ('to have breakfast') 3. *mettersi la giacca* ('to put a jacket on') 4. *avere lezione* ('to have a lesson') 5. *rifare il letto* ('to make the bed') 6. *mettere la musica* ('to put on some music') 7. *fare la doccia* ('to take a shower') 8. *mandare un messaggio* ('to send a message')
la mia casa ('my house')	1. *avere fame* ('to be hungry') 2. *preparare la cena* ('to prepare the dinner') 3. *sbagliare strada* ('to go the wrong way') 4. *trovare la strada* ('to find the right way') 5. *trovare casa* ('to find a house') 6. *affittare una casa* ('to rent a house') 7. *dividere un appartamento* ('to share an apartment') 8. *dividere una spesa* ('to share an expense')
I miei hobby ('my hobbies')	1. *suonare la chitarra* ('to play the guitar') 2. *fare sport* ('to do sport') 3. *fare shopping* ('to go shopping') 4. *ascoltare musica* ('to listen to music') 5. *dipingere quadri* ('to paint pictures') 6. *fare una foto* ('to take a photo') 7. *leggere un romanzo* ('to read a novel') 8. *vedere un film* ('to watch a film')
le mie ultime vacanze ('my most recent holidays')	1. *gustare i cibi* ('to taste food') 2. *visitare la città* ('to visit the city') 3. *ampliare le conoscenze* ('to expand knowledge') 4. *ricordare un'esperienza* ('to remember an experience') 5. *organizzare un viaggio* ('to organise a trip') 6. *prendere un treno* ('to take a train') 7. *fare la fila* ('to queue') 8. *fare la valigia* ('to prepare the suitcase')

Table 6.4 Cont.

Themes	Combinations
un'amicizia ('a friendship')	1. *raccontare una storia* ('to tell a story') 2. *diventare amico* ('to become friends') 3. *avere un dubbio* ('to have a doubt') 4. *chiedere un consiglio* ('to ask for advice') 5. *dare un consiglio* ('to give advice') 6. *ascoltare un consiglio* ('to listen to an advice') 7. *trovare una soluzione* ('to find a solution') 8. *cambiare opinione* ('to change opinion')
progetti per il futuro ('plans for the future')	1. *fare l'artista* ('to be an artist') 2. *fare un viaggio* ('to go on a trip') 3. *risparmiare soldi* ('to save money') 4. *fare esperienze* ('to have experiences') 5. *fare un esame* ('to sit an exam') 6. *avere un'idea* ('to have an idea') 7. *cambiare casa* ('to change houses') 8. *avere successo* ('to be successful')

involved in the study were all pre-intermediate students enrolled in Italian language courses. As a result, the linguistic data contained in the reference corpus of Italian used in this study (i.e. the PEC, Spina 2014) would not suit the learners' level without some form of adaptation. Third, it was not feasible to move the groups of 15 students from their classrooms to the IT lab of the university where all the computers were located. For these reasons, developing paper-based activities was deemed the most viable option.

In order to develop the experimental activities, linguistic data from the PEC were used. More specifically, concordance lines for each of the weekly word combinations (see Table 6.4.) were extracted from the corpus. A pattern analysis of the extracted concordance lines was performed in order to identify the presence of regularities with respect to form, meaning and structure. The activities were developed on the basis of the observed regularities. Groups of either 20, 15 or 10 sentences were selected to build the paper-based concordance-oriented activities, so that the regularities found in the pattern analysis could be visible in a representative way. As the corpus used was not tailored for pedagogical materials development, the following steps in adapting the corpus data were taken:

1. selection of sentences deemed suitable to pre-intermediate level learners, from which it is possible to infer the overall context of occurrence and meaning;
2. selection of sentences so that the observation of a pattern is possible;
3. cut/copy of the concordance lines into a two-column MS Word table;

4. separation of the two halves so that the verb and noun combination is centred;
5. elimination of spaces between a word and a punctuation mark or an apostrophe/quotation marks, etc.
6. transformation of word strings into sentences;
7. elimination of long subordinate clauses;
8. substitution of long expressions with single, simpler words so as to make the sentences fit into the table;
9. modification of verb tenses according to pre-intermediate proficiency level;
10. correction of errors and typos, which would not work well to model the language to the learners (e.g., *artcioli* instead of *articoli*; *cosi* instead of *così*; etc.);
11. if not enough occurrences of a word combination are found, integration with combinations that have a similar meaning and formal patterns and can be integrated into the activity.
12. attention to left and right cotexts, so that they are always logically linked (sometimes they are not, and devoid of a larger context become difficult to understand).
13. alignment of the text, combination in bold, numbering of each sentence.

The paper-based experimental activities reflected the most common errors found in LOCCLI. More specifically, they ranged from activities aimed at observing patterns of determiner usage in verb-noun combinations (by the far the largest error in the combinations produced by the learners represented in LOCCLI), to others focusing, for instance, on dealing with the differences between metaphorical and literal uses of word combinations. The activities included a variety of formats such as multiple-sentence gap fills, multiple-sentence matching, and multiple-sentence error correction. In all cases, the learners were exposed to multiple examples pertaining to a single verb-noun combination. All of the activities were sequenced so as to fit with the lesson in a meaningful way. As for the non-DDL activities, the activity types included single sentence gap-fills, single sentence matching, single word combination matching. The sample lesson plans provided in Appendix A and B show how the same set of learning aims were pedagogically operationalised in a different way, so as to either reflect DDL principles or not.

6.3.4 A data collection tool for the etic dimension: the phraseological competence test

Phraseological competence has been tested on the basis of a number of testing formats. For the purposes of the present study, we developed a two-part phraseological competence test, consisting of 32 multiple-choice items and 32 gap-fill items. The former used errors derived from LOCCLI as distractors (Gyllstad & Snoder, 2021; Marello, 2009), while the latter was based on sentences extracted from the Italian L1 corpus PEC. The total number of items forming the test was thus 64. Each multiple-choice item contained four options: one was the correct answer; one contained an error found in LOCCLI, regarding the selection of the verb collocate or the use of the determiner; one contained an error modeled on those found in LOCCLI; and the last option was 'none of these', following the recommendation contained in Jaèn (2009). According to Jaèn, the insertion of such an option can help reduce guessing, and it is recommended to make the option true at least 10% of the time over the total amount of items contained in the test. In our case, the option was made true four times. At each administration of the test, the order of presentation of the items was randomised. Furthermore, no corrective feedback was provided to the students after each administration of the test before the end of the study. Appendix C contains the full phraseological competence test developed and administered in the context of the present study.

6.3.5 A data collection tool for the emic dimension: the student questionnaire

As seen in Chapter 2, Mizumoto et al. (2016) developed and validated a thorough questionnaire tailored for eliciting learner attitudes and perceptions towards DDL activities. This tool represents an invaluable resource in the context on emic studies dealing with DDL effects, as it allows comparability among studies and systematicity. However, we chose not to use the questionnaire in the context of the present study for two reasons. First, many aspects contained in Mizumoto et al.'s questionnaire were not features of the pedagogical treatment that characterised the present study, and in turn many aspects that were present in the activities developed within the present study are not reflected in the items developed by Mizumoto et al. (2016). Second, as very little pedagogical experimentation has been conducted on DDL in Italian L2 contexts, we wanted to provide the students with the opportunity to share their insight and suggestions by means of open-ended questions, besides the likert-scale items. For these reasons, we decided to develop an ad hoc questionnaire, in order to cater for the specific characteristics of the present study.

The student questionnaire we developed sought to elicit perceptions related to how the two groups work on word combinations, whether with or without corpus-informed materials. The questionnaire was divided into two main parts. The first contained eight likert-scale items, while the second contained four open-ended questions. The eight likert-scale items were evenly divided into items regarding aspects of the DDL materials, and aspects regarding the lessons at a more general level (the focus on word combinations, the presence of group work, the usefulness of the homework assigned, etc.). The four open-ended questions sought to provide the students with more freedom to comment on the pedagogical experience that they had, while providing them with the chance to make suggestions in terms of ideas for future improvements. As a result, two versions of the questionnaire were administered: one version catered for the experimental group, containing eight likert-scale items on general aspects of the lessons, on word combinations and on more specific aspects related to the DDL activities, together with the four open-ended questions; the other version catered for the participants of the control group, as it contained only four likert-scale items (i.e. those pertaining to general aspects of the lessons) and the four open-ended questions. The likert-scale items were developed on the basis of a six-point scale. The scale contained the following values: 1 = 'totally disagree'; 2 = 'disagree'; 3 = 'partially disagree'; 4 = 'partially agree'; 5 = 'agree'; 6 = 'totally agree'.

When choosing whether to opt for an even- or an odd-numbered scale, we followed the recommendation contained in Dörnyei (2010): with an even-numbered scale, respondents are prevented from having the possibility of choosing a neutral middle option, thus being directed towards choosing one of the two ends of the scale. Each likert-scale item was conceived as an assertion regarding the perception of specific single aspects characterising the learning experience that the students engaged in. As for how the likert-scale items were worded, we followed Dörnyei (2010) once again, by wording them either positively or negatively, maintaining an even alternation between the two modes. As pointed out by Dörnyei (2010), the adoption of this criterion in the wording of the items should help prevent respondents from marking only one end of the scale. This happens when respondents assume that assertions about either negative or positive perceptions of the experience are systematically placed at the same end of one scale. The absence of such systematicity is thought to guide respondents towards a more careful reflection on the meaning of a specific item. In consideration of the fact that the questionnaire was not aimed at assessing the learners' reading comprehension skills in Italian, but sought to elicit their perceptions regarding the pedagogical intervention, the items of the questionnaire were presented in a bilingual form: Italian and Chinese. This choice preempted possible difficulties for the learners to understand the items in the questionnaire. The questionnaire was administered at the end of the pedagogical intervention. It may be viewed in Appendix D and E.

6.3.6 Data analysis

In this section we describe how the data analysis was conducted for each of the four research questions formulated in section 6.2. The first three research questions were addressed by analysing the collected data through mixed-effects modelling. As for the first research question, related to the overall effects of DDL activities on the development of phraseological competence as opposed to non-DDL activities, the data collected from the phraseological competence test was analysed by means of mixed-effects modelling (Cunnings, 2012; Cunnings & Finlayson, 2015; Linck & Cunnings, 2015). The independent variable was the teaching approach and had two levels: DDL and non-DDL. The dependent variables were the scores obtained by the students in the phraseological competence test, which were measured in terms of accuracy on the basis of two values: correct and incorrect. The second research question examines the role that semantic transparency and L1-L2 congruency play in DDL effects on phraseological competence development. Each of these properties were operationalised so that the items in the dataset could be coded accordingly.

Semantic transparency was coded on the basis of the annotations performed by 13 native Italian speakers, all of whom had passed at least one linguistics exam at MA level. Each annotator was asked to assign one of the following categories (Howarth, 1998, p. 47) to each item in the list of 64 verb + noun combinations used in the study:

(1) free combination: both words are used in their literal meaning and each one can be substituted without influencing the meaning of the other (e.g., *firmare una lettera / firmare un foglio / spedire una lettera*);
(2) collocation: one of the words is used in its literal meaning, while the other one is used in its specific sense (figurative or metaphorical), and the substitution of the word used in its literal sense would modify the meaning of the word used in its non-literal meaning (e.g., *prendere l'aereo / prendere una penna*);
(X) uncertain: cases in which neither (1) nor (2) are applicable.

Each annotator worked on an individually-randomised list of items and did not engage in any prior consensus-building discussion with the other annotators (Plonsky & Derrick, 2016, p. 13). Krippendorff's alpha was calculated to obtain a measure of inter-annotator agreement rate. The obtained value was 0.484, well below the minimum value that is acceptable for considering a multiple-rater annotation sufficiently consistent and thus reliable (i.e. alpha > 0.667). We then opted for removing the disputed data from the list (Loewen & Plonsky, 2015, pp. 90–91), until we reached a set of 32 combinations, yielding an alpha coefficient of 0.742. Table 6.5 contains the final list of combinations coded according to semantic transparency.

The property of L1-L2 congruency was then coded. To this end, two expert L1 Chinese speakers, with advanced competence in Italian, were asked to annotate the list of 64 combinations according to whether they had a literal and structural correspondence in Chinese. Both sets of annotations coincided, with the annotators feeling unsure about the same items, but ultimately taking the same final decisions. Table 6.6 lists the 64 items according to L1-L2 congruency.

The third research question, pertaining to the different dimensions of phraseological knowledge (i.e. definitional and transferable), was investigated by considering the first part of the competence test, consisting of multiple-choice items, as a reflection of definitional knowledge, and the second part of the competence test, consisting of gap-fill items, as a reflection of transferable knowledge. As for the fourth and last research question,

Table 6.5 List of semantically transparent and semantically opaque combinations

	Free combinations (semantically transparent)	Collocations (at least partially opaque)
1	affittare una stanza	avere un'idea
2	ascoltare la musica	dividere un appartamento
3	chiedere consigli	fare colazione
4	comprare un regalo	fare gli auguri
5	dipingere quadri	fare la fila
6	gustare i cibi	fare la spesa
7	leggere un romanzo	fare shopping
8	mandare un messaggio	fare una doccia
9	organizzare un viaggio	mettere la musica
10	organizzare una festa	prendere aria
11	preparare la cena	prendere il sole
12	pulire la casa	prendere il treno
13	raccontare una storia	prendere l'autobus
14	ricordare un'esperienza	rifare il letto
15	risparmiare soldi	
16	sbagliare strada	
17	suonare la chitarra	
18	visitare la città	

Table 6.6 List of congruent and incongruent combinations

	Congruent	Incongruent
1	Affittare una stanza	Avere [numero] anni
2	Amare lo sport	Avere fame
3	Ampliare le conoscenze	Avere fretta
4	Ascoltare musica	Dare consigli
5	Ascoltare un consiglio	Fare amicizia
6	Avere lezione	Fare colazione
7	Avere successo	Fare esperienze
8	Avere un dubbio	Fare una foto
9	Avere un'idea	Fare gli auguri
10	Cambiare casa	Fare la doccia
11	Cambiare opinione	Fare la fila
12	Chiedere consigli	Fare la spesa
13	Dipingere un quadro	Fare shopping
14	Diventare amico	Comprare un regalo
15	Dividere un appartamento	Fare un sorriso
16	Dividere una spesa	Fare un viaggio
17	Fare l'artista	Fare una gita
18	Fare sport	Fare un esame
19	Gustare il cibo	Fare una passeggiata
20	Leggere un romanzo	Fare le valigie
21	Mandare un messaggio	Mettere la musica
22	Organizzare un viaggio	Mettere la giacca
23	Organizzare una festa	Prendere aria
24	Preparare la cena	Prendere il sole

Table 6.6 Cont.

	Congruent	Incongruent
25	Pulire la casa	Prendere il treno
26	Raccontare una storia	Prendere l'autobus
27	Ricordare un'esperienza	Rifare il letto
28	Risparmiare soldi	Sbagliare strada
29	Spendere soldi	Trovare casa
30	Studiare [materia]	
31	Suonare la chitarra	
32	Trovare la strada	
33	Trovare una soluzione	
34	Vedere un film	
35	Visitare la città	

the data collected by means of the student questionnaire was analysed by identifying percentage of responses for each likert-scale point, with the addition of a trend line (for a discussion on whether to treat likert-scale item data as ordinal and/or interval data, see Hatch & Lazarton, 1991).

6.4 Chapter summary and conclusions

In this chapter we explored the different aspects involved in setting up a study design aimed at investigating DDL effects. We did so by making a series of choices of the basis of the range of choices presented in Chapter 4. We started by identifying a language area to focus on: phraseology. The centrality of phraseology for second language learning as a whole was sustained in light of a wealth of studies pointing in this direction and pertaining to diverse disciplines, such as corpus linguistics, psycholinguistics and language testing. We then chose to embark on a mixed-methods study design, seeking to integrate both etic data, pertaining to language gains and reflecting an external and objective perspective concerning language learning processes and mechanisms; and emic data, pertaining to leaner attitudes and perceptions related to the approach, reflecting a more internal and subjective perspective concerning the exposure to the approach.

The combination of the literature review on L2 phraseology and on DDL (see previous chapters) led to the formulation of four research questions. Each one looks at a specific aspect: DDL effects overall; DDL effects in relation to linguistic properties of the learning aims (i.e. semantic transparency and L1 congruency); DDL effects in relation to the cognitive properties of learning aims (i.e. dimension of phraseological knowledge); and DDL effects in relation to learner attitudes. We presented the method adopted in relation to the study design, the population and participant sample, the operationalisation of the DDL construct, the identification of learning aims, the development of learning materials, the construction of the phraseological competence test and how the data analysis will be conducted with respect to each of the four research questions formulated. Chapters 7 and 8 illustrate the findings related to the etic and emic perspectives respectively.

References

Altenberg, B. (1998). On the phraseology of spoken English: The evidence of recurrent word-combinations. In A.P. Cowie (Ed.), *Phraseology: Theory, analysis and applications* (pp. 101–122). Oxford University Press.

Altenberg, B., & Granger, S. (2001). The grammatical and lexical patterning of MAKE in native and non-native student writing. *Applied Linguistics*, 22(2), 173–195.

Bahns, J. (1993). Lexical collocations: A contrastive view. *ELT Journal*, 47(1), 56–63.

Bestgen, Y., & Granger, S. (2014). Quantifying the development of phraseological competence in L2 English writing: An automated approach. *Journal of Second Language Writing*, 26, 28–41.

Biskup, D. (1992). L1 influence on learners' renderings of English collocations. In L. Arnaud & H. Béjoint (Eds.), *Vocabulary and applied linguistics* (pp. 85–93). Macmillan.

Boers, F., Dang, T.C.T., & Strong, B. (2017). Comparing the effectiveness of phrase-focused exercises: A partial replication of Boers, Demecheleer, Coxhead, and Webb (2014). *Language Teaching Research*, 21(3), 362–380.

Boers, F., Demecheleer, M., Coxhead, A., & Webb, S. (2014). Gauging the effects of exercises on verb–noun collocations. *Language Teaching Research*, 18(1), 54–74.

Boers, F., & Webb, S. (2018). Teaching and learning collocation in adult second and foreign language learning. *Language Teaching*, 51(01), 77–89.

Boulton, A. (2008). DDL: Reaching the parts other teaching can't reach? In A. Frankenberg-Garcia (Ed.), *Proceedings of the 8th Teaching and Language Corpora Conference* (pp. 38–44). Associação de Estudos e de Investigação Científica do ISLA-Lisboa.

Boulton, A., & Cobb, T. (2017). Corpus use in language learning: A meta-analysis. *Language Learning*, 67(2), 348–393.

Bratankova, L. (2015). *Le collocazioni Verbo + Nome in apprendenti di italiano L2*. Unpublished PhD thesis. University for Foreigners of Perugia.

Bulté, B., & Housen, A. (2012). Defining and operationalising L2 complexity. In A. Housen, F. Kuiken, & I. Vedder (Eds.), *Dimensions of L2 Performance and Proficiency*, Volume 32 (pp. 21–46). Benjamins.

Choi, S. (2017). Processing and learning of enhanced English collocations: An eye movement study. *Language Teaching Research*, 21(3), 403–426.

Columbus, G. (2010). Processing MWUs: Are MWU subtypes psycholinguistically real? In D. Wood (Ed.), *Perspectives on formulaic language: Acquisition and communication* (pp. 194–212). Continuum.

Cunnings, I. (2012). An overview of mixed-effects statistical models for second language researchers. *Second Language Research*, 28(3), 369–382.

Cunnings, I., & Finlayson, I. (2015). Mixed effects modeling and longitudinal data analysis. In L. Plonsky (Ed.), *Advancing quantitative methods in second language* (pp. 159–181). Routledge.

De Mauro, T., & Voghera, M. (1996). Scala mobile. Un punto di vista sui lessemi complessi. In P. Benincà, G. Cinque, T. De Mauro, & N. Vincent (Eds.), *Italiano e dialetti nel tempo. Saggi di grammatica per Giulio C. Lepschy* (pp. 99–131). Bulzoni.

Dörnyei, Z., with Tatsuya Taguchi. (2010). *Questionnaires in second language research. construction, administration, and processing.* (2nd ed.). Routledge.

Durrant, P. (2014). Corpus frequency and second language learners' knowledge of collocations: A meta-analysis. *International Journal of Corpus Linguistics*, 19(4), 443–477.

Durrant, P., & Schmitt, N. (2009). To what extent do native and non-native writers make use of collocations? *IRAL – International Review of Applied Linguistics in Language Teaching*, 47(2), 157–177.

Durrant, P., & Schmitt, N. (2010). Adult learners' retention of collocations from exposure. *Second Language Research*, 26(2), 163–188.

Elia, A., D'Agostino, E., & Martinelli, M. (1985). Tre componenti della sintassi italiana: Frasi semplici, frasi a verbo supporto e frasi idiomatiche. In A. Franchi de Bellis & L.M. Savoia (Eds.), *Sintassi e morfologia della lingua italiana d'uso. Teorie e applicazioni descrittive* (pp. 311–325). Bulzoni.

Ellis, N.C. (2002). Frequency effects in language processing. *Studies in Second Language Acquisition*, 24(02), 143–188.

Ellis, N.C., Simpson-Vlach, R., Römer, U., O'Donnell, M.B., & Wulff, S. (2015). Learner corpora and formulaic language in second language acquisition research. In S. Granger, G. Gilquin, & F. Meunier (Eds.), *The Cambridge Handbook of Learner Corpus Research* (pp. 357–378). Cambridge University Press.

Erman, B., & Warren, B. (2000). The idiom principle and the open choice principle. *Text – Interdisciplinary Journal for the Study of Discourse*, 20(1), 29–62.

Fan, M. (2009). An exploratory study of collocational use by ESL students – A task based approach. *System*, 37(1), 110–123.

Farghal, M., & Obiedat, H. (1995). Collocations: A neglected variables in EFL. *IRAL – International Review of Applied Linguistics in Language Teaching*, 33(4), 315–331.

Firth, J.R. (1957). *Papers in linguistics 1934–1951*. Oxford University Press.

Forti, L., & Spina, S. (2019). Corpora for linguists vs. corpora for learners: Bridging the gap in Italian L2 learning and teaching. *EL.LE – Educazione Linguistica. Language Education*, 8(2), 349–362.

Gilquin, G. (2007). To err is not all. What corpus and elicitation can reveal about the use of collocations by learners. *Zeitschrift Für Anglistick Und Amerikanistick*, 55(3), 273–291.

Granger, S. (Ed.). (1998). *Learner English on computer*. Longman.

Groom, N. (2009). Effects of second language immersion on second language collocational development. In *Researching collocations in another language: Multiple interpretations* (pp. 21–33). Palgrave Macmillan.

Gyllstad, H., & Snoder, P. (2021). Exploring learner corpus data for language testing and assessment purposes: The case of Verb + Noun Collocations. In S. Granger (Ed.), *Perspectives on the L2 Phrasicon: The view from learner corpora* (pp. 49–71). Multilingual Matters.

Gyllstad, H., & Wolter, B. (2016). Collocational processing in light of the Phraseological Continuum Model: Does semantic transparency matter?: Collocational processing and semantic transparency. *Language Learning*, 66(2), 296–323.

Hasselgren, A. (1994). Lexical teddy bears and advanced learners: A study into the ways Norwegian students cope with English vocabulary. *International Journal of Applied Linguistics*, 4(2), 237–258.

Hatch, E., & Lazaraton, A. (1991). *The research manual: Design and statistics for applied linguistics*. Heinle & Heinle Publishers.

Henriksen, B. (2013). Research on L2 learners' collocational competence and development – A progress report. In C. Bardel, C. Lindqvist, & B. Laufer (Eds.), *L2 vocabulary acquisition, knowledge and use. New perspectives on assessment and corpus analysis. Eurosla Monographs Series, 2* (Vol. 2, pp. 29–56). EuroSLA.

Howarth, P.A. (1996). *Phraseology in English academic writing: Some implications for language learning and dictionary making*. Lexicografica.

Howarth, P.A. (1998). Phraseology and second language proficiency. *Applied Linguistics*, 19(1), 24–44.

Hunston, S. (2002). *Corpora in applied linguistics*. Cambridge University Press.

Jaén, M.M. (2009). A corpus-driven design of a test for assessing the ESL collocational competence of university students. *International Journal of English Studies*, 7(2), 127–148.

Ježek, E. (2016). *The lexicon: An introduction*. Oxford University Press.

Koya, T. (2005). *The acquisition of basic collocations by Japanese learners of English*. Unpublished PhD Thesis. Waseda University.

Laufer, B., & Waldman, T. (2011). Verb-noun collocations in second language writing: A corpus analysis of learners' English: Verb-noun collocations in L2 writing. *Language Learning*, 61(2), 647–672.

Lee, H., Warschauer, M., & Lee, J.H. (2018). The effects of corpus use on second language vocabulary learning: A multilevel meta-analysis. *Applied Linguistics*, 40(5), 721–753.

Li, J., & Schmitt, N. (2010). The development of collocation use in academic texts by advanced L2 Learners: A multiple case study approach. In D. Wood (Ed.), *Perspectives on Formulaic Language: Acquisition and Communication* (pp. 23–46). Continuum.

Licui, Z., Daichi, Y., & Haruyuki, K. (2019). Similarities and differences between native and non-native speakers' processing of formulaic sequences: A Functional Near-Infrared Spectroscopy (fNIRS) study. *Journal of Psycholinguistic Research*, 50, 397–416.

Linck, J.A., & Cunnings, I. (2015). The utility and application of mixed-effects models in second language research: Mixed-effects models. *Language Learning*, 65(S1), 185–207.

Lo Cascio, V. (2013). *Dizionario Combinatorio Italiano*. Benjamins.

Loewen, S., & Plonsky, L. (2015). *An A [to] Z of applied linguistics research methods*. Palgrave Macmillan.

Manning, C.D., & Schütze, H. (1999). *Foundations of statistical natural language processing*. MIT Press.

Marello, C. (2009). Distrattori tratti da corpora di apprendenti di italiano LS/L2. In E. Corino & C. Marello (Eds.), *VALICO. Studi di linguistica e didattica* (pp. 177–193). Guerra.

Masini, F. (2009). Combinazioni di parola e parole sintagmatiche. In E. Lombardi Vallauri & L. Mereu (Eds.), *Spazi linguistici. Studi in onore di Raffaele Simone* (pp. 191–209). Bulzoni.

Masini, F. (2012). *Parole sintagmatiche in italiano*. Caissa.

Meunier, F., & Granger, S. (Eds.). (2008). *Phraseology in foreign language learning and teaching*. Benjamins.

Mizumoto, A., Chujo, K., & Yokota, K. (2016). Development of a scale to measure learners' perceived preferences and benefits of data-driven learning. *ReCALL*, 28(02), 227–246.

Nation, P. (2020). The different aspects of vocabulary knowledge. In S. Webb (Ed.), *The Routledge Handbook of Vocabulary Studies* (pp. 15–29). Routledge.

Nesselhauf, N. (2003). The use of collocations by advanced learners of English and some implications for teaching. *Applied Linguistics*, 24(2), 223–242.

Nesselhauf, N. (2005). *Collocations in a learner corpus*. Benjamins.

Paquot, M. (2018). Phraseological competence: A missing component in university entrance language tests? Insights from a study of EFL learners' use of statistical collocations. *Language Assessment Quarterly*, 1–15.

Parkinson, J. (2015). Noun–noun collocations in learner writing. *Journal of English for Academic Purposes*, 20, 103–113.

Pellicer-Sánchez, A. (2017). Learning L2 collocations incidentally from reading. *Language Teaching Research*, 21(3), 381–402.

Plonsky, L., & Derrick, D.J. (2016). A meta-analysis of reliability coefficients in second language research. *The Modern Language Journal*, 100(2), 538–553.

Rescher, N. (1998). *Complexity: A philosophical overview*. Transaction Publishers.

Sag, I.A., Baldwin, T., Bond, F., Copestake, A., & Flickinger, D. (2002). Multiword expressions: A pain in the neck for NLP. In A. Gelbukh (Ed.), *Computational Linguistics and Intelligent Text Processing*, Vol. 2276 (pp. 1–15). Springer.

Simone, R., & Masini, F. (2007). Support nouns and verbal features: A case study from Italian. *Verbum*, 1–2, 143–172.

Sinclair, J.M. (1991). *Corpus, concordance, collocation*. Oxford University Press.

Siyanova, A., & Schmitt, N. (2007). Native and nonnative use of multi-word vs. One-word verbs. *IRAL – International Review of Applied Linguistics in Language Teaching*, 45(2), 119–139.

Siyanova-Chanturia, A. (2015). Collocation in beginner learner writing: A longitudinal study. *System*, 53, 148–160.

Sonbul, S., & Schmitt, N. (2013). Explicit and implicit lexical knowledge: Acquisition of collocations under different input conditions: Explicit and implicit lexical knowledge. *Language Learning*, 63(1), 121–159.

Spina, S. (2010). The Dici project: Towards a dictionary of Italian collocations integrated with an online language learning platform. *Proceedings of ELex 2009. eLexicography in the 21st century. New challenges, new applications*. 22–24 October 2009, Presses universitaires de Louvain.

Spina, S. (2014). Il Perugia Corpus: Una risorsa di riferimento per l'italiano. Composizione, annotazione e valutazione. *Proceedings of the First Italian Conference on Computational Linguistics CLiC-It 2014 & the Fourth International Workshop EVALITA 2014*, 1, 354–359.

Spina, S. (2015). Phraseology in academic L2 discourse: The use of multi-words units in a CMC university context. In E. Castello, K. Ackerley, & F. Coccetta (Eds.), *Studies in Learner Corpus Linguistics: Research and Applications for Foreign Language Teaching and Assessment* (pp. 279–294). Peter Lang.

Spina, S. (2016). Learner corpus research and phraseology in Italian as a second language: The case of the DICI-A, a learner dictionary of Italian collocations. In B. Sanromán Vilas (Ed.), *Collocations Cross-Linguistically. Corpora, Dictionaries* and *Language Teaching (Mémoires de la Société Néophilologique de Helsinki)* (pp. 219–244). Société Néophilologique.

Spina, S. (2019). The development of phraseological errors in Chinese learner Italian: A longitudinal study. In A. Abel, A. Glaznieks, V. Lyding, & N. Lionel (Eds.). *Widening the scope of learner corpus research. Selected papers from the Fourth Learner Corpus Research Conference* (pp. 95–119), Presses universitaires de Louvain.

Spina, S., & Siyanova-Chanturia, A. (2018). *The longitudinal corpus of Chinese learners of Italian (LOCCLI)*. Poster presented at the 13th Teaching and Language Corpora conference, University of Cambridge.

Szudarski, P., & Carter, R. (2016). The role of input flood and input enhancement in EFL learners' acquisition of collocations: L2 input types and acquisition of collocations. *International Journal of Applied Linguistics, 26*(2), 245–265.

Tiberii, P. (2012). *Dizionario delle collocazioni. Le combinazioni delle parole in italiano*. Zanichelli.

Tognini Bonelli, E. (2001). *Corpus Linguistics at Work*. Benjamins.

Urzì, F. (2009). *Dizionario delle Combinazioni Lessicali*. Convivium.

Van Lancker Sidtis, D. (2012). Two-track mind: Formulaic and novel language support a dual-process model. In M. Faust (Ed.), *The handbook of the neuropsychology of language* (pp. 342–367). Wiley-Blackwell.

Vietri, S., Franchi de Bellis, A., & Savoia, L.M. (1985). On the study of idiomatic expressions in Italian. In *Sintassi e morfologia della lingua italiana d'uso. Teorie e applicazioni descrittive* (pp. 373–389). Bulzoni.

Vilkaitė, L. (2016). Are nonadjacent collocations processed faster? *Journal of Experimental Psychology: Learning, Memory, and Cognition, 42*(10), 1632–1642.

Vilkaitė, L., & Schmitt, N. (2019). Reading collocations in an L2: Do collocation processing benefits extend to non-adjacent collocations? *Applied Linguistics, 40*(2), 329–354.

Voghera, M. (1994). Lessemi complessi: Percorsi di lessicalizzazione a confronto. *Lingua e Stile, 29*(2), 185–214.

Voghera, M. (2004). Polirematiche. In M. Grossmann & F. Rainer (Eds.), *La formazione delle parole in italiano* (pp. 56–69). Niemeyer.

Wang, Y. (2016). *The idiom principle and L1 influence. A contrastive learner-corpus study of delexical verb+noun collocations*. Benjamins.

Webb, S. (Ed.). (2019). *The Routledge handbook of vocabulary studies*. Routledge.

Webb, S., Newton, J., & Chang, A. (2013). Incidental learning of collocation. *Language Learning, 63*(1), 91–120.

Wolter, B., & Gyllstad, H. (2011). Collocational links in the L2 mental lexicon and the influence of L1 intralexical knowledge. *Applied Linguistics, 32*(4), 430–449.

Wolter, B., & Gyllstad, H. (2013). Frequency of input and L2 collocational processing: A comparison of congruent and incongruent collocations. *Studies in Second Language Acquisition, 35*(03), 451–482.

Wolter, B., & Yamashita, J. (2015). Processing collocations in a second language: A case of first language activation? *Applied Psycholinguistics, 36*(05), 1193–1221.

Wolter, B., & Yamashita, J. (2018). Word frequency, collocational frequency, L1 congruency, and proficiency in L2 collocational processing: What accounts for L2 performance? *Studies in Second Language Acquisition, 40*(2), 395–416.

Wood, D. (2020). Classifying and identifying formulaic language. In S. Webb (Ed.), *The Routledge Handbook of Vocabulary Studies* (pp. 30–45). Routledge.

Wray, A. (2002). *Formulaic language and the lexicon*. Cambridge University Press.
Wray, A. (2008). *Formulaic language: Pushing the boundaries*. Oxford University Press.
Yamashita, J., & Jiang, N. (2010). L1 Influence on the acquisition of L2 collocations: Japanese ESL users and EFL learners acquiring English collocations. *TESOL Quarterly*, 44(4), 647–668.
Zaninello, A., & Nissim, M. (2010). Creation of lexical resources for a characterisation of multiword expressions in Italian. *Proceedings of the Seventh Conference on International Language Resources and Evaluation*, 654–661.

7 How data-driven learning impacts language gains

This chapter presents and discusses the findings related to the etic component of the study described in Chapter 6. More specifically, it will illustrate how DDL impacts language gains over time in relation to the development of phraseological competence. It will do so by looking at how phraseological competence develops over time in the context of a DDL and a non-DDL approach to learning collocations. It will then focus on the influence that specific properties of the target combinations exert on competence development in the two conditions. Finally, it will also consider different dimensions of phraseological knowledge, to see whether differences are observable through this other perceptive. The findings are interpreted in light of the study design and in relation to the most recent literature on effects-oriented empirical DDL research.

7.1 Overall DDL effects over time

The research questions addressed in this chapter are:

1. How does phraseological competence develop over time when comparing a DDL approach with a non-DDL approach?
2. How does a DDL/non-DDL approach influence the development of phraseological competence over time, with respect to certain specific properties of the learning aims (i.e. semantic transparency and L1-L2 congruency)?
3. How does a DDL/non-DDL approach influence the development of phraseological competence over time, with respect to different dimensions of phraseological knowledge (i.e. definitional vs. transferable)?

7.1.1 Descriptive overview

In Figure 7.1 we see the measures of central tendency and the distribution values for both the DDL and non-DDL groups in the form of boxplots. The visualised data refer to the total number of correct answers obtained in the four tests administered to both groups. We notice that both groups display

DOI: 10.4324/9781003137320-7

How data-driven learning impacts language gains 141

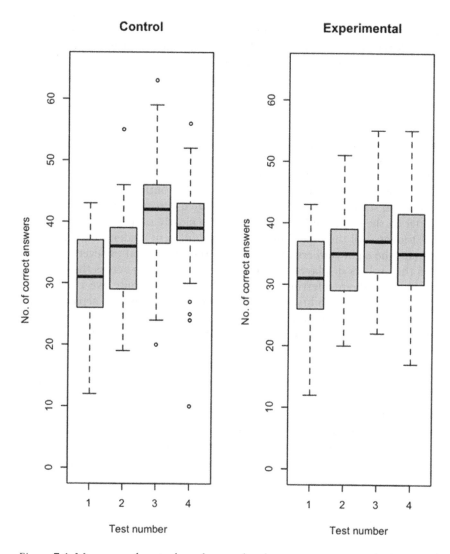

Figure 7.1 Measures of central tendency related to correct answers in DDL and non-DDL group.

a U-shaped pattern, with correct answers increasing steadily up to Test 3 and then slightly decreasing in Test 4, though without reaching a level that is below Test 2. We can also notice a considerable variation in the control group, especially in relation to the number of outliers, which increase as we progress from Test 1 through to Test 4. Less variation is visible in the experimental groups, where no outliers are present.

Outliers require special attention as they are 'extreme observations', which 'may exert very strong influence upon the results of ensuing analyses' (Raykov & Marcoulides, 2008, p. 69). The literature indicates two main ways to treat outliers. First, it is necessary to ensure that the data are correct and not a consequence of manual errors. Second, it is necessary to examine the nature of the data points constituting the outliers. Knowing the nature of the outliers will put the researcher in the position to decide whether they can be kept in the analysis, or whether they will need to be removed. Following the indications provided in the literature, we will now have a closer look at the outliers found in our data. Figure 7.2 shows the eight outliers labelled with the letters of the Latin alphabet, so as to be more readily identifiable, while Table 7.1 matches the outliers with the students, in order to see how the outliers are distributed across them. Outliers b and d refer to the same student (138656), who clearly outperforms the rest of the students. All the other outliers refer to different students each time. As a result, the eight outliers that we found refer to a total of seven students. Had the outliers displayed a more skewed distribution across the learners, say most of them referring to one or two of them only, we could have considered the possibility of removing them and running a separate analysis considering only these values. This would have allowed us to analyse the processes unfolding in relation to a particular subgroup of our sample. However, as the distribution is not skewed, we are in a position to keep the outliers in our dataset.

Although an initial descriptive overview is useful to get a first indication of what is happening in the data we collected, it remains insufficient. It is not able to tell us whether, given similar conditions, we may observe the same phenomena in a different sample of participants. In other words, no inferences can be made. In order to do this, while considering a number of variables, we proceed with an analysis based on mixed-effects modelling.

7.1.2 Modelling DDL effects over time

We built a model including condition (control and experimental) and time (a, b, c, d) as fixed effects. The values a, b, c, d stand respectively for 'test number 1', 'test number 2', 'test number 3', 'test number 4' respectively. All time points included random effects of participants and items were included. To account for varying effects of the predictors on the participants and on the items random slopes were also included (Baayen et al., 2008). By including random slope, we are able to estimate the fixed effects concerning by-subject and by-item variability, thus minimising the chance of Type I errors (Matuschek et al., 2017). Value 'a' was considered as the baseline. Model selection was based on a backward selection approach, starting from the maximal level of interactivity and then gradually eliminating non-significant

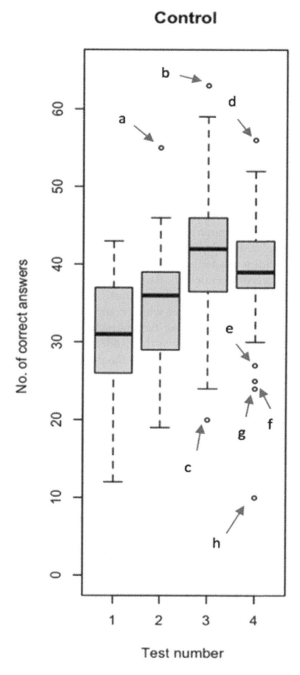

Figure 7.2 Identification of outliers in control group.

Table 7.1 Outliers across subjects

OUTLIER	TEST	SCORE	SUBJECT ID
a	2	55	138758
b	3	63	138656
c	3	19	139009
d	4	56	138656
e	4	27	139007
f	4	25	138776
g	4	24	139004
h	4	10	138769

predictors, keeping only the factors displaying significance in interaction, but not when they appear significant as individual predictors (Gries, 2013, p. 260). We will now provide a summary of the model selection process, and then show the estimates related to the final model.

The analysis started with a model (model 1) containing condition and time as fixed effects. As recommended in Barr, Levy, Scheepers, & Tily (2013), a maximal random effects structure was adopted. All the factors that could determine variation within the model which could not be controlled for were included as random effects. These factors included participants, classes and test items. An interaction term was then added between the fixed effects in order to see whether this would improve the model fit (model 2). The likelihood ratio test indicated that the interaction term did improve the model fit significantly in comparison to model 1, $\chi2(3) = 25.31$, $p < .001$. When comparing the various models, we also considered the Akaike Information Criterion (AIC). This value indicated the amount of variance left unexplained by the model (Cunnings, 2012, p. 374). When comparing model 1 and model 2 on the basis of this value, we found that model 2 left a slightly inferior amount of variance unexplained. This means that there is an inter-dependence between time and condition which produces an effect that is not predictable by predictors alone. For all of these reasons, we selected model 2, and moved onto the modelling of random effects structure. We thus started by adding the random slope of condition on participants, class, and items. We considered the various different combinations: in model 3, the slope was added only on participants; in model 4, it was added on participants and class; in model 5, on participants, class and items; in model 6, on class and items; in model 7, on items only; in model 8, on class only. All models converged. A series of likelihood ratio tests were conducted between the various models. Models 6 and 7 turned out to be significantly better than the other ones, $\chi2(0) = 17.2746$, $p < .001$ and $\chi2(0) = 17.2748$, $p < .001$ respectively. The two models were not significantly different. However, model 7 displayed the lowest AIC value, and was thus the model that we selected. In order to observe possible variance in the effect of condition on

Table 7.2 Overall DDL effects: fixed effects and interactions of final model

	Estimate	Std. Error	z value	Pr(>|z|)	
(Intercept)	0.23963	0.27444	0.873	0.382588	***
CONDITIONEXP	0.05129	0.27487	0.187	0.851973	******
TIME2-1	0.53413	0.06658	8.022	1.04e-15	*
TIME3-2	0.66896	0.06770	9.881	< 2e-16	***
TIME4-3	-0.35048	0.07446	-4.707	2.51e-06	*
CONDITIONEXP:TIME2-1	-0.18781	0.09429	-1.992	0.046395	
CONDITIONEXP:TIME3-2	-0.33348	0.09198	-3.626	0.000288	
CONDITIONEXP:TIME4-3	0.22534	0.09917	2.272	0.023069	

class, we added a nesting term to class. This, however, did not improve the model fit, $\chi2(0) = 0$, p < 1. Model 7 is thus our final model. The formula of the model is:

ACCURACY ~ CONDITION * TIME + (1 | STUDENT_ID) + (1 | CLASS) + (1 + CONDITION | ITEM_ID)

Table 7.2 shows the coefficients of the final model. We see that there are no significant effects of condition on the intercept (*Estimate* = 0.23963, *SE* = 0.27444, *p* = 0.382588). This means that, overall and without considering any specific properties of the learning aims, the development of phraseological competence in the two groups was not influenced by the difference in teaching conditions. As for interactions, the only significant positive estimate concerns the interaction between condition and the test4-test3 contrast (*Estimate* = 0.22534, *SE* = 0.09917, *p* = 0.023069). This contrast related to the four-week timeframe where no lessons were held.

In Figure 7.3, we see a visual representation of the fixed effects. The U-shaped pattern present in both conditions is visible: the predicted probabilities of accuracy increase steadily up to point c, and then decrease at point d, without reaching values that are lower than point b. In Figure 7.4 we can see how variation pans out in the two conditions. The control group seems to exhibit a much higher degree of variation in comparison to the experimental group. In Table 7.3 we see the values concern variance in the random effects. The largest values are those related to ITEM_ID, which includes a slope of condition. In comparison to items, the variance in participants (STUDENT_ID) and class (CLASS) are considerably lower.

To be meaningful, a mixed-effects model needs to meet certain assumptions. These can be investigated by means of a series of diagnostic plots assessing linearity (i.e. the deviations of the observed from the predicted values in the model), homoskedasticity (i.e. indicates that the variance in the data is similar across the predicted values in the model), and normality of

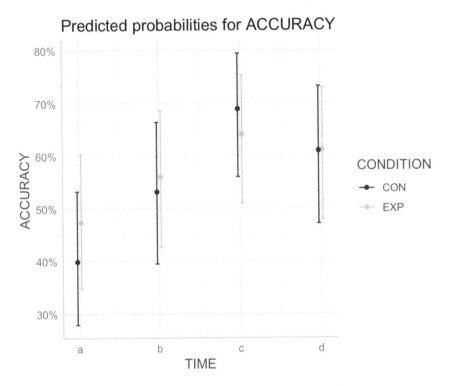

Figure 7.3 Overall DDL effects: plot of fixed effects across conditions.

residuals (i.e. indicating the normal distribution of residuals) (Winter, 2020, pp. 109–115). Linearity can be assessed by visually inspecting residual plots. The plots that we generated show lines that are mostly linear, despite the presence of some elements of non-linearity. Homoskedasticity was assessed visually by verifying the presence of a uniform distribution of the residual plot. The distribution was, indeed, mostly uniform. Finally, a histogram and a q-q plot enabled us to check for normality of residuals. In both graphs, the predicted values do not seem to fit a normal distribution perfectly. We then calculated R^2 values in order to determine the amount of variance that the final selected model is able to explain. The values are visible in Table 7.4.

How R^2 values should be interpreted, as well as the extent to which they can be informative in regards to the quality of a model, are widely discussed issues (Winter, 2020, pp. 109–155). Nevertheless, what we see in Table 7.4 is that R^2m, indicating the variance explained by the fixed effects alone, is considerably lower that R^2c, indicating the variance explained by the whole model, including the random effects. The variance explained by the whole model is, in fact, 41/46%, while the variance explained by the fixed effects alone is 0.2 %. This may indicate that the fixed effects alone that are

How data-driven learning impacts language gains   147

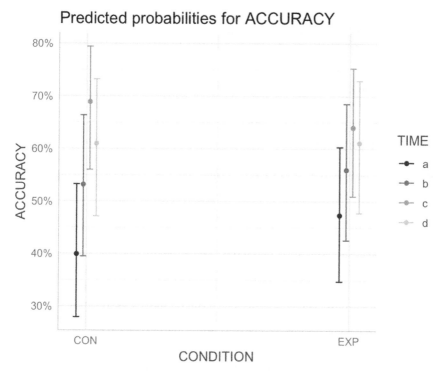

Figure 7.4 Overall DDL effects: plot of fixed effects in each condition.

Table 7.3 Overall DDL effects: random effects values of final model

Groups	Name	Variance	Std.Dev	Corr
STUDENT_ID	(Intercept)	0.26497	0.5148	-0.45
ITEM_ID	(Intercept)	2.44067	1.5623	
	CONDITIONEXP	0.06282	0.2506	
CLASS	(Intercept)	0.13164	0.3628	

Table 7.4 Overall DDL effects: R^2 values of final model

	R^2m	R^2c
theoretical	0.02032565	0.4606379
delta	0.01812351	0.4107311

included in the model cannot adequately capture the variation in the model, without considering the random effects. As indicated also by the assumption of linearity not being fully met, this may indicate the need to consider other fixed effects, to be integrated within the model.

7.2 DDL effects through the lens of semantic transparency and L1 congruency

In this section we explore the effects of DDL on phraseological competence development, through the lens of learning aim properties. More specifically, the results relate to how these effects can be viewed from the perspective of semantic transparency and L1-L2 congruency. Generalised mixed-effects modelling was conducted for both properties.

7.2.1 Semantic transparency

We now proceed with modeling DDL effects from the perspective of the role that semantic transparency may play. We consider the set of 32 combinations previously identified (see section 6.3.6). We start with model 1, where the variable of item type is included as a fixed effect. The variable contains two levels: opaque and transparent. A maximal random effects structure, containing participants, class and item IDs was also fitted. We then moved to model 2, which contained interaction terms on all factors. None of them, however, was significant. We thus returned to model 1, moving on to the modelling of the random effects structure.

A random slope of condition was added on all terms, taking into account all the possible combinations: in model 3, we added a slope on participants only; in model 4, on participants and class; in model 5, on participants, class and items; in model 6, on class and items; in model 7, on items only; in model 8, on class only. We performed a likelihood ration test in order to compare the goodness of fit of the models. The test indicated that model 6 and model 7 were significantly better fits in comparison to the other models, $\chi^2(0) = 12.4852, p < .001$ and $\chi^2(0) = 12.4993, p < .001$ respectively. In order to select one of the two models, we looked at the AIC values. These indicated model 7 as the one with the least amount of variance unexplained, even though the difference was quite small (12019 vs. 12022). Once again, the best model fit is the model with a slope of condition on the random effect of items. A nesting term on class was added in model 9, but this did not improve model fit. As a result, our final model is model 7, with the following formula:

ACCURACY ~ CONDITION + TIME + ITEM_TYPE +
(1 | STUDENT_ID) + (1 | CLASS) + (1 + CONDITION | ITEM_ID)

The regression coefficients of the model can be seen in Table 7.5. Condition has a negative estimate in relation to the intercept, but it is not significant.

How data-driven learning impacts language gains 149

Table 7.5 DDL effects related to semantic transparency: fixed effects and interactions of final model

	Estimate	Std. Error	z value	Pr(>|z|)	
(Intercept)	1.28430	0.41170	3.119	0.00181	**
CONDITIONEXP	-0.03635	0.25635	-0.142	0.88723	
TIME2-1	0.38730	0.06599	5.180	2.22e-07	***
TIME3-2	0.33418	0.06452	5.270	1.36e-07	***
TIME4-3	-0.10655	0.06941	-1.535	0.12474	
ITEM_TYPEtransparent	-1.14938	0.48503	-2.370	0.01780	*

Time contrasts are all significant, with only the 3–4 time contrast showing a negative estimate. This means that it affects accuracy negatively. Item type shows a significant negative estimate in relation to transparent items, indicating that opaque combinations produce significantly higher predicted probabilities of accuracy (*Estimate* = -1.14938, *SE* = 0.48503, *p* = 0.01780). In this model, condition is non-significant.

Figure 7.5 allows a visual inspection of the model predictors. We can notice that very similar U-shaped patterns occur in both conditions and in relation to both item types. Retention rates in the two conditions are also quite similar. If we then look at overall language gains, the values appear much more similar between the conditions as opposed to when considering overall DDL effects. In Table 7.6 we see the values related to random effects in the model. Again, we can observe that the largest variance is connected to item ID.

Model assumptions were checked visually via diagnostic plots. In the case of linearity and normality, we observe patterns that are similar to those observed in relation to the overall DDL effects. For homoskedasticity, on the other hand, the data is sparser. Finally, the R^2 values for the model were calculated and are visible in Table 7.7. As can be seen, they are slightly higher than the overall model in relation to marginal R^2. The variance explained by the fixed effects alone is now slightly higher (0.7/0.6%).

7.2.2 L1 congruency

We now turn to modelling DDL effects from the perspective of L1-L2 congruency. In order to do so, we returned to the original dataset containing the full set of 64 items. Model 1 contained time, condition and item type 2 as fixed effects. Item type 2 contained two levels: congruent and incongruent. We then added interactions on all terms, thus creating a maximal level of interactivity, to see whether these would improve model fit (model 2). The only interaction that was not significant was the three-way interaction between all terms (TIME2-1 contrasts: *Estimate* = 0.23101, *SE* = 0.18179, *p* = 0.2038; TIME3-2 contrasts: *Estimate* = -0.09916, *SE* = 0.17905,

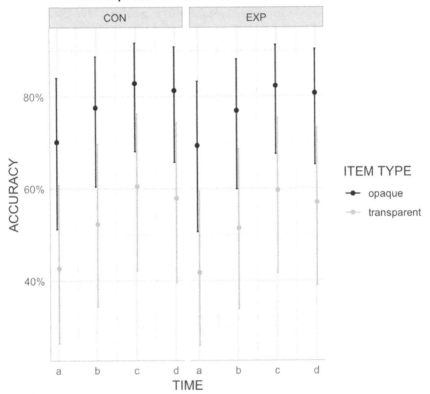

Figure 7.5 DDL effects related to semantic transparency: plot of fixed effects.

Table 7.6 DDL effects related to semantic transparency: random effects of final model

Groups	Name	Variance	Std.Dev	Corr
STUDENT_ID	(Intercept)	0.26518	0.5150	
ITEM_ID	(Intercept)	1.98905	1.4103	
	CONDITIONEXP	0.08444	0.2906	-0.35
CLASS	(Intercept)	0.11232	0.3351	

Table 7.7 DDL effects related to semantic transparency: R^2 values of final model

	R^2m	R^2c
theoretical	0.06670448	0.4468217
delta	0.05803966	0.3887802

p = 0.5797; TIME4-3 contrasts: *Estimate* = -0.01579, *SE* = 0.19147, p = 0.9343). As a result, we kept only the two significant interactions in the model (model 3). This model proved to be a significantly better fit than model 1, $\chi^2(6)$ = 39.906, p < .001.

We then moved on to the random effects structure, by adding slopes of condition on each of the random effects. In model 4, the slope was added only on participants; in model 5, on participants and class; in model 6, on participants, class and items; in model 7, on class and items; in model 8, on items only; in model 9, on class only. Model 5 had convergence problems, so the likelihood ratio test was conducted only among models 4, 6, 7, 8 and 9. Model 7 and 8 resulted as the models fitting significantly better, $\chi^2(2)$ = 16.680, p < .001 and $\chi^2(0)$ = 16.073, p < .001 respectively. In order to select one of the two, we looked at the AIC value. Model 8 turned out to be the preferred one, as it had a lower AIC value (23939 compared to 23943). Next, we added a nesting term of condition on class to see whether this would improve model fit (model 10), but this did not significantly improve model fit. As a result, model 8 is selected as our final model, with the following formula:

ACCURACY ~ (CONDITION * TIME) + (TIME * ITEM_TYPE2) + (1 | STUDENT_ID) + (1 | CLASS) + (1 + CONDITION | ITEM_ID)

Table 7.8 contains the regression coefficients for fixed effects and interactions. In the first case, we see that incongruent combinations have a significant positive estimate on the intercept, larger than opaque combinations seen in the previous paragraph (*Estimate* = 1.02829, *SE* = 0.24697, p = 3.13e-05). This indicates that incongruent combinations are generally learned better in both conditions, and the result is highly significant. In terms of interactions, the most highly significant ones are between the time3-2 contrast and condition (*Estimate* = -0.32482, *SE* = 0.09189, p = 0.000408), and between the time3-2 contrast and item type 2 (*Estimate* = -0.34282, *SE* = 0.09002, p = 0.000140): this indicates that the strongest interactions are present when comparing test 2 to test 3, and in both cases the estimate is negative. The second largest interaction values are detected in the time 4-3 contrast, with respect to the interaction with condition (*Estimate* = 0.21721, *SE* = 0.09894, p = 0.028138) and item type 2 (*Estimate* = 0.20817, *SE* = 0.09554, p = 0.09554). In both cases, the estimates are positive.

Figure 7.6 shows the fixed effects graphically. We notice the presence of a pattern which is not U-shaped. Such a pattern is observable in relation to incongruent combinations in the experimental condition. This indicates the possible presence of better retention rates and little loss during the four weeks of no lessons. If we observe the difference between points c and d in congruent combinations, we notice a smaller difference in the experimental groups compared to the control group.

Table 7.8 DDL effects related to L1 congruency: fixed effects and interactions of final model

	Estimate	Std. Error	z value	Pr(>|z|)	
(Intercept)	-0.22460	0.27913	-0.805	0.421025	
CONDITIONEXP	0.04964	0.27199	0.183	0.855179	
TIME2-1	0.47042	0.07755	6.066	1.31e-09	***
TIME3-2	0.80595	0.07616	10.582	< 2e-16	***
TIME4-3	-0.43255	0.08236	-5.252	1.50e-07	***
ITEM_TYPE2non-congruent	1.02829	0.24697	4.164	3.13e-05	***
CONDITIONEXP:TIME2-1	-0.18528	0.09457	-1.957	0.050089	.
CONDITIONEXP:TIME3-2	-0.32482	0.09189	-3.535	0.000408	***
CONDITIONEXP:TIME4-3	0.21721	0.09894	2.195	0.028138	*
TIME2-1:ITEM_TYPE2non-congruent	0.15445	0.09131	1.692	0.090725	.
TIME3-2:ITEM_TYPE2non-congruent	-0.34282	0.09002	-3.807	0.000140	***
TIME4-3:ITEM_TYPE2non-congruent	0.20817	0.09554	0.09554	0.09554	*

We now turn to the random effects values, which are visible in Table 7.9. Once more, we can see that the largest proportion of variance is related to Item ID, which contains a random slope. In order to check the assumptions of the model, we looked once more at linearity, homoskedasticity and normality. In each of these cases, we observe very similar patterns to those seen previously for the overall model. In terms of explanatory power of the model, the R^2 values remained very similar to what was observed in the semantic transparency model. The values can be seen in Table 7.10.

7.3 DDL effects and dimensions of phraseological knowledge

In this section, we explore the effects of DDL on the development of phraseological competence from the perspective of the dimension of phraseological knowledge. To do so, we look at the effects of DDL on accuracy in the two groups of participants, by including the variable of test part in the modelling as one of the fixed effects. Test part referred to either the multiple-choice of the gap fill items section, which elicited phraseological knowledge related to the definitional and transferable dimension respectively. Model 1 contained time, condition and test part as fixed effects, and had a maximal random effects structure including participants, items and class. In model 2, we added interaction terms between all predictors in order to see whether this would improve model fit. This three-way interaction was however non-significant

How data-driven learning impacts language gains   153

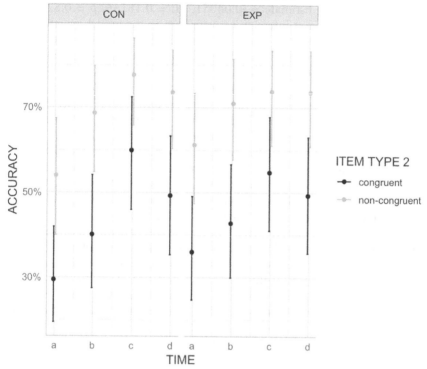

Figure 7.6 DDL effects related to L1 congruency: plot of fixed effects.

Table 7.9 DDL effects related to L1 congruency: random effects values of final model

Groups	Name	Variance	Std.Dev	Corr
STUDENT_ID	(Intercept)	0.26491	0.5147	
ITEM_ID	(Intercept)	1.85952	1.3636	
	CONDITIONEXP	0.06187	0.2487	-0.40
CLASS	(Intercept)	0.12971	0.3602	

Table 7.10 DDL effects related to L1 congruency: R^2 values of final model

	R^2m	R^2c
theoretical	0.06707142	0.4354240
delta	0.05950334	0.3862925

154 *How data-driven learning impacts language gains*

(TIME2-1 contrasts: Estimate = -0.25756, SE = 0.17971, p = 0.151799; TIME3-2 contrasts: Estimate = -0.20961, SE = 0.17536, p = 0.231954; TIME4-3 contrasts: Estimate = -0.04051, SE = 0.18736, p = 0.828830). Only the two significant interactions were kept in the model, which led to model 3. Model 3 was then compared to model 1 in order to see which of the two exhibited a better fit. Model 3 turned out to be the better model, $\chi^2(6) = 32.554, p < .001$.

Next, we moved to random effects structure. First, slopes of condition were added on each of the random effects terms. As a result, model 4 included a slope on participants only; model 5, on participants and class; model 6, on participants, class and items; model 7, on class and items; model 8, on items only; model 9, on class only. According to the likelihood ratio test conducted to compare all the models, the two models showing significantly better fits were models 7 and 8, $\chi^2(0) = 17.4284, p < .001$ and $\chi^2(0) = 17.4288, p < .001$ respectively. The two models did not display any significant differences between them. As a result, we conducted a comparison between the respective AIC values. The comparison indicated model 8 as the model containing the least amount of variance unexplained (23960 compared to 23964). We then added a nesting term of condition on class (model 10), to see whether this improved model fit. The likelihood ratio test, however, still indicated model 8 as the best model fit, $\chi^2(0) = 0.4424, p < .001$. Our final model is thus model 8, which has the following formula:

ACCURACY ~ (CONDITION * TIME) + (TIME * TEST_PART) + (1 | STUDENT_ID) + (1 | CLASS) + (1 + CONDITION | ITEM_ID)

In Table 7.11 we see the coefficients for fixed effects and interaction. We can notice that the dimension of phraseological knowledge is not a significant

Table 7.11 DDL effects related to dimensions of phraseological knowledge: fixed effects and interactions of final model

	Estimate	Std. Error	z value	Pr(>|z|)	
(Intercept)	0.33993	0.28912	1.176	0.239693	***
CONDITIONEXP	0.05122	0.27497	0.186	0.852235	***
TIME2-1	0.41471	0.08148	5.090	3.59e-07	***
TIME3-2	0.69539	0.08260	8.419	< 2e-16	*
TIME4-3	-0.30541	0.09018	-3.387	0.000707	***
TEST_PARTTRA	-0.19948	0.18730	-1.065	0.286871	*
CONDITIONEXP:TIME2-1	-0.18945	0.09438	-2.007	0.044721	*
CONDITIONEXP:TIME3-2	-0.33305	0.09192	-3.623	0.000291	
CONDITIONEXP:TIME4-3	0.22489	0.09919	2.267	0.023377	
TIME2-1:TEST_PARTTRA	0.22882	0.09017	2.538	0.011162	
TIME3-2:TEST_PARTTRA	-0.04171	0.08858	-0.471	0.637713	
TIME4-3:TEST_PARTTRA	-0.09114	0.09392	-0.970	0.331814	

How data-driven learning impacts language gains 155

predictor in the model (*Estimate* = -0.19948, *SE* = 0.18730, *p* = 0.286871). One the other hand, all time effects are once again highly significant. The interaction between condition and time3-2 contrast is the one exhibiting the highest values (*Estimate* = -0.33305, *SE* = 0.09192, *p* = 0.000291), followed by interactions between condition and time2-1 contrasts (*Estimate* = -0.18945, *SE* = 0.09438, *p* = 0.044721), condition and time4-3 contrasts (*Estimate* = 0.22489, *SE* = 0.09919, *p* = 2.267) and time2-1 contrasts and test part (*Estimate* = 0.22882, *SE* = 0.09017, *p* = 0.011162). Time4-3 contrasts exhibit different patterns compared to other contrasts in all cases, with the exception of the item part interactions.

In Figure 7.7 we see how the patterns related to definitional and transferable dimensions of phraseological knowledge mostly overlap in both conditions. Although the differences are minimal and non-significant, we can notice that definitional knowledge seems to attract slightly better accuracy rates compared to transferable knowledge.

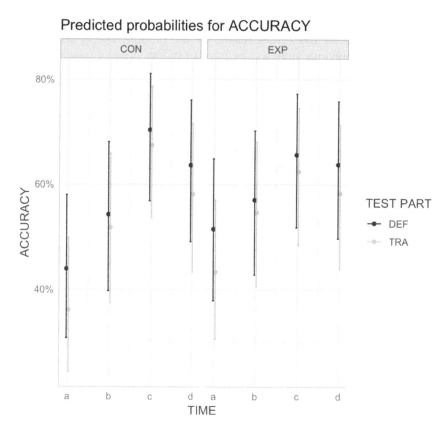

Figure 7.7 DDL effects related to dimensions of phraseological knowledge: plot of fixed effects.

Table 7.12 DDL effects related to dimensions of phraseological knowledge: random effect values of final model

Groups	Name	Variance	Std.Dev	Corr
STUDENT_ID	(Intercept)	0.26526	0.5150	
ITEM_ID	(Intercept)	2.38512	1.5444	
	CONDITIONEXP	0.06303	0.2511	-0.46
CLASS	(Intercept)	0.13154	0.3627	

Table 7.13 DDL effects related to dimensions of phraseological knowledge: R^2 values of final model

	R^2m	R^2c
theoretical	0.02234182	0.4568210
delta	0.01990430	0.4069812

Table 7.12 shows the values related to the random effects structure. Similarly to the previous analyses, we have a random slope of condition on item ID, displaying a very large variance. Once more, we checked for the assumptions being met, and obtained a similar picture to most of cases seen previously for the overall effects model.

Table 7.13 contains the R^2 values. As can be seen, these now decrease in comparison to the analysis conducted with the linguistic properties of semantic transparency and L1 congruency as predictors, getting closer to the model obtained in the general analysis on overall DDL effects. Now, once more, the variance explained by the whole model is 49/45%.

7.4 Discussion of findings

When analysing overall DDL effects over time, the first finding emerging is that the pedagogy involved in DDL activities does not produce significant differences with respect to non-DDL activities. Both the DDL and the non-DDL groups in the study develop phraseological competence in very similar ways, in terms of predicted probabilities of accuracy. This finding can be interpreted in light of at least three factors: study length, study design, participant sample (level and L1 background).

The first factor we will consider is study length. The length of the study was 13 weeks. It involved one one-hour lesson a week, which was taught for eight weeks in every class of students involved in the study. About 25 minutes in each lesson were actually devoted to DDL activities, while the remainder of each lesson involved introductory and practice activities. The specific context in which the study was carried out (i.e. Marco Polo and

Turandot Italian language course run at the University for Foreigners of Perugia, Italy) did not allow us to extend the timeframe of the study any further. The lessons took place within the scheduled lesson time of other teachers' language courses. As a result, we took up one hour a week from each language course, which consisted of four hours a day, five days a week. The flipside of not being able to take up more than one hour a week from each course was that we were able to involve a large number of classes, and thus a large number of participants. With eight classes of students, we were able to create a participant cohort of 123 students, which is high if we consider the average number of students involved in empirical DDL studies. As reported in Boulton & Cobb (2017), the mean number of total participants in studies including a control group is 57, that is less than half of the total number of participants in the present study. The advantage of including a high number of participants in an empirical study is that of being able to observe variation over time and over student groups (i.e. classes). However, a high number of participants should imply a consistent exposure to the approach being evaluated. But how consistent and how long should this exposure be? According to the meta-analysis conducted by Lee et al. (2018), a minimum amount of ten DDL sessions is the threshold that is needed in an empirical study in order to increase the probabilities of observing significant benefits of DDL in comparison to other approaches, with respect to language gains. This confirms the empirical impact that a restricted amount of exposure to DDL, due to difficulties in logistics and teaching context involved, may have in terms of the nature of obtainable findings. Although analogy-based inferencing is a common and implicit everyday practice, gaining awareness of this practice in a second language learning context requires time. From the state of awareness, even more time will then be needed in order to extend the strategy to other learning contexts while gradually developing autonomy in doing so. Lower-proficiency learners, such as those involved in the present study, may need even more time and support. As a result, the lack of differences between the DDL and non-DDL groups in the study may be a consequence of the restrictions that the study faced, which did not allow to reach the exposure threshold needed in order to allow development of awareness and impact on language gains.

The second factor which might explain the results of the study relates to how the study was designed. As both Boulton & Cobb (2017) and Lee et al. (2018) highlight, a between-groups design, such as the one employed in the present study, makes it difficult to detect significant differences between the two groups involved in a relatively short time span. Within-groups designs, in which each participant is exposed to each different condition involved in the study are more likely to produce significant findings in a shorter amount of time. A between-groups design, claim Cobb and Boulton (2015), makes it more difficult to detect differences in two groups, as 'almost any kind of instruction is likely to lead to some effect' (Cobb & Boulton, 2015, p. 491, in reference to Hattie, 2009 and Oswald & Plonsky, 2010). When two groups of participants are exposed to two different pedagogical treatments, this introduces a high degree of variation in the comparison, which would require a long time to make specific and distinctive patterns emerge. Although all the necessary measures were taken to ensure the absence of significant differences between the two groups at the beginning of the study, we are still dealing with two groups of different individuals, and each group will be characterised by a specific kind of internal variation. When a single group of participants is exposed to different conditions, as in within-groups designs, numerous advantages arise: inter-learner variation relates solely to how they respond to both approaches, and not to their individual responses to a single approach; individual development can be monitored in relation to both approaches; at the emic level, learner attitudes can be particularly useful as they can express their opinion in relation to both of the approaches they were exposed to, thus being able to indicate pros and cons of each.

A third factor possibly influencing the findings of the study concerns the nature of the participant sample in terms of proficiency level and L1 background. The learners involved in the study belonged to a pre-intermediate proficiency level. At the time of the study, no learner-friendly corpus for Italian was available, whereas today we have the Italian version of SkELL (Baisa & Suchomel, 2014), which can usefully be used with learners in the form of hands-on DDL activities (Boulton, 2012; Pérez-Paredes et al., 2012). In order to make corpus data suitable for the learner population involved in the present study, a series of paper-based DDL activities was developed, on the basis of pre-selected concordance lines and corpus data adaptation (see par. 6.3.3.2. for details). The adaptation was required as the L1 Italian corpus that was used was a reference corpus mainly built for researchers rather than for learners (Forti & Spina, 2019). The activities did produce a positive effect on language gains through times, but these effects were not significantly different when compared to more traditional activities. In other words, DDL activities were not able to reach 'the parts other teaching can't reach' (Boulton, 2008). This leads us to hypothesise that the pedagogical development of the activities may not have been perfectly respondent to the learners' needs in terms of their proficiency level. While, as we shall see, no comment from the end-of-course questionnaire points at the linguistic difficulty of the corpus data contained in the concordance lines, we can assume this to be a potential issue. In order for DDL to be more effective than other approaches or methods, its suitability for a specific population of learners must be ensured. Suggestions on the use of graded corpora, for instance, go in this direction (Allan, 2009).

Furthermore, a more extensive knowledge of the teaching context may be helpful in successfully designing a series of DDL activities. The learners involved in the study were learners enrolled in Italian language courses managed by teachers employed by the University for Foreigners of Perugia. They were not students in direct contact with the researcher conducting the study. The cases in which a researcher is, at the same time, conducting a DDL study as well as teaching a second/foreign language in one or more classrooms would be ideal to foster sensitivity to the context. Collaboration between DDL researchers and language teachers can also have beneficial effects on DDL materials design, in the cases where a researcher is not also a language teacher, a situation that occurs quite commonly. The level of the participants involved may also play a role. The meta-analyses conducted by Mizumoto & Chujo (2015), Boulton & Cobb (2017) and Lee et al. (2018) all indicate that DDL is generally more effective with higher proficiency learners. This finding, however, in most cases reflects the use of computer-based DDL, where the corpora being used with the learners are not corpora that were developed *for* the learners. DDL activities can certainly be developed in a way that meets learner needs at different proficiency levels. This is a key aspect that will need to be kept in consideration for future research on DDL effects.

Another aspect of the participant sample considered in this study which may have affected the findings is L1 background. In this study, L1 background was homogenous, as all participants were L1 Chinese speakers. This is a positive aspect as it allows us to isolate possible patterns characterising a specific learner group. Forti (2019a) attempts to identify some possible differences between a population of L1 Chinese learners in comparison to a population of L1 (Belgian) French learners, on the basis of their attitudes towards DDL activities. The fact that the Belgian students reported considerably lower initial difficulties in working with concordance lines may indicate that this kind of population could benefit from DDL activities in a shorter timeframe compared to L1 Chinese learners.

Despite the several factors which might explain the lack of significant differences between DDL and non-DDL pedagogy, other phenomena emerge from the findings. All the models we constructed show a U-shaped learning patterns. This reflects not only the literature on L2 phraseology development (see section 6.1.), but also the literature on second language acquisition and human development at large (Gass & Selinker, 2008). Learners gradually increase their accuracy over time. However, when tested with a delayed test, which is generally administered some time after the end of a lesson series, learners exhibit slightly lower accuracy levels. These levels, though, do not go as low as the third-last test that was administered. When looking at all the models we developed, we notice only one case in which the pattern does not resemble a U-shape, but is rather more linear, with a gradual increase of the predicted probabilities of accuracy continuing all the way through to the delayed test. It is the case of the congruency model (see Figure 7.6), in which we can see that timepoint d, which corresponds to Test 4, does not decrease as what we observed in all the other models. Why could this be? While incongruent combinations are learned significantly better in both conditions, their retention rate in the DDL condition seems to be markedly better when compared to the non-DDL condition. This would indicate that the learners in the DDL group tend to retain what they worked on in class better than their peers in the non-DDL group. This pattern is visible also in the overall effects model, as well as in the dimensions of knowledge model. While in these two cases we notice U-shaped learning curves, we may also notice that the differences between timepoints c and timepoints d, corresponding to the differences in tests 3 and 4, are much smaller in the DDL groups rather than in the non-DDL groups. These differences in retention rates could be explained as a result of the way in which DDL activities were developed. The structured observation of multiple examples pertaining to a single combination increases the frequency of input of that combination, and this may determine, as an immediate effect, a comparative improvement in terms of retention rates. The increased frequency of input is also combined with the typographical enhancement of the input, through the KWIC format. Both the increased frequency of input and the input enhancement may determine better retention rates through improved memorisation. This improvement might manifest itself before any observable effect at the level of language gains. While not reaching a comparatively higher competence level with respect to their peers, the learners exposed to DDL engage in collaborative problem-solving activities characterised by a higher cognitive load, which may also be responsible for better retention rates. The relationship between retention rates and language gains may be fruitfully explored in further studies.

The semantic transparency model for DDL effects revealed, as for the other models, no significant effects in relation to experimental condition. Nevertheless, on its own, semantic transparency was a significant predictor in the development of phraseological competence. Opaque combinations, in fact, displayed significantly higher predicted probabilities of accuracy in both the DDL and non-DDL conditions. This general finding, which goes beyond the scope of DDL effects-oriented research, does not seem to be in line with what we know about the role of semantic transparency in the development of L2 phraseological competence. Wang (2016) and Nesselhauf (2005), for example, assume that combinations, of the verb+noun type in particular, are likely to be more difficult to learn because of their increased chance, compared to other combinations types, of exhibiting a certain degree of semantic opacity in relation to the verb collocate or the whole combinations. A semantically opaque or partially opaque combination will not lend itself to be decoded on the sole basis of the single units it is made of. On these grounds, both Wang (2016) and Nesselhauf (2005) conduct specific analyses on how verb+noun combinations are used by second language learners of English. They do not, however, include a systematic comparison between semantically transparent and semantically opaque combinations, in order to see whether there is an actual difference in learning difficulty. Nevertheless, the assumption of semantic opacity being a potential source of difficulty for language learners in partially corroborated by the psycholinguistic study conducted by Gyllstad & Wolter (2016). In this study, both L1 and L2 speakers of English exhibit processing costs when confronted with opaque combinations, as opposed to transparent ones. The phenomenon was observed in terms of reaction times and accuracy rates. In their experiment, Gyllstad and Wolter systematically compare semantically transparent and semantically opaque verb + noun combinations. This way, they are able to observe the processing dynamics characterising the two types of combinations. Their study points out that there may be an increased difficulty for learners to gain competence concerning non-transparent word combinations.

In our models, opaque combinations are significantly learned better in all conditions. This finding could contain the effect of a variable that was not controlled for, namely, phrasal frequency. Durrant (2014)'s meta-analysis on the role of frequency and MI on phraseological knowledge showed that learners tend to be more sensitive to frequency rather than MI. However, as shown in Forti (forthcoming), as phrasal frequency of combinations increases, accuracy decreases for both opaque and transparent. As a result, the increase in phrasal frequency does not seem to be an explanatory factor for this finding. Other quantitative measures and qualitative properties may, however, be considered in future studies. Finally, the DDL effects models based on semantic transparency do not display any significant differences between the two conditions in relation to retention rates. The differences between timepoints c and d are in fact quite similar in both conditions. This sets the semantic transparency model somewhat apart from the other models that were constructed, suggesting the presence of other variables at play, which would be worthy of investigation.

As for congruency, some interesting patterns were observed. The final model displayed a highly significant estimate for the items that were coded with this property. In particular, combinations classified as incongruent show a significantly higher predicted probability of accuracy, when compared to combinations classified as congruent. The effect is much stronger than for semantic transparency, which can be seen by the plots overlapping much less than in the semantic transparency model. Once again, condition is not a significant predictor. Nevertheless, as mentioned earlier, this model shows the effect of DDL on retention rates more starkly than in other models. The longitudinal pattern characterising the development of competence in incongruent combinations displays, in fact, a mostly linear trajectory. This linearity suggests minimal or no loss in terms of accuracy, over the time span of weeks following the end of the lessons.

The literature on phraseological competence development indicates incongruent combinations as generally more difficult to learn in comparison to congruent ones. An early study by Biskup (1992), however, indicates that in cases of genetically distant L1s and L2s, the errors produced by an adverse influence of the L1 tend to be fewer than those involving genetically closer L1s and L2s. Learners that have an L1 background that is closer to the L2 being learned will tend to take more risks, thus determining a higher chance of committing errors. The L1s considered by Biskup were German and Polish, while the L2 was English. The findings of our study involving

Chinese learners of Italian might reflect Buskup's findings. Incongruent combinations might be learned with a higher degree of accuracy in comparison to congruent ones, as incongruency will be characterised by more memorable lexical co-selections, based on the fact that those combinations adopt lexical choices that the learners would not find in the own L1. Furthermore, according to Yamashita & Jiang (2010), the adverse influence of an L1 is likely to increase in a FL context, rather than in a SL one. Our study involved learners who were situated in a SL context. This factor may have been key in increasing the frequency of input if incongruent combinations, thus allowing the learners to manage the potential obstacle of L1-L2 incongruency successfully. This is confirmed by the study presented in Forti (2019b): when modeling phrasal frequency in combination with L1-L2 congruency, a significant interaction between the two factors emerges. As phrasal frequency increases, so does accuracy, for both the DDL and non-DDL groups. As for what was mentioned with regards to the semantic transparency model, the case of L1-L2 congruency also lends itself to further investigations related to the possible presence of other variables at play. The insertion of other variables into the models might provide a fuller explanation of why we observe such a striking difference in accuracy between congruent and incongruent combinations, and why incongruent combinations display better retention rates in the DDL groups.

Our study also considered two different dimensions of phraseological knowledge, namely the definitional and the transferable. These were reflected in the two different parts of the phraseological competence test that was administered to all participants over 4 weeks. The multiple-choice section of the test elicited the initial, more superficial kind of phraseological knowledge, while the gap-fill part concerned the more in-depth kind of combinations knowledge. The former is generally associated with receptive knowledge, while the latter to productive knowledge. These two different dimensions of phraseological knowledge have been addressed by using the two testing formats mentioned in order to elicit definitional and transferable knowledge respectively (Jaén, 2009; Koya, 2005). Previous SLA studies have found that receptive/definitional knowledge generally develops earlier and more easily in comparison to productive/transferable knowledge. However, when reviewing the literature concerning DDL specifically, we find that the DDL approach seems to be usually more effective in developing in-depth knowledge of combinations. In our study, this does not seem to be the case. The variable pertaining to dimension of collocational knowledge is not a significant predictor, though it does produce very mildly significant interactions with time and condition. This finding may be explained by at least two factors. First, the amount of exposure to DDL may not have been sufficient to determine significant observable differences at the level of dimensions of phraseological knowledge. Second, the differences may have been difficult to notice as different sets of combinations were addressed in the two different parts of the test. This may require a longer timeframe in order to hope for visible differences. Examining different knowledge dimensions on the basis on the same set of combinations may have provided significant results in a shorter amount of time.

7.5 Chapter summary and conclusions

In this chapter, we illustrated and discussed the findings of a study on DDL effects in relation to the development of phraseological competence over time. We specified why phraseology was selected as the area of interest in the study, being a central component in the development of language competence overall. Phraseological competence data was collected over 13 weeks, on the basis of a between-groups design. The collected accuracy data was analysed with mixed effects modelling and contrast coding. No significant differences were found in relation to language gains when comparing DDL to non-DDL groups. Furthermore, the study found that the development of phraseological competence follows a U-shaped learning pattern in all models and in both conditions (DDL and non-DDL), with the exception of incongruent combinations in the experimental condition. In this case, in fact, we noticed a more linear pattern in relation to timepoints 3 and 4. When restricting the focus on the differences between timepoints 3 and 4, we see that this difference is consistently narrower in the experimental condition in all four models, in comparison to the control condition. The only exception concerns the semantic transparency model: in this case, in fact, the differences are not observable. Opaque and incongruent combinations exhibit higher predicted probabilities of accuracy in all models.

The explanatory power of the models, expressed by marginal and condition R-squared values, was markedly higher when considering the whole model (i.e. including both the fixed effects and the random effects, rather than considering the fixed effects only): the amount of variance explained by the whole model went from a minimum of 38% to a maximum of 46%. As for the different dimensions of phraseological knowledge, no significant effects emerged. The findings were interpreted with reference to the length and design of study, the nature of the participant sample, the type of DDL materials developed, and the type of data elicitation tool used.

References

Allan, R. (2009). Can a graded reader corpus provide 'authentic' input?'. *ELT Journal*, 63, 23–32.

Baayen, R.H., Davidson, D.J., & Bates, D.M. (2008). Mixed-effects modeling with crossed random effects for subjects and items. *Journal of Memory and Language*, 59(4), 390–412.

Baisa, V., & Suchomel, V. (2014). SkELL: Web interface for English language learning. *Eighth Workshop on Recent Advances in Slavonic Natural Language Processing*, 63–70.

Barr, D.J., Levy, R., Scheepers, C., & Tily, H.J. (2013). Random effects structure for confirmatory hypothesis testing: Keep it maximal. *Journal of Memory and Language*, 68(3), 255–278.

Biskup, D. (1992). L1 influence on learners' renderings of English collocations. In L. Arnaud & H. Béjoint (Eds.), *Vocabulary and applied linguistics* (pp. 85–93). Macmillan.

Boulton, A. (2008). DDL: Reaching the parts other teaching can't reach? In A. Frankenberg-Garcia (Ed.), *Proceedings of the 8th Teaching and Language Corpora Conference* (pp. 38–44). Associação de Estudos e de Investigação Científica do ISLA-Lisboa.

Boulton, A. (2012). Hands-on / hands-off: Alternative approaches to data-driven learning. In J. Thomas & A. Boulton (Eds.), *Input, Process and Product: Developments in Teaching and Language Corpora* (pp. 152–168). Masaryk University Press.

Boulton, A., & Cobb, T. (2017). Corpus use in language learning: A meta-analysis. *Language Learning*, 67(2), 348–393.

Cobb, T., & Boulton, A. (2015). Classroom applications of corpus analysis. In D. Biber & R. Reppen (Eds.), *The Cambridge Handbook of English Corpus Linguistics* (pp. 478–497). Cambridge University Press.

Durrant, P. (2014). Corpus frequency and second language learners' knowledge of collocations: A meta-analysis. *International Journal of Corpus Linguistics*, 19(4), 443–477.

Forti, L. (forthcoming). Data-driven learning effects on the development of Italian L2 phraseological competence: the combined role of semantic transparency and frequency. In H. Tyne & S. Spina, *Applying corpora in teaching and learning Romance languages*, Benjamins.

Forti, L. (2019a). Learner attitudes towards data-driven learning: Investigating the effect of teaching contexts. In F. Meunier, J. Van de Vyver, L. Bradley, & S. Thouësny (Eds.), *CALL and complexity – short papers from EUROCALL 2019* (pp. 137–143). Research-publishing.net.

Forti, L. (2019b). Modeling data-driven learning effects through the properties of the learning aims: a combined view of frequency and L1 congruency in collocations. Poster presented at 2019 EuroCALL conference 2019 'CALL and complexity', Université catholique de Louvain.

Forti, L., & Spina, S. (2019). Corpora for linguists vs. corpora for learners: Bridging the gap in Italian L2 learning and teaching. *EL.LE – Educazione Linguistica. Language Education*, 8(2), 349–362.

Gass, S.M., & Selinker, L. (2008). *Second language acquisition. An introductory course*. Routledge.

Gries, S.T. (2013). *Statistics for linguistics with R: A practical introduction* (2nd ed.). De Gruyter Mouton.

Gyllstad, H., & Wolter, B. (2016). Collocational processing in light of the phraseological continuum model: Does semantic transparency matter?: Collocational processing and semantic transparency. *Language Learning*, 66(2), 296–323.

Hattie, J. (2009). *Visible learning: A synthesis of meta-analyses relating to achievement*. Routledge.

Jaén, M.M. (2009). A corpus-driven design of a test for assessing the ESL collocational competence of university students. *International Journal of English Studies*, 7(2), 127–148.

Koya, T. (2005). *The acquisition of basic collocations by Japanese learners of English*. Unpublished PhD Thesis. Waseda University.

Lee, H., Warschauer, M., & Lee, J.H. (2018). The effects of corpus use on second language vocabulary learning: A multilevel meta-analysis. *Applied Linguistics, 40*(5), 721–753.

Matuschek, H., Kliegl, R., Vasishth, S., Baayen, H., & Bates, D. (2017). Balancing Type I error and power in linear mixed models. *Journal of Memory and Language, 94*, 305–315.

Mizumoto, A., & Chujo, K. (2015). A meta-analysis of data-driven learning approach in the Japanese EFL Classroom. *English Corpus Studies, 22*, 1–18.

Nesselhauf, N. (2005). *Collocations in a learner corpus*. Benjamins.

Oswald, F., & Plonsky, L. (2010). Meta-analysis in second language research: Choices and challenges. *Annual Review of Applied Linguistics, 30*, 85–110.

Pérez-Paredes, P., Sánchez-Tornel, M., & Calero, J. M. A. (2012). Learners' search patterns during corpus-based focus-on-form activities: A study on hands-on concordancing. *International Journal of Corpus Linguistics, 17*(4), 482–515.

Raykov, T., & Marcoulides, G.A. (2008). *Introduction to applied multivariate analysis*. Routledge.

Wang, Y. (2016). *The Idiom Principle and L1 Influence. A contrastive learner-corpus study of delexical verb+noun collocations*. Benjamins.

Winter, B. (2020). *Statistics for linguists: An Introduction Using R*. Routledge.

Yamashita, J., & Jiang, N. (2010). L1 influence on the acquisition of L2 collocations: Japanese ESL users and EFL learners acquiring English collocations. *TESOL Quarterly, 44*(4), 647–668.

8 How learners react to data-driven learning

After exploring DDL effects on the development of phraseological competence over time, we now turn to DDL effects on learner attitudes. We will do so through the analysis of data collected by means of an end-of-course student questionnaire, which was administered at the end of the pedagogical intervention described in the previous chapters. Data collected from both the experimental and the control group will be examined. Specific features of DDL will be looked at in terms of how the students perceived them. Furthermore, approaching a phraseology-based series of lessons will constitute the focus of our investigation, as it will take on a comparative outlook, with the attitudes of learners exposed to DDL materials and those who were not placed side to side. The findings are discussed in light of the current literature on emic perspectives related to DDL.

8.1 Data collection and analysis

The research question explored here is the following:

> 4. What are the learners' overall attitudes towards DDL activities?

A total of 82 responses were collected, 50 from the DDL groups, and 32 from the non-DDL groups. We will illustrate the data in two parts. First, we present data collected from both groups, in relation to the perceived usefulness of the phraseology-based lessons (i.e. the focus on word combinations, peer-work, receiving feedback on homework, working on eight combinations in one hour) and to more general aspects (i.e. what was enjoyed the most/the least, how they would describe the experience with three adjectives, and whether they have any suggestions for future re-runs of the lesson series). Second, we report on the items that were formulated with specific reference to the DDL activities, and were thus addressed only by the experimental group.

DOI: 10.4324/9781003137320-8

8.2 Working on word combinations: learner perceptions from DDL and non-DDL groups

8.2.1 Likert-scale items

In this section we look at how work on word combinations was perceived by both the DDL and non-DDL groups. More specifically, the likert-scale items which both groups were asked to evaluate relate to the perceived usefulness of the experience in relation to four different aspects of the lessons. Table 8.1 presents the results related to likert-scale item 1, 'Studying word combinations was useful'. The table shows data concerning to both groups. As we can see, both groups display similar trends. In the DDL group, over 90% of respondents either agreed or totally agreed with the claim, while just over 80% did so in the non-DDL group. The most frequently selected value in both groups was 'totally agree' (DDL group: 60%; non-DDL group: 53,1%). A small percentage in the non-DDL group totally disagreed with the claim. Overall, both groups perceive the lessons focused on word combinations as useful.

Table 8.2 displays the results related to likert-scale item 2, 'Working with my peers slowed down my learning process'. As may be seen, both groups exhibit the same pattern, with most respondents selecting 'disagree' in relation to the claim. The trend line, however, is not as steep as in the previous graphs. The most frequently selected value in both groups is 'disagree' (DDL group: 42%; non-DDL group: 37.5%). A total of 32% of the respondents in the DDL group agreed, to various extents, with the claim, as did 37.5% of those in the non-DDL group. While, overall, most of the respondents did

Table 8.1 Perceptions of DDL vs. non-DDL groups on phraseology-based language course (likert-scale items) – Item 1

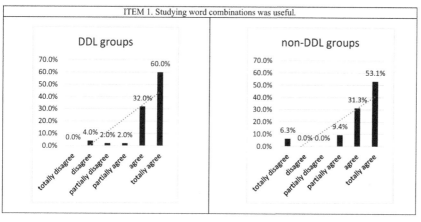

168   *How learners react to data-driven learning*

Table 8.2 Perceptions of DDL vs. non-DDL groups on phraseology-based language course (likert-scale items) – Item 2

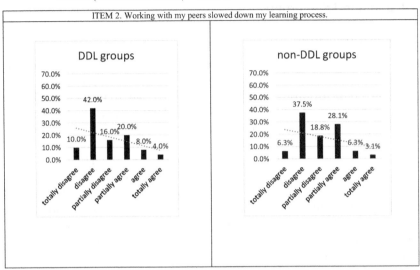

not perceive group work as slowing down their learning process, about one third, from both groups, did.

In Table 8.3, participants responded to the claim contained in likert-scale item 3, 'The feedback received on my homework helped me to improve my writing'. Both groups exhibit very similar trend lines, with most responses being concentrated in the upper part of the scale. A total of 96% in the DDL group and a total of 90.7% in the non-DDL group, in fact, perceived the feedback received on how to use word combinations in writing as useful in terms of improving their writing skills. The most frequently selected value in both groups is 'totally agree' (DDL group: 62%; non-DDL group: 53.1%).

Table 8.4 shows the data pertaining to likert-scale item 4, 'Engaging in didactic activities on eight word combinations in one hour was too challenging'. As can be seen, once again both groups show very similar perceptions along the likert-scale cline. A total of 90% of the respondents in the DDL group disagree, to various extents, with the claim, as do most of the respondents in the non-DDL group (84.4%). The most frequently selected value in both groups is 'disagree' (DDL group: 46%; non-DDL group: 40.6%).

8.2.2 Open-ended questions

We now turn to the open-ended questions proposed in the second part of the questionnaire. The purpose of these questions was to gather a broader view of learner perceptions concerning the phraseology-based lessons. Once again, we compare DDL groups to non-DDL groups. The percentages are

Table 8.3 Perceptions of DDL vs. non-DDL groups on phraseology-based language course (likert-scale items) – Item 3

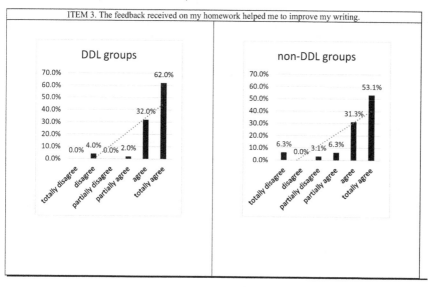

Table 8.4 Perceptions of DDL vs. non-DDL groups on phraseology-based language course (likert-scale items) – Item 4

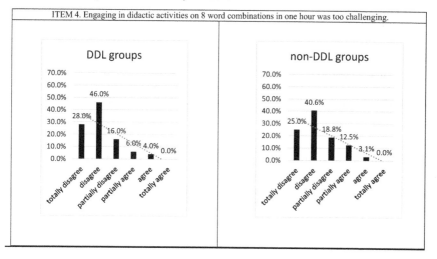

calculated on the basis of the number of responses given. This takes into consideration also the cases in which more than one answer is given for the single question. Question 1 asked the learners the following: 'What did you enjoy the most in the course?'. The top most frequent responses in both groups are the same. The most recurring response was 'learning word

170 *How learners react to data-driven learning*

Table 8.5 Perceptions of DDL vs. non-DDL groups on phraseology-based language course (open-ended questions). Question 1

QUESTION 1. *What did you enjoy the most in the course?*

DDL group			non-DDL group		
	Themes	Occ. (%)		Themes	Occ. (%)
1	Learning word combinations	18 (31,0%)	1	Learning word combinations	17 (41,4%)
2	Playing games / competitions among different class teams	8 (13,8%)	2	Playing games / competitions among different class teams	8 (19,5%)
3	Speaking / working with my peers	7 (12,1%)	3	Speaking / working with my peers	7 (17,1%)
4	Everything	5 (8,6%)	4	Practising the language more	3 (7,3%)
5	The comments on the homework and the writing practice involved	5 (8,6%)	5	Everything	2 (4,9%)
6	The teacher (nice / patient)	5 (8,6%)	6	The activities	2 (4,9%)
7	All activities and the homework	4 (6,9%)	7	The enjoyable atmosphere	1 (2,4%)
8	The groups of sentences	4 (6,9%)	8	Writing and matching sentences	1 (2,4%)
9	Nothing	1 (1,7%)		tot	41
10	Speaking about my own experience	1 (1,7%)			
	tot	58			

combinations' (DDL group: 31%; non-DDL group: 41.4%). The second most recurring response was 'playing games/competitions among different class teams' (DDL group: 13.8%; non-DDL group: 19.5%). Finally, the third most recurring response was 'Speaking / working with my peers' (DDL group: 12.1%; non-DDL group: 17.1%). Other aspects that were appreciated in the DDL group include the comments on the homework and the writing practice involved in doing the homework, the rapport with the teacher, and working with concordances. The non-DDL group, on the other hand, enjoyed practising the language and the activities in general. The data is shown in Table 8.5.

Table 8.6 displays the data related to Question 2: 'What did you enjoy the least in the course?'. If we look at the DDL group compared to the non-DDL group, we notice that the first two positions are the same: 'Nothing' (i.e. everything was good; DDL group: 37.2%; non-DDL group: 46.4%)

Table 8.6 Perceptions of DDL vs. non-DDL groups on phraseology-based language course (open-ended questions). Question 2

QUESTION 2. *What did you enjoy the least in the course?*

DDL group		non-DDL group	
Themes	Occ. (%)	Themes	Occ. (%)
1 Nothing / I liked everything	16 (37,2%)	1 Nothing / I liked everything	13 (46,4%)
2 Too many tests and never an explanation / I don't like tests / Tests are not important	8 (18,6%)	2 Too many tests and never an explanation / I don't like tests / Tests are not important	4 (14,3%)
3 Time was too short	5 (11,6%)	3 Too many games	2 (7,1%)
4 Reading many sentences with the same combination is confusing	3 (7,0%)4	4 The first part of the course	1 (3,6%)
5 Working with my peers	3 (7,0%)	5 Too many word combinations	1 (3,6%)
6 Playing games	2 (4,7%)	6 Learning only word combinations	1 (3,6%)
7 The homework	2 (4,7%)	7 Sometimes activities are too slow	1 (3,6%)
8 Learning only word combinations	1 (2,3%)	8 Sometimes activities are too fast, no time to talk	1 (3,6%)
9 Sometimes activities are too slow	1 (2,3%)	9 Not enough combinations in one hour	1 (3,6%)
10 Sometimes activities are too fast, no time to talk	1 (2,3%)	10 Playing easy games	1 (3,6%)
11 Searching for the error in a sentence	1 (2,3%)	11 Some combinations were too difficult for my current level of Italian	1 (3,6%)
Total	43	12 Some activities were boring	1 (3,6%)
		Total	28

and 'Too many tests and never an explanation/I don't like tests/Tests are not important' (DDL group: 18.6%; non-DDL group: 14.3%). Five respondents in the DDL group claimed that time was too short, and three claimed that they found reading groups of sentences with the same combination confusing. In both groups, some respondents found the activities either too fast or too slow, and did not enjoy the games.

172 *How learners react to data-driven learning*

Table 8.7 Perceptions of DDL vs. non-DDL groups on phraseology-based language course (open-ended questions). Question 3

QUESTION 3. *Choose three adjectives to describe the course.*

DDL group		non-DDL group	
Adjectives	Occ. (%)	Adjectives	Occ. (%)
Interesting	35 (30.1%)	Interesting	18 (20.5%)
Useful	30 (26.5%)	Useful	17 (19.3%)
Energic / Active	7 (6.2%)	Joyful/Happy	10 (11.4%)
Joyful/Happy	5 (4.4%)	Relaxing	8 (9.1%)
Wonderful	5 (4.4%)	Easy	5 (5.7%)
Necessary / Fundamental / Significant / Important	5 (4.4%)	Energic / Active	4 (4.5%)
Enjoyable	4 (3.5%)	Practical	3 (3.4%)
Fun	3 (2.7%)	Well-paced	2 (2.3%)
Boring	2 (1.7%)	Casual	2 (2.3%)
Difficult	2 (1.7%)	Fun	2 (2.3%)
Effective	2 (1.7%)	Nice	2 (2.3%)
Relaxing	2 (1.7%)	Light	1 (1.1%)
Short	2 (1.7%)	Helpful	1 (1.1%)
Tiring	2 (1.7%)	Functional	1 (1.1%)
Clear	1 (0.9%)	Complete	1 (1.1%)
Complete	1 (0.9%)	Good	1 (1.1%)
Easy	1 (0.9%)	Difficult	1 (1.1%)
Good	1 (0.9%)	Pleasant	1 (1.1%)
Responsible	1 (0.9%)	Productive	1 (1.1%)
Unforgettable	1 (0.9%)	Competitive	1 (1.1%)
Unique	1 (0.9%)	Free	1 (1.1%)
Total	113	Detailed	1 (1.1%)
		Effective	1 (1.1%)
		Excellent	1 (1.1%)
		Courageous	1 (1.1%)
		Wonderful	1 (1.1%)
		Total	88

In Question 3, the participants were asked to choose three adjectives to describe the course. Table 8.7 shows the list of adjectives chosen by the two groups, starting from the most frequent ones. As we can see, the first two positions in the lists are occupied by the same adjectives, namely 'interesting' (DDL group: 30.1%; non-DDL group: 20.5%) and 'useful' (DDL group: 26.5%; non-DDL group: 19.3%). Eight of the adjectives that follow are present in both lists with different percentages: 'energic/happy', 'joyful/happy', 'wonderful', 'relaxing', 'good', 'fun', 'complete', 'easy'. Overall, most of the adjectives chosen by both groups are positive. The only exceptions are found mostly in the DDL group, and they include the following adjectives: 'boring' (DDL group: 1.7%), 'difficult' (DDL

Table 8.8 Perceptions of DDL vs. non-DDL groups on phraseology-based language course (open-ended questions). Question 4

QUESTION 4. *Other ideas or suggestions.*

DDL group		non-DDL group	
Themes	Occ. (%)	Themes	Occ. (%)
Extend the activities into a story or a dialogue with other students, so that we get freer practice	3 (12%)	More help and more time for oral production	6 (27,3%)
Contextualise in real life so that we can remember more effectively	3 (12%)	Nothing	5 (22,7%)
Less of the same tests	3 (12%)	Have more time	2 (9,1%)
Meet every week / More of this course	3 (12%)	We could learn more word combinations related to everyday life and more difficult ones.	2 (9,1%)
Eight combinations per lesson could be increased to ten / more combinations	2 (8%)	Strange to speak in Italian with fellow Chinese students. It would be better to be in course with a mixed L1 background.	1 (4,5%)
Have lessons outside	2 (8%)	Eight combinations per lesson could be increased to ten / more combinations	1 (4,5%)
More games	2 (8%)	The first part should have been faster	1 (4,5%)
I don't want to do the homework	1 (4%)	More tests	1 (4,5%)
Lessons can go faster	1 (4%)	More grammar	1 (4,5%)
Longer lessons	1 (4%)	More activities	1 (4,5%)
More exercises and explanations	1 (4%)	More games	1 (4,5%)
More feedback on the tests	1 (4%)	tot	22
More grammar	1 (4%)		
More homework and tests	1 (4%)		
Tot	25		

group: 1.7%; non-DDL group: 1.1%), 'short' (DDL group: 1.7%), 'tiring' (DDL group: 1.7%).

In Question 4, the participants were asked to express additional ideas in relation to the course and provide suggestions for future possible re-runs. Table 8.8 shows the answers. Both groups express the need for more time dedicated to freer practice with their peers, with the non-DDL group

174 *How learners react to data-driven learning*

making specific reference to the need for more oral production (DDL group: 12%; non-DDL group: 27.3%). Both groups express the wish for more time dedicated to this course in general. More specifically, in both groups participants ask for more games, more explanations and feedback, more grammar, and more tests. Furthermore, three participants from the DDL group and two from the non-DDL group make the suggestion to contextualise the activities in real-life contexts, so as to make the combinations more memorable. The following extended comment is made by a participant from the non-DDL group: 'It is strange to speak in Italian with fellow Chinese students. It would be better to be in a course with a mixed L1 background'.

8.3 Working on word combinations through DDL activities: learner perceptions from DDL groups

This section looks at the findings related to the questionnaire items which reflected, more closely, some of the specific features characterising the DDL pedagogical intervention. The items considered here are likert-scale items 5 to 8. Figure 8.1 shows the findings related to likert-scale item 5, 'Reading groups of sentences containing the same combination confused me'. As we can see, the responses are almost evenly distributed across the six likert-scale points. We notice, however, a slight upward trend towards the agreeing end of the scale, with most of the respondents (58%) claiming that they either 'partially agree', 'agree' or 'totally agree' with the statement. The most frequently selected value out of all values provided is 'partially agree' (26%).

Figure 8.2 shows the findings related to likert-scale item 6, 'The observation of groups of sentences containing the same combination has helped me to understand how to use that combination in the future'. Here we see a steady upward trend line signalling the presence of most selected values in the upper part of the scale. The most selected value is 'totally agree' (46%). The vast majority of respondents (92%) selected either 'totally agree', 'agree' (40%) or 'partially agree' (6%).

Figure 8.3 illustrates the findings concerning likert-scale item 6, 'The groups of sentences will help me make fewer errors in the future'. Once again, we see a steady upward trend line towards the agreeing end of the scale. The most frequently selected value is 'agree' (46%), followed by 'totally agree' (36%) and 'partially agree' (12%). Only 4% of the respondents selected 'partially disagree', and 2% selected 'disagree'.

Figure 8.4 shows the findings concerning the final likert-scale items proposed to the students: 'A new smartphone application with groups of sentences for word combinations would be useless'. Here we see a downward trend line, indicating a concentration of selection in the lower part of the scale. The most frequently selected value is 'disagree' (32%), followed by 'totally disagree' (28%) and 'partially agree'/'partially disagree' (14% each). A total of 12% of the respondents selected either 'agree' or 'totally agree'.

How learners react to data-driven learning 175

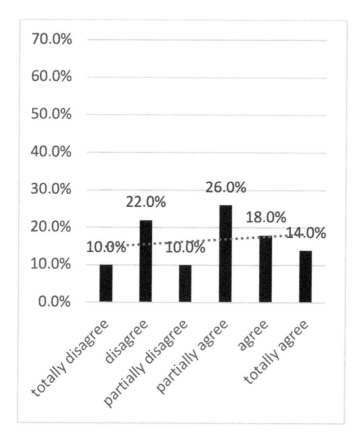

Figure 8.1 Perceptions of DDL groups on phraseology-based language course (likert scale items). Item 5. Reading groups of sentences containing the same combination confused me.

8.4 Discussion of findings

The likert-scale items and open-ended questions addressed to both the DDL and non-DDL groups usefully shed light on the different ways in which the phraseology-based lesson series was perceived in the two groups. When asked whether they found working on word combinations (as opposed to working on single words at a time) useful, the DDL group expressed more confidence in responding positively. A total of 94% of the respondents responded positively, with a distribution of 60% responding that they 'totally agree' with the assertion 'Studying word combinations was useful', as opposed to 53.1% in the non-DDL group, 32% responding 'agree', as opposed to 31.3% in the non-DDL group, and 2% responding 'partially agree', as opposed to 9.4% in the non-DDL group. The 94% of positive

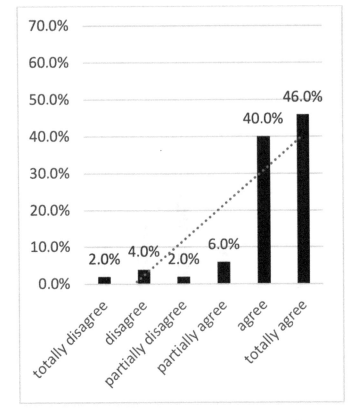

Figure 8.2 Perceptions of DDL groups on phraseology-based language course (likert scale items). Item 6. The observation of groups of sentences containing the same combination has helped me to understand how to use that combination in the future.

responses that we obtain by merging the percentages related to the values 'partially agree', 'agree' and 'totally agree' contrasts with a value of 83.8% in the non-DDL group. We observe a difference of 10.2%. Furthermore, 6.0% of respondents from the non-DDL groups selected 'totally disagree' with respect to the proposed assertion, while none of the respondents did the same from the DDL groups. These differences might indicate a beneficial effect of corpus-based materials in fostering the perceived usefulness of studying word combinations. The fact that learners are exposed to multiple examples referred to a single word combination has the potential of igniting frequency effects which will then foster learning through association mechanisms and guided attention processes (Ellis, 2002; Schmidt, 2012). Observing the numerous examples of a word combination can, in fact, create the optimal conditions to raise awareness in relation to the patterned

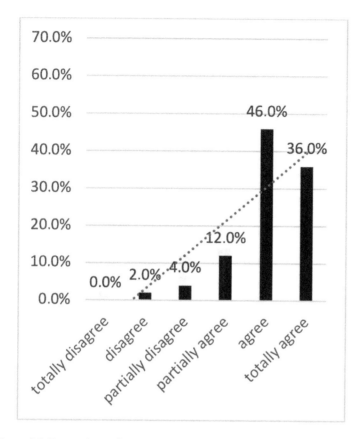

Figure 8.3 Perceptions of DDL groups on phraseology-based language course (likert scale items). Item 7. The groups of sentences will help me make fewer errors in the future.

nature of language use (Boulton, 2012; Hunston, 2019; Hunston & Francis, 2000). The enhancement of the perceived usefulness of learning word combinations through the use DDL materials can be explained not only by the nature of the linguistic data that learners engage with, as opposed to traditional materials, but also with the discovery-based pedagogy underlying it. Working with peers to identify a pattern, in the context of a gamified lesson, can increase motivation which will then influence the perceived benefits of working on a certain learning aim. Peer-work was present also in the non-DDL activities, though in that case the aim was not to identify patterns in a concordance, but to conduct a given activity successfully. The differences in aims characterising the two series of activities might contribute to the explanation of why the perceived benefits of learning word combinations is more prominent in the DDL group.

178 How learners react to data-driven learning

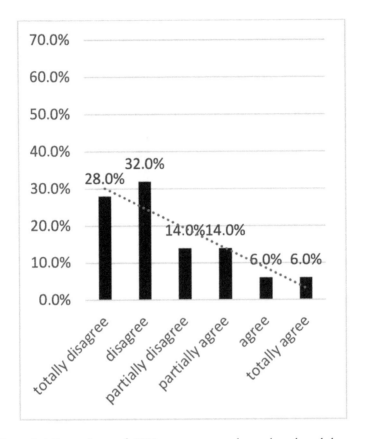

Figure 8.4 Perceptions of DDL groups on phraseology-based language course (likert scale items). Item 8. A new smartphone application with groups of sentences for word combinations would be useless.

In the second likert-scale item, learners from both the DDL and non-DDL groups are asked to express their degree of agreement/disagreement with respect to the following assertion: 'Working with my peers slowed down my learning process'. In both groups, most learners mostly 'disagree': 42% in the DDL group and 37.5% in the non-DDL group. If we pull together all the values on the 'disagreeing' end of the likert scale, we obtain 68% for the DDL group and 62.6% for the non-DDL group. The values are quite similar, with a slightly higher value for the DDL group. This might be explained in connection with item 5 of the questionnaire, which was specifically directed at the DDL groups and asserted the following: 'Reading groups of sentences containing the same combination confused me'. Here, most of the respondents selected 'partially agree' (26%). Overall, 42% selecting one of three values from the 'disagreeing' end of the scale, while 58% selected one of the three values from the 'agree' end of the scale. The initial difficulty in working with concordances is well attested in previous empirical studies (Chambers, 2007). These difficulties may be due to the format in which the linguistic material is presented (i.e. concordance lines), as well as to the language itself that is contained in the concordance lines (Cheng et al., 2003). In the present study, concordance lines extracted from the PEC (Spina, 2014) were preselected and numerous adjustments were needed in order to make them suitable for the learners involved in the study (see section 6.3.3.2). It is possible that the adjustments were to some extent insufficient to effectively adapt the concordance data to the abilities of the learners. Furthermore, no preliminary information had been given to the learners in the DDL group regarding corpora or corpus linguistics in general. Another aspect that may have influenced the initial difficulty in working with concordance lines is the possible information overload, deriving from being exposed to multiple examples for a single word combination, an activity type with a considerable element of novelty for the learners (Yoon & Hirvela, 2004). Since working with concordances involved peer work, it is possible that these two aspects interacted in the DDL group, thus leading to slightly higher values in the DDL group when asked about whether peer work slowed them down. Individual differences in managing concordance-based work may be starker in comparison to those related to more commonly known activity types, such as single-sentence gap fills, single-sentence matching exercises, and so on. These differences may have emerged within these single DDL groups in each classroom, thus determining the perception of 'being slowed down'.

The third likert-scale item proposed to both groups was the following: 'The feedback received on my homework helped me to improve my writing'. The highest values in both groups were 'totally agree', though the learners from the DDL group expressed more confidence in this respect (62% vs. 53.1%). If we pull together the values pertaining to the 'agreeing' end of the scale, we obtain a total 96% for the DDL group and 90.7% for the non-DDL group, and notice a slight difference between the groups. Feedback was provided indirectly in the form of supported guidance to foster self-correction. An error was typically underlined, and indications to self-correct the error were provided (Lim & Renandya, 2020). The form of the feedback reflected the scaffolding provided within the DDL activities. The fact that the DDL group perceived a higher degree of usefulness related to the indirect written feedback provided might depend on their higher familiarity with the feedback format, due to the DDL activities they had engaged in. The structure of DDL activities, characterised by the different phases of a guided-discovery process, might have an effect on how positively and accurately the feedback received from the teacher is perceived.

In the fourth likert-scale item provided in the questionnaire, the cohort of participants had to express their agreement in relation to the following assertion: 'Engaging in didactic activities on eight word combinations in one hour was too challenging'. In this case, the highest percentages in both groups were observed with regards to the value 'disagree' (46% in the DDL group vs. 40.6% in the non-DDL group). Overall, if we unify the three likert-scale points of the 'disagreeing' end of the scale if we obtain 90% for the DDL group and 84.4% for the non-DDL group. Once again, we notice a slight difference between the two groups: the number of word combinations which each lesson was based on was considered less challenging in the DDL group, rather than in the non-DDL group. Why could this be? The lessons based on DDL activities were inevitably more uniform in terms of the pedagogical activity formats proposed, as they were all characterised by having multiple examples for each word combination, while the non-DDL activities were more varied in nature. Not having to switch rapidly from one format to the next within the space of a single lesson may have been beneficial for DDL learners in terms of quantity of learning aims addressed. Learners may navigate more easily through the patterns of different word combinations if the pedagogical task types remain fairly similar, namely the constant availability of multiple examples, in our case. As a result, they may deal more easily with the heavier cognitive load that is involved in DDL activities, thus perceiving the numerosity of the learning aims less problematic in comparison to the participants in the non-DDL groups. Working memory, namely the maintenance of 'relevant information in storage while processing and incorporating incoming information to create a coherent understanding of a text' (Shin, 2020, p. 873), may also play a role in the numerosity of learning aims addressable through either DDL or non-DDL activities.

The group of open-ended questions was presented to both participant groups. When asked about what they enjoyed the most in the course, the most frequent answer in both groups referred to the fact that the lessons involved learning word combinations (31% in the DDL group; 41.4% in the non-DDL group). Playing games and working with peers were respectively the second and third most frequent answers in the groups. It is interesting to note that the different approaches used in the two groups did not emerge starkly in these answers. More particularly, the novelty of the DDL approach, involving activities based on multiple examples for single word combinations, does not seem to have been perceived as a major factor in the enjoyment of the lessons. Only 6.9% of the participants from the DDL group, in fact, mentioned that the presence of groups of sentences in the activities was the aspect they enjoyed the most in the lessons. This might be explained by the fact that no explicit reference to the nature of DDL was made prior to the commencement of the lessons, nor was it made throughout the lessons. Despite the fact that the DDL group was systematically exposed to concordance lines, the actual notion of concordance line was not introduced in the lessons. While receiving explicit training on corpora prior to engaging in DDL activities is not necessarily linked benefits on language gains (Lee et al., 2018), a greater awareness of how DDL activities are constructed may have a positive impact on the learners' ability to identify the tools that are helping them learn, namely the concordance lines extracted from a corpus. The fact that no prior training was conducted in the present study may explain the limited awareness related to how DDL activities were developed and how they differed form more traditional activities. At the same time, only few of the participants may have answered that they enjoyed the groups of sentences simply because most the others did not.

In the second open-ended question, we asked what the participants enjoyed the least. The vast majority in both groups responded that there was nothing they particularly disliked in the course (37.2% in the DDL group; 46.4% in the non-DDL group). What comes second in the list of most frequent responses for both groups is having to sit multiple tests throughout the course, without receiving any feedback (18.6% in the DDL group; 14.3%). The phraseological competence test was used to elicit data pertaining to the development of phraseological competence throughout the 13 weeks of the study. The test was administered in a pen-and-paper format. The items of the test were the same each time was their order was randomised at each administration. No feedback was given in order to avoid effects on intermediate tests. One final round of feedback was provided at the end of the lessons. Having to sit a test multiple times and receiving no feedback can indeed be frustrating. A gamified version of the test, for example through Socrative or Kahoot, could have had a different effect on the learners, and may have stimulated a higher degree of motivation in taking the test. A sense of challenge could have ignited their willingness to take the same test every four weeks. The positive effects of gamified language assessment and testing are increasingly being attested in the literature, both in terms of improved attitudes towards assessment (Attali & Arieli-Attali, 2015; Garland, 2015), as well as in terms of potential positive washback effects on learning motivation (Pitoyo et al., 2020). Gamified language assessment could very well be a way to go for the elicitation of longitudinal etic data in empirical studies on DDL effects.

The third open-ended question asked both groups to choose three adjectives to describe the course. The majority of learners in both groups provided a wide range of positively connotated adjectives, such as 'interesting', 'useful' and 'joyful'. Some of the adjectives that were found in the responses from the DDL group and not in those from the non-DDL group include 'necessary/fundamental/significant/important' (n=5; 4.4%), 'boring' (n=2; 1.7%), 'short' (n=2; 1.7%), 'tiring' (n=2; 1.7%), 'clear' (n= 1; 0.9%). While the numbers are low, it is interesting to notice how the aspect related to the 'importance' of the experience emerges in the DDL group and not in the non-DDL group. Learners may have intuited the novelty of the approach and the usefulness of being exposed to it. This might be in line with the fact that some of the respondents thought the lesson series was too short. It is possible that the perceived novelty of the approach triggered curiosity and willingness to proceed further and learn more about the approach. Two participants claimed the experience was 'boring', while none of the participants in the non-DDL group claimed the same. This may be a consequence of the short amount of time that was available to conduct the study which, together with the initial difficulty entailed in working with concordance lines, may have hindered the possibility of making things more interesting for everyone in the long run. The time factor is a major one in the observation of potentially beneficial effects of DDL on language competence, as sustained in Mizumoto and Chujo (2015), Boulton and Cobb (2017) and Lee et al. (2018). Without having the opportunity to try DDL extensively over time, the risk of it being perceived as boring can always be present.

In the last open-ended question, participants were asked to provide ideas and suggestions to improve the course, in case of future re-runs. The DDL group provided a wider range of responses in comparison to the non-DDL group. Both groups, however, expressed the need for an extension of the activities into freer language practice with their peers (12% in the DDL group; 27.3% in the non-DDL group). This perspective ties in with the need for DDL to be normalised into general teaching practices (Chambers & Bax, 2006; Pérez-Paredes, 2019), not only at the level of the syllabus, but also at the level of the different stages of a single lesson. Lessons lasting longer than one hour certainly have the potential of extending the work on the corpus into freer language production practices, using the corpus work as a basis for experimentation.

As for the likert-scale items specifically focusing on features of the proposed DDL activities, and thus directed at the learners in the DDL group only, we already discussed the perceived initial confusion that many learners expressed in relation to working with groups of sentences containing the same word combination. This aspect was addressed by likert scale item 5. If we consider different teaching contexts, we might get different answers. Forti (2019), for example, explored the attitudes of a group of Belgian students who engaged in a small range of DDL activities in the space of a one two-hour lesson. Despite the very short exposure to DDL, students largely disagreed with the assertion 'Reading groups of sentences containing the same combination confused me'. The trendline emerging from the responses given by the Belgian learners signals an opposite trend compared to the Chinese learners, despite the latter having been exposed to DDL activities for a much longer time. Difference in L1 background, when considering homogeneous groups of learners, may play a role in how working with concordance lines in perceived. As for the Chinese L1 group, it is interesting to observe how their attested initial confusion did not prevent them to express a perceived usefulness of the activities in terms of increased understanding of how the combination works, and in terms of a perceived higher degree of confidence concerning future uses of the combination.

In likert scale item 6, in fact, learners were asked to express their agreement in relation to the assertion 'The observation of groups of sentences containing the same combination has helped me to understand how to use that combination in the future'. Most learners responded that they totally agreed with the assertion (46%). Overall, a total of 92% of the respondents claimed that they agreed, to some extent, with the assertion. This response might be related to the beneficial effects of activities with a high cognitive load, which lead to potentially higher awareness levels in relation to the language items in the corpus data the learners engaged with (Boulton, 2012; Lee et al., 2020). Nevertheless, when in likert scale item 7 asked to express their degree of agreement with the assertion 'The groups of sentences will help me make fewer errors in the future most of the learners', most of the respondents (46%) selected 'agree', while a slightly lower percentage (36%) selected 'totally agree'. Overall, 94% of the students believe that having worked with concordance lines is likely to prevent them from making errors in the future. The hiatus between comprehension and performance could explain the slightly lower percentage related to the 'totally agree' values, with respect to the 'agree' values. Learners need opportunities to experiment with the language, in order to gain confidence and put the generalisations emerging from DDL activities to the test. The perceptions of Belgian students explored in Forti (2019) were fairly similar, with the higher proficiency level group exhibiting higher confidence in the usefulness of the approach, and with respect to the prospect of possibly making fewer errors in future, as a result of engaging in DDL activities. This finding may indicate a possible influence of proficiency level on how DDL activities are perceived by learners, in connection to the etic dimension related to language gains according to proficiency level, which is explored in the meta-analyses conducted by Mizumoto & Chujo (2015), Boulton & Cobb (2017) and Lee et al. (2018).

Finally, in likert scale item 8, learners were asked to express their degree of agreement in relation to the following assertion: 'A new smartphone application with groups of sentences for word combinations would be useless'. While the lessons did not involve an explanation of how such a smartphone application for learning Italian could actually look like, the question aimed at eliciting attitudes towards this future possibility, in light of recent studies exploring the affordances of a mobile-based DDL (Burston, 2013; Meurice & Van de Vyver, 2017; Pérez-Paredes et al., 2019). Most of the respondents (32%) selected the 'disagree' value, followed by those who selected 'totally disagree' (28%) and 'partially disagree' (14.0%). The prospect of bringing DDL closer to the community of Italian L2 learners through MALL could be fruitful. It would foster increasingly greater autonomy in the use of a corpus, while creating the conditions to normalise its use in language learning practices, both as a language pattern discovery tool, as well as a tool for self-correction. However, possible differences between different learner communities need to be considered. Forti (2019), in fact, shows mixed findings for Belgian students: the elementary level group of learners involved in the study largely agreed with the assertion, as the total percentage of 'agreeing' values was 70%. The intermediate level group of Belgian learners displayed a more evenly distributed range of perceptions, which lead to the emergence

184 *How learners react to data-driven learning*

of a balanced trend line, with no stark orientation towards either end of the likert scale.

8.5 Chapter summary and conclusions

This chapter described the findings pertaining to the end-of-course questionnaire eliciting emic data on learner attitudes towards the pedagogical intervention. The questionnaire (see Appendix D and E) was divided into likert-scale items and open-ended questions. The DDL groups responded to a questionnaire with eight likert-scale items, including four items addressing specific DDL features in the activities that they engaged in, and four open-ended questions, while the non-DDL groups responded to a questionnaire with four likert-scale items (those addressing DDL features were excluded) and four open-ended questions. The chapter placed the two groups side to side with respect to reactions concerning the phraseology-oriented lessons that both groups engaged in. Both groups found learning word combinations useful, though the DDL group appears more confident in this respect. Furthermore, they mostly enjoyed working in groups or pairs, although in both cases the groups did not display a sharp preference or enjoyment for group or pair work. The helpfulness of the feedback provided on the phraseology-oriented homework was perceived in both groups, though more starkly in the DDL group. In terms of the level of challenge involved in working on eight combinations in one hour, slightly higher scores were elicited from the non-DDL group as opposed to the DDL group, though both exhibited fairly similar trend lines.

As for the open-ended questions, what both groups enjoyed the most was learning word combinations, followed by playing games and working with their peers. Most of the students in both groups reported that there was nothing in particular that they did not like or enjoy. However, having to sit regular tests and receiving no explanation afterwards was mentioned by students from both groups as a negative aspect on the lessons. When asked to describe the course with three adjectives, the top two adjectives from both groups were 'interesting' and 'useful', followed by 'energic/active' and 'joyful/happy' in the DDL group, and by 'joyful/happy' and 'relaxing' in the non-DDL group. When asked for ideas and suggestions to improve the lessons, both groups expressed the need for more and freer oral practice, and for a clearer connection of the activities with their everyday lives.

As for the likert-scale items specifically focusing on DDL features, a good number of participants admitted being confused by reading groups of sentences. A total of 58% of participants agreed, to various extents, with the assertion 'Reading groups of sentences containing the same combination confused me'. Nevertheless, the vast majority (92%) of students agreed with the assertion 'The observation of groups of sentences containing the same combination has helped me to understand how to use that combination in the future'. Furthermore, most of them deemed the concordance-based activities useful to help them make fewer errors in the future. Lastly, most of them (74%) consider potentially useful a smartphone application with groups of sentences for word combinations.

Potential differences in learner groups with different L1 background should be considered, as indicated in Forti (2019). Furthermore, a greater emphasis on learner perceptions in DDL would help in its spread and normalisation within teaching contexts. Investigating learner perceptions towards DDL, in fact, is key in gaining insight into how DDL practices may be developed to be increasingly closer to learner needs and expectations. They are also pivotal in designing new learner-friendly corpus exploration tools that are able to bridge the gap between 'corpora for linguists' vs. 'corpora for learners' gap (Forti & Spina, 2019).

References

Attali, Y., & Arieli-Attali, M. (2015). Gamification in assessment: Do points affect test performance? *Computers & Education*, *83*, 57–63.

Boulton, A. (2012). Language awareness and medium-term benefits of corpus consultation. *Proceedings of Eurocall 2009 Conference: New Trends in CALL- Working Together*, 39–46.

Boulton, A., & Cobb, T. (2017). Corpus use in language learning: A meta-analysis. *Language Learning*, *67*(2), 348–393.

Burston, J. (2013). Mobile-assisted language learning: A selected annotated bibliography of implementation studies 1994–2012. *Language Learning & Technology*, *17*(3), 157–224.

Chambers, A. (2007). Popularising corpus consultation by language learners and teachers. *Language and Computers*, *61*(1), 3–16.

Chambers, A., & Bax, S. (2006). Making CALL work: Towards normalisation. *System*, *34*(4), 465–479.

Cheng, W., Warren, M., & Xun-feng, X. (2003). The language learner as language researcher: Putting corpus linguistics on the timetable. *System*, *31*(2), 173–186.

Ellis, N.C. (2002). Frequency effects in language processing. *Studies in Second Language Acquisition*, *24*(02), 143–188.

Forti, L. (2019). Learner attitudes towards data-driven learning: Investigating the effect of teaching contexts. In F. Meunier, J. Van de Vyver, L. Bradley, & S. Thouësny (Eds.), *CALL and complexity – short papers from EUROCALL 2019* (pp. 137–143). Research-publishing.net.

Garland, C.M. (2015). *Gamification and implications for second language education: A meta analysis*. Unpublished MA Thesis, St. Cloud University.

Hunston, S. (2019). Patterns, constructions, and applied linguistics. In S. Hunston & F. Perek (Eds.) *Constructions in Applied Linguistics. International Journal of Corpus Linguistics*, *24*(3), 324–353.

Hunston, S., & Francis, G. (2000). *Pattern Grammar*. Benjamins.

Lee, H., Warschauer, M., & Lee, J.H. (2018). the effects of corpus use on second language vocabulary learning: A multilevel meta-analysis. *Applied Linguistics*, *40*(5), 721–753.

Lee, H., Warschauer, M., & Lee, J. H. (2020). toward the establishment of a data-driven learning model: Role of learner factors in corpus-based second language vocabulary learning. *The Modern Language Journal*, 104(2), 345–362.

Lim, S. C., & Renandya. (2020). Efficacy of written corrective feedback in writing instruction: A meta-analysis. *The Electronic Journal for English as a Second Language*, 24(3), 1–26.

Meurice, A., & Van de Vyver, J. (2017, January 12). *TELL-OP app: When data-driven learning meets mobile learning*. BAAHE conference 2017, Université catholique de Louvain.

Mizumoto, A., & Chujo, K. (2015). A meta-analysis of data-driven learning approach in the Japanese EFL classroom. *English Corpus Studies*, 22, 1–18.

Pérez-Paredes, P. (2019). A systematic review of the uses and spread of corpora and data-driven learning in CALL research during 2011–2015. *Computer Assisted Language Learning*, 35(1–2), 36–61.

Pérez-Paredes, P., Ordoñana Guillamón, C., Van de Vyver, J., Meurice, A., Aguado Jiménez, P., Conole, G., & Sánchez Hernández, P. (2019). Mobile data-driven language learning: Affordances and learners' perception. *System*, 84, 145–159.

Pitoyo, M.D., Sumardi, S., & Asib, A. (2020). Gamification-based assessment: The washback effect of Quizizz on students' learning in higher education. *International Journal of Language Education*, 1–10.

Schmidt, R.W. (2012). Attention, awareness, and individual differences in language learning. In W.M. Chan (Ed.), *Proceedings of CLaSIC 2010, Singapore, December 2-4* (pp. 721–737). National University of Singapore, Centre for Language Studies.

Shin, J. (2020). A meta-analysis of the relationship between working memory and second language reading comprehension: Does task type matter? *Applied Psycholinguistics*, 41(4), 873–900.

Spina, S. (2014). Il Perugia Corpus: Una risorsa di riferimento per l'italiano. Composizione, annotazione e valutazione. *Proceedings of the First Italian Conference on Computational Linguistics CLiC-It 2014 & the Fourth International Workshop EVALITA 2014*, 1, 354–359.

Yoon, H., & Hirvela, A. (2004). ESL student attitudes toward corpus use in L2 writing. *Journal of Second Language Writing*, 13(4), 257–283.

9 Conclusions and future prospects

This chapter concludes the book's journey. It does so by summarising the main findings of the study presented in the book in relation to each of the research questions that were formulated. It then discusses the need to connect DDL research to SLA research evidence pertaining to the specific learning aims selected for a particular DDL intervention. It also addresses the theme of theory and theorisation in DDL research, by highlighting how theory has been integrated in DDL research so far, and the role that theory could have in future DDL studies. The methodology involved in DDL research is also outlined, in terms of how it can be expanded and refined, in light, for example, of what the study presented in the book demonstrated. Finally, the ways in which the book seeks to contribute to the field of Italian language learning research and pedagogy are illustrated, and potential avenues for future research suggested.

9.1 Investigating DDL effects on Italian L2 phraseological competence development: a summary

In this book, we have explored the effects of DDL in the context of Italian L2 phraseological competence development. We have done so by adopting two perspectives: one based on the impact that DDL may have on language gains, the other based on the attitudes that DDL may produce in learners exposed to corpus-based activities. As for the first perspective, we formulated three research questions. We initially explored the overall effects of DDL on language gains, by comparing a group of L1 Chinese learners who had engaged in paper-based DDL activities for eight weeks with another group of L1 Chinese learners who had engaged in non-DDL activities, focusing on the same learning aims. More specifically, we asked:

1. How does phraseological competence develop over time when comparing a DDL approach with a non-DDL approach?

We found U-shaped learning curves in both groups, with no significant differences between them. We noticed, however, possibly better retention

DOI: 10.4324/9781003137320-9

rates in the DDL group. Although DDL does not seem to determine significantly higher language gains in comparison to other approaches, it does seem to create the conditions for more memorable and long-term learning. We then moved onto a more fine-grained analysis, by considering certain properties of the learning aims. Much of the literature on phraseology learning and processing points at the influence that several properties have in the development of phraseological competence over time and with reference to different proficiency levels (Altenberg & Granger, 2001; Gyllstad & Wolter, 2016; Nesselhauf, 2005; Wang, 2016; Wolter & Yamashita, 2018). So we first considered the possible influence of properties such as semantic transparency and L1-L2 congruency. More specifically, we formulated the following research question:

2. How does a DDL/non-DDL approach influence the development of phraseological competence over time, with respect to certain specific properties of the learning aims (i.e. semantic transparency and L1-L2 congruency)?

We found that opaque and incongruent combinations have higher predicted probabilities of accuracy in both groups, with respect to transparent and congruent combinations. We also found that although the U-shaped learning curve is present in most cases, incongruent combinations display a more linear pattern, with improved predicted probabilities of accuracy four weeks after the end of the lessons, in comparison to the other categories (semantically opaque, semantically transparent, and congruent combinations). As a result, DDL might be most useful to learn combinations that are incongruent.

We then focused on a cognitive property of the learning aims, namely the dimension of phraseological knowledge, and we formulated the following research question:

3. How does a DDL/non-DDL approach influence the development of phraseological competence over time, with respect to different dimensions of phraseological knowledge (i.e. definitional vs. transferable)?

The findings showed no significant differences between the two groups. However, definitional knowledge appeared to be characterised by slightly higher accuracy rates with respect to transferable knowledge, despite that fact that DDL is usually found to be more effective in the development of transferable knowledge.

Moving on to the second perspective of the study, focused on the attitudes of learners exposed to DDL activities in comparison to those who were exposed to non-DDL ones, we formulated the following research question:

4. What are the learners' overall attitudes towards DDL activities?

We found that although learners experienced some initial difficulties in relation to working with concordances, they ultimately found the approach useful in helping them to learn word combinations and the ways in which they may be used in context. Furthermore, learners indicated the need for a better integration between DDL activities and other activities in which they can use language more freely, even in connection with everyday communicative situations.

9.2 The need to connect DDL research with SLA research evidence

Whether DDL works or not is not only a matter of language context, proficiency level of the learners or the specific characteristics of a proposed DDL activities, but also a matter of the aim at which DDL is directed. If we consider specific learning aims, such as the development of lexical, syntactic, or phraseological competence, we have a wealth of research evidence at our disposal informing us on how specific linguistic subsystems are acquired by second language learners. In this respect, meta-analyses, in particular, are useful in gaining a general and systematic perspective.[1] Knowing how learners deal with certain learning aims, with particular reference to the main difficulties they encounter, is crucial in devising an empirical study seeking to evaluate DDL effects on language learning. If it is true that DDL has the potential of providing learners with unique resources for better understanding of how a language works, then it is pivotal to know in which areas of language learning DDL would be most needed.

In our study, we considered the research evidence stemming from learner corpus research and psycholinguistics. From this body of research, we gleaned some of the properties which seem to influence the development of phraseological competence in L2 learners. The compositionality of phraseological units, for example, has been addressed in both corpus-based and psycholinguistic studies. The fact that verb + noun (object) combinations are frequently non-semantically transparent at the level of the verb collocate has been seen as a possible challenge for second language learners, even at advanced levels of proficiency (Altenberg & Granger, 2001; Wang, 2016), although the psycholinguistic evidence related to how semantic transparency is processed by L1 and L2 speakers does not identify any significant differences between the two (Gyllstad & Wolter, 2016). This means that, overall, second language learners may need a learning approach that is effective in addressing such potential difficulties.

Another property that we addressed in our study was that of L1-L2 congruency. The ways in which the L1 may influence second language competence development have been classified into various types and a call for more rigorous conceptualisation and operationalisation of such influences has been made (Jarvis, 2000, 2010). L1 influence is certainly a major theme in SLA research as a whole: how can DDL come into play in terms of pedagogical practices that are able to accompany the learner towards a closer relationship with the target language? Finally, we considered the different dimensions of phraseological knowledge. In particular, we identified definitional knowledge as the knowledge corresponding to the initial and receptive phases of learning, and transferable knowledge as the knowledge corresponding to the more in-depth and productive phases of learning (Jaén, 2009; Koya, 2005). With the increased frequency of input that characterises concordance-based DDL activities, a more in-depth knowledge of word combinations would be expected, as the numerous contexts of occurrences are examined throughout a DDL activity. It would thus make sense to investigate more widely whether this is actually the case, since the literature points at the fact that in-depth and productive knowledge of lexis in general tends to arrive later than the initial and more receptive knowledge. Concordance-based DDL activities may indeed be beneficial in helping learners develop in-depth knowledge more quickly.

Overall, the opportunity of connecting DDL research with SLA research evidence lies in the chance of addressing, though the investigation of DDL effects, the learners' actual needs. DDL may be beneficial for numerous a priori reasons (e.g., it provides numerous examples, authentic examples, etc.), but can it really get to what the learners need the most and are unable to get from other approaches? Devising a learner-needs-driven DDL research agenda certainly involves considering the emic dimension of SLA research evidence. How do learners feel about the language learning process in general? How do they react towards novel teaching and learning approaches and to the use of technology? What are their expectations and needs in this respect? In order to answer these questions, we must look at the research evidence beyond the strict domain of research on DDL. What we know about second language acquisition, from the perspective of language gains and learner attitudes, can very usefully nurture and drive DDL research. This would be helpful in deciding what DDL should be used for, which necessities its principles would most likely satisfy.

9.3 The need to connect DDL research with SLA theories

Recent years have seen an increased interest in connecting DDL research with SLA theories. Cobb (1999) showed how DDL reflects principles pertaining to constructivist theory, how the learner can be a 'scientist' sifting through the wealth of empirical evidence provided by a corpus on language use, and how this approach can lead to more longer-term forms of understanding and learning. Flowerdew (2015) then pointed at the possible limitations of a purely constructivist view of DDL, as not all learners may be equipped for autonomous discovery-based learning. Learners may need to be more guided towards autonomy, through mediation and scaffolding. As a result, Flowerdew turns to sociocultural theory (Vygotsky, 1934), and points out the value in associating corpus exploration practices with an interactive dialogue that the learner can initiate on his/her own, or develop with peers or with the teacher. This way, cognition is progressively reshaped according to the different negotiating phases involved in the interaction, which will have both a mediating and a scaffolding function. Furthermore, Flowerdew (2015) situates DDL within the domain of the noticing hypothesis (Schmidt, 2012), according to which learning implies the conscious noticing of forms and regularities in the language input that a learner is exposed to. Noticing a pattern clearly ties in with the mediating practices conceptualised in the sociocultural theory and is characteristic of typical corpus-based pedagogical activities. However, as pointed out in Boulton & Vyatkina (2021, p. 82), these theories have been called upon to 'attempt to justify the approach after the event'.

O'Keeffe (2020) has broadened the perspective by highlighting how new and different theoretical questions may be addressed by DDL research. Cognitive variables and degrees of mediations may be investigated within the theoretical framework of usage-based models of language learning and in relation to long-standing SLA debates such as the interface between implicitness vs. explicitness in language learning.

The mechanisms of DDL can thus benefit from a deeper theoretical grounding. At the same, research on DDL can be beneficial for second language acquisition theories, other than being informed by it. When addressing the question 'what needs to be explained by theories in SLA?', Van Patten et al. (2020) take inspiration from Michael Long's article *The least a second language acquisition theory needs to explain* (Long, 1990) to identify ten main observations that are claimed as needing to be explained:

Observation 1. Exposure to input is necessary for L2 acquisition.
Observation 2. A good deal of L2 acquisition happens incidentally.
Observation 3. Learners come to know more than what they have been exposed to in the input.
Observation 4. Learners' output (speech) often follows predictable paths with predictable stages in the acquisition of a given structure.
Observation 5. Second language learning is variable in its outcome.
Observation 6. Second language learning is variable across linguistic subsystems.
Observation 7. There are limits to the effects of frequency on L2 acquisition.
Observation 8. There are limits on the effects of a learner's L1 on L2 acquisition.
Observation 9. There are limits on the effects of instruction on L2 acquisition.
Observation 10. There are limits on the effects of output (learner production) on language acquisition.

(Van Patten et al., 2020, pp. 10–12)

Each of these observations which the various contemporary theories on second language acquisition attempt to explain can be usefully addressed in DDL research. While most researchers agree that input plays a key role in second language acquisition, not all agree that it is sufficient (observation 1). How can input be conceptualised and structured? How can learners engage with input? How do different kinds of input impact learning? As DDL involves a particular kind of input exposure and input interaction, many different operationalisations of the input may be explored and investigated empirically. The theme of incidental learning is also a central one in SLA (observation 2). What is learned through DDL beyond the object of the explicit focus during the activities? How does DDL foster incidental learning over time?

DDL may have a lot to say in terms of how the input can be organised and how learners can interact with it, but can it also account for what learners seem to learn beyond the input they are exposed to through DDL (observation 3)? The idea that learners are able to acquire features of a language that they are not taught and that are not present in the input they are exposed to is generally referred to as the 'Poverty of the Stimulus' argument, which in turn sustains the key role of innateness in language learning. But is the input necessarily 'poor' or 'poorer' than what a learner may be able to acquire?

One theme that seems to be overlooked in DDL research so far is how corpus work affects the learner's output in terms of speech production over time. Learners' speech seems to follow predictable paths and stages when acquiring a given structure (observation 4). How does explicit instruction through DDL affect the developmental stages of language learning? Variability in language learning is another major theme in second language acquisition theory. Language learning varies in terms of outcome, as not all learners reach the same competence in the target language, even when they have been exposed to the language under the same conditions (observation 5). Individual differences may come into play, for example. Variation in outcomes when investigating DDL effects has been observed but seldom explained.

Language learning varies also in terms of linguistic subsystems, as a learner may develop higher competence in the syntax rather than in the sound system, for example (observation 6). What influences such variability? How can DDL address such variability? Frequency of input is one the main features of concordance-based DDL and is also present in a number of SLA theories. However, it is claimed that frequency effects on L2 acquisition have limits (observation 7). Which factors modulate the impact of frequency on learning? Which features of DDL can enhance the effects of frequency in order to counterbalance its potential limitations? Another major theme in SLA research is L1 influence. It has been observed that L1 influence interacts with other factors and varies across learners (observation 8). What role can DDL have in the influence of the mother tongue on second language learning? SLA research also deals with the role of instruction on L2 acquisition. More specifically, it has been observed that instruction is no guarantee of acquisition and that it may be even detrimental to language acquisition (observation 9). How does DDL respond to that? DDL is, of course, an instructional approach which aims to develop into a set of skills and resources that the learner can use autonomously and independently from the teacher and the teaching context. Can this particular aspect of DDL cover the potential limitations of instruction of language learning? Finally, SLA addresses the issue pertaining to the role of language production on language acquisition. Whether producing the language has an effect on language learning is debated and it is held that there are constraints on the role of language production (observation 10). Can DDL influence the interplay between language production and language learning? Can it explain the potential discrepancies between the two? All in all, grounding DDL theoretically can help DDL explain at least some of the ten observations we just illustrated. In this sense, DDL research can not only be more theory-driven but its findings can also be theory-nurturing.

9.4 Reflecting on DDL empirical research methods

Researching DDL effects is a methodologically interdisciplinary endeavour. While historically stemming from corpus linguistics, DDL branches into language pedagogy as it merges the use of corpus data in the classroom with a specific kind of pedagogy. It is, in fact, mostly oriented at inductive and discovery-based forms of learning, leaning towards a growing degree of autonomy on the part of the learner. Setting out to evaluate the effects that DDL produces on the development of language competence and language attitudes will then require a multifaceted set of methodological skills. We will need to design a pedagogical empirical study and then develop empirical data elicitation tools. In our case, these were the phraseological competence test, for the etic dimension, and the end-of-course student questionnaire, for the emic dimension. Designing a mixed-methods study has the advantage of addressing broad research questions from different perspectives (Riazi, 2017). However, different data elicitation tools will require different skills, both in terms of how they are constructed, as well as in terms of the statistical knowledge needed to analyse the data obtained through them. The evaluation of DDL effects will then require knowledge in how pedagogical materials can be developed and insight into how DDL principles may be reflected in pedagogical activities.

If setting up an empirical DDL study requires competencies in such diverse fields, doing it rigorously is certainly a challenge but also a need of the field. In their 30-year review of DDL studies, Boulton and Vyatkina notice that 'statistical analyses have frequently been insufficiently robust and reporting practices non-standard' (Boulton & Vyatkina, 2021, p. 82). In Chapter 4 we illustrated how the various methodological challenges in investigating DDL may be addressed. In terms of the participant sample, our study involved a sample which was above the average size that is normally found in DDL studies, though variation within the sample was still observed. The sampling method moved one step away from the convenience sampling that is usually found in DDL studies, as it introduced a judgment-sampling criterion (see section 6.3.2). Furthermore, the sample was drawn from a homogeneous population of learners in terms of the L1, and it involved learners of a language other than English. The vast majority of DDL studies refers to English as the target language (Forti & Jablonkai, 2020), and although an increase in studies dealing with languages other than English has been observed (Vyatkina, 2020), much more research is needed and called for in order to identify the challenges and develop the necessary tools for assessing the spread of DDL in different language learning contexts.

Study length is another aspect that is frequently addressed in the 'conclusion' sections of DDL studies (Boulton & Vyatkina, 2021). Calls for longer study durations are made, but the studies covering extended periods of time, and which, most importantly, collect data pertaining to the delayed effects of DDL are still rare. If the ultimate goal of DDL is to make learners increasingly more autonomous, then study designs with multiple delayed post-tests should become the norm. Our study included one delayed test, which was able to elicit improved retention rates particularly evident in relation to one specific situation: incongruent combinations in the DDL group. However, longer-term designs would certainly shed new light on the effects of DDL over time. Future meta-analyses could focus on delayed data only, but multiple studies going in this direction would be needed first.

In sum, the study presented in this book reflects on the possibility of extending the methodological foundation that has characterised DDL research so far. It does so in several ways. First, it focuses on a language other than English. Second, it combines etic and emic dimensions, so as to gain comprehensive insight into DDL effects. The only empirical studies on DDL in an Italian L2 domain had focused on aspects related to learner attitudes and processes involved in working with corpus data (Kennedy & Miceli, 2001, 2010, 2016). Then, it takes into account some specific linguistic properties of the learning aims, in an attempt to merge the research evidence available from other fields (learner corpus research, psycholinguistics) into the research on DDL effects. It also included cognitive properties, pertaining to different dimensions of phraseological knowledge (definitional, transferable). It then adopts a longitudinal design, with a delayed data collection point aimed at evaluating retention rates. Finally, it analyses etic data through mixed-effects modelling and contrast coding, a statistical technique which is gaining popularity in second language research at large, but still seems to be rare in DDL research.

9.5 Contributing to Italian language learning studies and pedagogy

In tracing the history of studies discussing corpus use in the Italian L2 teaching/learning domain, we found a total of 26 publications covering an almost 30-year timeframe (see section 2.5). Empirical studies seeking to evaluate the effects of DDL on language gains and the development of learner attitudes and learner processes have, however, been very few so far. Pedagogical resources on how corpora may be used in the Italian L2 context, and/or ready-made corpus-based activities for the Italian L2 classroom are still largely missing. And learner-friendly corpus exploration tools for Italian are only starting to appear (Baisa & Suchomel, 2014) and no research on these or news of pedagogical implementation are available yet.

This book seeks to participate in the decade-long conversation on the role that corpora can have in Italian L2 learning and teaching contexts, by considering different perspectives. First, it charts the territory of corpus use for Italian L2 learning, so as to have a comprehensive view of where we are at with respect to DDL for English, which is still the main target language characterising DDL practices and research. It then provides a response to the calls for larger implementation of corpora in the Italian L2 domain by both researching its effects empirically, and by illustrating the principles behind the development of corpus-based materials. It shows how corpus data may be used directly, to create paper-based DDL activities, but also indirectly, to create language competence tests and/or activities reflecting test formats (multiple choice, gap-fill, etc.).

Researchers in second language acquisition, focusing on Italian L2, can not only learn about the potential of corpora in second language learning and teaching practices, but also how their effects can be evaluated. Similar or different methods may be adopted in future studies so that the empirically-founded knowledge base on corpora in Italian L2 settings can be expanded and our understanding improved. Teachers and pedagogical materials' developers can gain insight from this book into novel ways of creating materials and conducting activities and can, in turn, provide insights into DDL activities design for researchers. This will help define DDL as a pedagogical construct, and the measurement of its effects can become increasingly more relevant for real-world teaching contexts. The introduction of DDL-related modules in Italian L2 teacher training programs and university degrees focused on teaching Italian as a second language can certainly go in the direction of cross-fertilising the teaching and research domains. Developing effective DDL materials and activities requires a greater collaboration between language teachers and researchers, and this is especially true in a context such as the Italian one where the conversation on the potential of corpora in language teaching is still sparse.

9.6 Looking ahead

Many future directions for DDL research as a whole and for DDL in the Italian context may be traced. The methodology involved in conducting DDL research would certainly benefit from more extended timeframes in the data-collection process, in order to capture delayed effects and assess the claim according to which corpora can be a useful resource for learners to be used autonomously whenever needed. Participant samples identified through criteria different from the convenience criterion would certainly provide DDL studies with greater robustness, as would the inclusion of learners from contexts other than academic and from a range of age groups (Crosthwaite, 2020). As for the aspects of DDL being investigated, an updated systematic review of learner perceptions and learner attitudes is desirable, as the last one published reflects research from about 20 years ago (Chambers, 2005). Gaining insight from learners in relation to DDL materials and activities can help the teacher-researcher enormously in designing subsequent materials and activities to be evaluated. DDL can be effective only if it is able to meet the needs of the learners. Another aspect that should gain more space in DDL research relates to the processes involved in DDL activities. Data deriving from keylogging and screen-recording is still limited (Pérez-Paredes et al., 2012), while data revealing the psycholinguistic processes involved in searching patterns in a concordance, for instance, are still missing. Eye-tracking studies, in this respect, could represent an insightful avenue for future research, as pointed out previously (O'Keeffe, 2020).

In terms of corpus resources, while some corpora built initially for researchers have incorporated useful tools to make them more learner-friendly (Lyding et al., 2013), we still need corpora specifically created for learners, and possibly suitable for a range of proficiency levels (Forti & Spina, 2019). Corpora for learners could have a significant impact on the probabilities of making DDL practices a normalised habit for the learners, even outside of the classroom. The possibilities related to mobile-DDL would also need to be explored at a greater length (Meurice & Van de Vyver, 2017; Pérez-Paredes et al., 2019), as this too could foster learner autonomy. The pedagogical potential of a wider range of corpus types could also be explored. So far, the corpora used in DDL activities have mostly been written corpora of the target language (Boulton & Vyatkina, 2021). This trend is understandable both because of the wider availability of written corpora, in comparison to spoken corpora, and because of the tendency to use corpora as a model source for the target language. However, expanding the scope of corpus use in language pedagogy by including, to a larger extent, also learner corpora (Ackerley, 2017) and spoken corpora (Aston, 2015), can be crucial in improving our understanding of the full scope of corpus uses in second language pedagogy. The normalisation of DDL activities in second language teaching practices is also a key aspect in improving the study of DDL effects (Pérez-Paredes, 2019).

As for the specific context of Italian L2 learning and teaching, the knowledge and experience accumulated over years of DDL research focused on English is immensely useful. Nevertheless, the development of pedagogical activities based on corpora for Italian L2 learning is key to nurture research on DDL for Italian, and necessary to explore how DDL can actually meet the needs of teachers and learners. Bridging the research-teaching gap can be hugely beneficial for both research and teaching practices. The development of the Italian version of SkELL (Baisa & Suchomel, 2014), the first learner-friendly corpus exploration tool for Italian, is certainly promising for corpus integration in teaching practices, and also for designing studies seeking to evaluate the effects that this new tool may produce on learners of Italian. It is our hope that this book sparks a renewed interest in the potential of corpora for Italian language learning and we look forward to more intense exchanges between the research and the teaching communities. After all, as Tim Johns famously claimed, 'research is too important to be left to the researchers' (Johns, 1991, p. 3).

Note

1 A list of research syntheses and meta-analyses compiled by Luke Plonsky may be found at this page: https://lukeplonsky.wordpress.com/bibliographies/meta-analysis/ (last accessed: 22/08/2022).

References

Ackerley, K. (2017). Effects of corpus-based instruction on phraseology in learner English. *Language Learning & Technology*, 21(3), 195–216.

Altenberg, B., & Granger, S. (2001). The grammatical and lexical patterning of MAKE in native and non-native student writing. *Applied Linguistics*, 22(2), 173–195.

Aston, G. (2015). Learning phraseology from speech corpora. In A. Boulton & A. Lenko-Szymanska (Eds.), *Multiple affordances of language corpora for data-driven learning* (pp. 65–84). Benjamins.

Baisa, V., & Suchomel, V. (2014). SkELL: Web interface for English language learning. *Eighth Workshop on Recent Advances in Slavonic Natural Language Processing*, 63–70.

Boulton, A., & Vyatkina, N. (2021). Thirty years of data-driven learning: Taking stock and charting new directions. *Language Learning and Technology*, 25(3), 66–89.

Chambers, A. (2005). Integrating corpus consultation in language studies. *Language Learning and Technology*, 9(2), 111–125.

Cobb, T. (1999). Applying constructivism: A test for the learner-as-scientist. *Educational Technology Research and Development*, 47(3), 15–31.

Crosthwaite, P. (Ed.). (2020). *Data-driven learning for the next generation: Corpora and DDL for pre-tertiary learners*. Routledge.

Flowerdew, L. (2015). Data-driven learning and language learning theories: Whither the twain will meet. In *Multiple affordances of language corpora for data-driven learning* (pp. 15–36). Benjamins.

Forti, L., & Jablonkai, R. (2020, August 19). *Data-driven learning for languages other than English: Charting the territory*, Poster presentation. 2020 EuroCALL conference, 'CALL for widening participation', Copenhagen/Online.

Forti, L., & Spina, S. (2019). Corpora for linguists vs. corpora for learners: Bridging the gap in Italian L2 learning and teaching. *EL.LE – Educazione Linguistica. Language Education, 8*(2), 349–362.

Gyllstad, H., & Wolter, B. (2016). Collocational processing in light of the phraseological continuum model: Does semantic transparency matter?: Collocational processing and semantic transparency. *Language Learning, 66*(2), 296–323.

Jaén, M.M. (2009). A corpus-driven design of a test for assessing the ESL collocational competence of university students. *International Journal of English Studies, 7*(2), 127–148.

Jarvis, S. (2000). Methodological rigor in the study of transfer: Identifying L1 influence in the interlanguage lexicon. *Language Learning, 50*(2), 245–309.

Jarvis, S. (2010). Comparison-based and detection-based approaches to transfer research. *EuroSLA Yearbook, 10*, 169–192.

Johns, T. (1991). Should you be persuaded – Two examples of data-driven learning materials. *Classroom Concordancing, English Language Research Journal 4*, 1–13.

Kennedy, C., & Miceli, T. (2001). An evaluation of intermediate students' approaches to corpus investigation. *Language Learning & Technology, 5*(3), 77–90.

Kennedy, C., & Miceli, T. (2010). Corpus-assisted creative writing: Introducing intermediate Italian learners to a corpus as a reference resource. *Language Learning & Technology, 14*(1), 28–44.

Kennedy, C., & Miceli, T. (2016). Cultivating effective corpus use by language learners. *Computer Assisted Language Learning, 30*(1–2), 91–114.

Koya, T. (2005). *The acquisition of basic collocations by Japanese learners of English*. Unpublished PhD Thesis. Waseda University.

Long, M.H. (1990). The least a second language acquisition theory needs to explain. *TESOL Quarterly, 24*, 649–666.

Lyding, V., Borghetti, C., Dittmann, H., Nicolas, L., & Stemle, E. (2013). Open corpus interface for Italian language learning. In *Proceedings of ICT for Language Learning, 6th Edition, Florence (Italy)* (p. 7). Libreriauniversitaria.it Edizioni.

Meurice, A., & Van de Vyver, J. (2017, 12 January). *TELL-OP app: When data-driven learning meets mobile learning*. BAAHE conference 2017, Université catholique de Louvain.

Nesselhauf, N. (2005). *Collocations in a learner corpus*. Benjamins.

O'Keeffe, A. (2020). Data-driven learning – a call for a broader research gaze. *Language Teaching, 54*(2), 259–272.

Pérez-Paredes, P. (2019). A systematic review of the uses and spread of corpora and data-driven learning in CALL research during 2011–2015. *Computer Assisted Language Learning, 35*(1–2), 36–61.

Pérez-Paredes, P., Ordoñana Guillamón, C., Van de Vyver, J., Meurice, A., Aguado Jiménez, P., Conole, G., & Sánchez Hernández, P. (2019). Mobile data-driven language learning: Affordances and learners' perception. *System, 84*, 145–159.

Pérez-Paredes, P., Sánchez-Tornel, M., & Calero, J.M.A. (2012). Learners' search patterns during corpus-based focus-on-form activities: A study on hands-on concordancing. *International Journal of Corpus Linguistics, 17*(4), 482–515.

Riazi, A.M. (2017). *Mixed methods research in language teaching and learning.* Equinox.

Schmidt, R.W. (2012). Attention, awareness, and individual differences in language learning. In W.M. Chan (Ed.), *Proceedings of CLaSIC 2010, Singapore, December 2–4* (pp. 721–737). National University of Singapore, Centre for Language Studies.

VanPatten, B., Keating, G.D., & Wulff, S. (2020). *Theories in second language acquisition* (3rd ed.). Routledge.

Vyatkina, N. (2020). Corpora as open educational resources for language teaching. *Foreign Language Annals, 52*(2), 359–370.

Vygotsky, L.S. (1934). *Thought and language, revised and expanded edition.* The MIT Press.

Wang, Y. (2016). *The idiom principle and L1 influence. A contrastive learner-corpus study of delexical verb+noun collocations.* Benjamins.

Wolter, B., & Yamashita, J. (2018). Word frequency, collocational frequency, L1 congruency, and proficiency in L2 collocational processing: What accounts for L2 performance? *Studies in Second Language Acquisition, 40*(2), 395–416.

Appendix A
Sample experimental lesson plan and activities (week 4)
(lesson plan)

Lezione 4_E

Data: 17, 18, 19 aprile	Durata: 45 minuti
Obiettivi di apprendimento: avere fame preparare la cena sbagliare strada trovare la strada trovare casa affittare un appartamento (o una stanza) dividere un appartamento dividere una spesa	

Materiali:
    1. Compiti per casa corretti.
    2. Test stili di apprendimento.
    3. Dispense con le attività del giorno.
    4. Compito per casa 4.
    5. Fogli compito per casa 1, 2, 3 per eventuali assenti che lo chiedessero.	

Svolgimento della lezione 4_E

Minuti	Attività e procedure	Obiettivi
2	Presenze (usa solo memoria per esercitare il riconoscimento di ogni studente) Resitituisci compiti corretti e raccogli compiti per casa svolti. (dare a tutti indirizzo mail e contatto WeChat) Dare test stili di apprendimento a chi non l'aveva fatto. Distribuire le dispense del giorno, chiedendo di aprire alla pagina con la prima attività.	Ricordare i nomi di tutti.
4	Giusto o sbagliato? *Su questa pagina c'è una lista di 24 combinazioni, con o senza errori. Ditemi quante sono le combinazioni giuste e quante quelle sbagliate. Avete 3 minuti. Chi si avvicina di più, vince.*	Per richiamare alla memoria e consolidare quanto visto le settimane precedenti.
2	Parola mancante. *Su questa pagina ci sono 8 frasi, ma in ogni frase manca una parola: qual è?*	Per introdurre le combinazioni della settimana.
25	Lavoro su concordanze.	Per guidare verso l'osservazione di regolarità d'uso delle combinazioni all'interno delle concordance fornite.
10	Riordina le parole. *Su questa pagina trovate 8 frasi, ma le parole in queste frasi non sono nel posto giusto. Rimettere le parole al loro posto.*	Per riutilizzare e consolidare le caratteristiche d'uso delle combinazioni viste finora.
1	Assegnazione compito per casa. *Su questo foglio ci sono le otto combinazioni che abbiamo fatto oggi. (Insegnante rilegge le otto combinazioni). Per la prossima settimana, scrivete un dialogo tra voi e un'altra persona con queste 8 combinazioni. Quando avete finito, date un titolo al dialogo. Prima di iniziare a scirvere il dialogo, scrivete il contesto, il posto dove le due persone stanno parlando. Per esempio, potete scrivere: 'siamo in un bar, la mattina presto, e c'è molta confusione intorno a noi'. Qual è la prima cosa che si scrive in un dialogo?* (elicita 'nome della persona che parla seguito da due punti').	

Minuti	Attività e procedure	Obiettivi
5	Attività finale: indovina la combinazione	Per concludere la lezione in modo allegro, riutilizzando le combinazioni del giorno e quelle della settimana precedente.
	Sono incluse le combinazioni del giorno e quelle della settimana precedente, dunque 16 in totale, in forma di cartoncini singoli in un sacchetto, che a turno ogni studente prende e deve far indovinare alle squadre attraverso il mimo.	

(Handout with activities)

Lezioni con Luciana

Settimana 4

Giusto o sbagliato? Metti ogni combinazione nella colonna giusta.

1. Fare amicizia
2. Dare un sorriso
3. Avere 25 anni
4. Studiare l'economia
5. Innamorare lo sport
6. Fare passeggiata
7. Prendere il sole
8. Fare una gita
9. Prendere l'aria
10. Avere fretta
11. Pulire casa
12. Spendere soldi
13. Fare le spese
14. Prendere l'autobus
15. Fare colazione
16. Vestire la giacca
17. Avere lezione
18. Rifare il letto
19. Prendere la musica
20. Fare doccia
21. Mandare un messaggio
22. Organizzare una festa
23. Fare auguri
24. Fare un regalo

Combinazioni giuste:	Combinazioni sbagliate:

Soluzione:

Combinazioni giuste: 14!	Combinazioni sbagliate: 10!
1. Fare amicizia 2. Avere 25 anni 3. Prendere il sole 4. Fare una gita 5. Avere fretta 6. Pulire casa 7. Spendere soldi 8. Prendere l'autobus 9. Fare colazione 10. Avere lezione 11. Rifare il letto 12. Mandare un messaggio 13. Organizzare una festa 14. Fare un regalo	1. Dare un sorriso (fare un sorriso) 2. Studiare l'economia (studiare economia) 3. Innamorare lo sport (amare lo sport) 4. Fare passeggiata (fare una passeggiata) 5. Prendere l'aria (prendere aria) 6. Fare le spese (fare spese) 7. Vestire la giacca (mettere la giacca) 8. Prendere la musica (mettere o ascoltare la musica) 9. Fare doccia (fare la doccia) 10. Fare auguri (fare gli auguri)

Componi le 8 combinazioni di questa settimana:

1. VEAEERFAM
A _ _ _ _ F _ _ _

2. RRAERCANAEEPPAL
P _ _ _ _ _ _ _ _ L _ C _ _ _

3. TESSRBAAGRIDLAA
SB _ _ _ _ _ _ _ L _ ST _ _ _ _

4. AVTLSATROAAREDR
TR _ _ _ _ _ L _ S _ _ _ _ _

5. RNVEURAOTNPTPRAOMTAAE
T _ _ _ _ _ _ U _ AP _ _ _ _ _ _ _ _ _ _

6. TANFNFTEAAZRUTAAIS
AF _ _ _ _ _ _ _ _ U _ _ S _ _ _ _ _

7. MVETOIURNDRNEEIPDAPAAT
DI _ _ _ _ _ _ U _ AP _ _ _ _ _ _ _ _ _ _

8. NPEAVESUAIRDDSIE
DI _ _ _ _ _ _ U _ _ SP _ _ _

208   Appendix A

1	Passavo le giornate vagando per questa bellissima. Non avevo	**fame**. Bevevo l'acqua fresca delle fontanelle.
2	'Caterina. E pronto a tavola'. 'Non ho	**fame**, grazie'. 'Ti prego tesoro, vieni'.
3	'Ti ho lasciato da parte le polpette'. 'Grazie, ma non ho	**fame**'.
4	Non voglio essere solo._ **Ho** un'infinita	**fame** d'amore.
5	Non avevo	**fame**, quindi sono entrata in un negozio di dischi.
6	La nuova squadra ha	**fame** di cose nuove.
7	Quando torna da lavoro, **ha** sempre	una **fame** incredibile.
8	**Ho**	**fame** ma non riesco a mangiare.
9	'Li vedi quelli lì? **Hanno** sempre	**fame**'.
10	'Io ho	una **fame** pazzesca, voi?'
11	'Vuoi mangiare qualcosa?' 'Grazie, ho mangiato un panino fuori e non ho	**fame**'.
12	L'opinione pubblica ha	**fame** di notizie.
13	'E mezzogiorno passato. **Ho**	**fame**, voi no?'
14	Appena entro in casa ho già	**fame**.
15	Le persone **hanno**	**fame** di giustizia.

1. In quali frasi c'è un articolo tra *avere* e *fame*?
2. Che tipo di articolo è?
3. In queste frasi, che cosa c'è dopo la parola *fame*?

Insieme ai tuoi compagni di squadra, scrivi qui sotto le risposte e spiega quando si usa l'articolo tra *avere* e *fame*.

....
....
....

4. n quali frasi *avere fame* non 6 riferito al cibo
5. Se non 6 riferito al cibo, a cosa si riferisce la combinazione?
6. In queste frasi, che parole ci sono dopo *fame*?

Insieme ai tuoi compagni di squadra, scrivi qui sotto le risposte e spiega quando la combinazione *avere* + *fame* non si riferisce al cibo.

....
....
....

Appendix A

Scrivi la parola che manca in ogni gruppo di frasi:

1. ....

Si è fatto molto tardi, devo	la cena.
Poi sono andata in cucina per	una cena veloce.
La mamma aveva passato it pomeriggio a	la cena.
Quel giorno sono tornata a casa prima per	una cena speciale.
Ho appena finito di	la cena.

2. ....

Ma qui dove siamo? Forse abbiamo	strada.
Quando non hai impegni di lavoro, anche	strada è Bello.
Ammettiamolo: hai	strada.
Era stata un'avventura straordinaria,	strada in quelle notti buie.
Ho capito di aver	strada.

3. ....

Prova a	la strada giusta.
Come	la strada di casa in mezzo a gente che non capisce?
Finalmente ho	la strada e it numero di casa tùa.
Dobbiamo	la strada migliore per uscire da questa crisi.
Non più	la strada.

Appendix A 211

4. ....

Abbiamo trovato	in	bellissimo, vicino al mare.
Forse riusciamo a trovate	un	in cui c'è posto anche per i nostri cugini.
Ho trovato	un	in centro da condividere con altri studenti.
Lucia ha trovato	un	troppo piccolo per ospitare anche i genitori
Alla fine, siamo riusciti a trovare	un	in via Vignoli.

5. ....

Se hai bisogno di un posto per dormire, posso		una stanza a casa mia.
Ho		una stanza in un quartiere bruttissimo.
Chi ha una stanza vuota in casa, può		la stanza.
Matteo		una stanza molto grande in un appartamento con altre due ragazze.
Quella famiglia non		stanze agli studenti.

6. ....

L'amica che		l'appartamento con una ragazza spagnola, Pilar.
Mi piacerebbe moltissimo		l'appartamento con me si è trasferita a Milano.
Spero che altri amici vorranno dividere		l'appartamento con altri colleghi.
C'era anche Carlo, con cui dividevo		l'appartamento con noi.
		lo stesso appartamento.

7. ....

Nessuno di voi due ha voluto	la spesa.
A pranzo qualcuno cucinava e poi si	le spese.
Se organizziamo un gruppo di viaggio, possiamo	le spese.
Visto the abbiamo case vicine, usiamo lo stesso wi-fi e	le spese.
Possiamo viaggiare con una sola macchina e poi	le spese della benzina.

Soluzioni:

1. preparare
2. sbagliare
3. trovare
4. appartamento
5. affittare
6. dividere
7. dividere

Appendix A

Rimetti le parole nell'ordine giusto:

1. a Andiamo una ho cena, pazzesca! fame

   ....

2. abbiamo sbagliato Forse siamo? strada. Dove

   ....

3. cena. Mentre una la preparo ti io doccia, tu fai

   ....

4. trovi ti strada. tua tu che Desidero la

   ....

5. mare. Abbiamo appartamento un trovato bellissimo al vicino

   ....

6. Vorrei all'università. vicino stanza una affittare

   ....

7. con un dividere appartamento piacerebbe Mi colleghi. altri molto

   ....

8. tutte viaggio insieme, le Quando un dividiamo spese. facciamo

   ....

Soluzione:

1. Andiamo a cena, ho una fame pazzesca!

2. Dove siamo? Forse abbiamo sbagliato strada.

3. Mentre tu ti fai una doccia, io preparo la cena.

4. Desidero che tu ti trovi la tua strada.

5. Abbiamo trovato un bellissimo appartamento vicino al mare.

6. Vorrei affittare una stanza vicino all'università.

7. Mi piacerebbe molto dividere un appartamento con altri colleghi.

8. Quando facciamo un viaggio insieme, dividiamo tutte le spese.

Appendix B
Sample control lesson plan and activities (week 4)
(Lesson plan)

Lezione 4_C

Data: 17, 18, 19 aprile	Durata: 45 minuti
Obiettivi di apprendimento: avere fame preparare la cena sbagliare strada trovare la strada trovare casa affittare un appartamento (o una stanza) dividere un appartamento dividere una spesa	
Materiali: 1. Compiti per casa corretti. 2. Test stili di apprendimento. 3. Dispense con le attività del giorno. 4. Compito per casa 4. 5. Fogli compito per casa 1, 2, 3 per eventuali assenti che lo chiedessero.	

Appendix B 217

Svolgimento della lezione 4_C

Minuti	Attività e procedure	Obiettivi
2	Presenze (usa solo memoria per esercitare il riconoscimento di ogni studente) Resitituisci compiti corretti e raccogli compiti per casa svolti. (dare a tutti indirizzo mail e contatto WeChat) Dare test stili di apprendimento a chi non l'aveva fatto. Distribuire le dispense del giorno, chiedendo di aprire alla pagina con la prima attività.	Ricordare i nomi di tutti.
4	Giusto o sbagliato? *Su questa pagina c'è una lista di 24 combinazioni, con o senza errori. Ditemi quante sono le combinazioni giuste e quante quelle sbagliate. Avete 3 minuti. Chi si avvicina di più, vince.*	Per richiamare alla memoria e consolidare quanto visto le settimane precedenti.
2	Combinazioni anagrammate Parola mancante. *Su questa pagina ci sono 8 frasi, ma in ogni frase manca una parola: qual è?*	Per introdurre le combinazioni della settimana.
10	Riordina le parole. *Su questa pagina trovate 8 frasi, ma le parole in queste frasi non sono nel posto giusto. Rimettere le parole al loro posto.* Inventa una frase. Per ogni combinazione, inventa una frase.	Per riutilizzare e consolidare le caratteristiche d'uso delle combinazioni viste finora.
1	Assegnazione compito per casa. *Su questo foglio ci sono le otto combinazioni che abbiamo fatto oggi. (Insegnante rilegge le otto combinazioni). Per la prossima settimana, scrivete un dialogo tra voi e un'altra persona con queste 8 combinazioni. Quando avete finito, date un titolo al dialogo. Prima di iniziare a scirvere il dialogo, scrivete il contesto, il posto dove le due persone stanno parlando. Per esempio, potete scrivere: 'siamo in un bar, la mattina presto, e c'è molta confusione intorno a noi'.*	

218 Appendix B

Minuti	Attività e procedure	Obiettivi
	Qual è la prima cosa che si scrive in un dialogo? (elicita 'nome della persona che parola seguito da due punti').	
5	Attività finale: indovina la combinazione	Per concludere la lezione in modo allegro, riutilizzando le combinazioni del giorno e quelle della settimana precedente.
	Sono incluse le combinazioni del giorno e quelle della settimana precedente, dunque 16 in totale, in forma di cartoncini singoli in un sacchetto, che a turno ogni studente prende e deve far indovinare alle squadre attraverso il mimo.	

(Handout with activities)

Lezioni con Luciana

Settimana 4

Giusto o sbagliato? Metti ogni combinazione nella colonna giusta.

1. Fare amicizia
2. Dare un sorriso
3. Avere 25 anni
4. Studiare l'economia
5. Innamorare lo sport
6. Fare passeggiata
7. Prendere il sole
8. Fare una gita
9. Prendere l'aria
10. Avere fretta
11. Pulire casa
12. Spendere soldi
13. Fare le spese
14. Prendere l'autobus
15. Fare colazione
16. Vestire la giacca
17. Avere lezione
18. Rifare il letto
19. Prendere la musica
20. Fare doccia
21. Mandare un messaggio
22. Organizzare una festa
23. Fare auguri
24. Fare un regalo

Combinazioni giuste:	Combinazioni sbagliate:

Soluzione:

Combinazioni giuste: 14!	Combinazioni sbagliate: 10!
1. Fare amicizia 2. Avere 25 anni 3. Prendere il sole 4. Fare una gita 5. Avere fretta 6. Pulire casa 7. Spendere soldi 8. Prendere l'autobus 9. Fare colazione 10. Avere lezione 11. Rifare il letto 12. Mandare un messaggio 13. Organizzare una festa 14. Fare un regalo	15. Dare un sorriso (fare un sorriso) 16. Studiare l'economia (studiare economia) 17. Innamorare lo sport (amare lo sport) 18. Fare passeggiata (fare una passeggiata) 19. Prendere l'aria (prendere aria) 20. Fare le spese (fare spese) 21. Vestire la giacca (mettere la giacca) 22. Prendere la musica (mettere o ascoltare la musica) 23. Fare doccia (fare la doccia) 24. Fare auguri (fare gli auguri)

Appendix B 223

Componi le 8 combinazioni di questa settimana:

1. VEAEERFAM
A _ _ _ _ F _ _ _

2. RRAERCANAEEPPAL
P _ _ _ _ _ _ _ _ L _ C _ _ _

3. TESSRBAAGRIDLAA
SB _ _ _ _ _ _ _ L _ ST _ _ _ _

4. AVTLSATROAAREDR
TR _ _ _ _ _ L _ S _ _ _ _ _

5. RNVEURAOTNPTPRAOMTAAE
T _ _ _ _ _ _ U _ AP _ _ _ _ _ _ _ _ _ _

6. TANFNFTEAAZRUTAAIS
AF _ _ _ _ _ _ _ U _ _ S _ _ _ _ _

7. MVETOIURNDRNEEIPDAPAAT
DI _ _ _ _ _ _ U _ AP _ _ _ _ _ _ _ _ _ _

8. NPEAVESUAIRDDSIE
DI _ _ _ _ _ _ U _ _ SP _ _ _

Appendix B

Soluzione:

1. AVERE FAME

2. PREPARARE LA CENA

3. SBAGLIARE STRADA

4. TROVARE LA STRADA

5. TROVARE UN APPARTAMENTO

6. AFFITTARE UNA STANZA

7. DIVIDERE UN APPARTAMENTO

8. DIVIDERE UNA SPESA

In ogni frase, manca una parola. La parola può essere un verbo, un articolo o un nome. Scrivi la parola che manca.

1. 'Caterina. È pronto a tavola'. 'Non _____ fame, grazie'.

2. Vado a preparare _____ cena. Stasera ho ospiti.

3. Quando non hai impegni di lavoro, anche _____ strada è bello.

4. A volte, è difficile _____ la strada giusta.

5. Finalmente, ho _____ un appartamento da condividere con altre quattro persone.

6. Riccardo aveva _____ l'appartamento dell'ultimo piano a uno studente di medicina.

7. Quando vivevo a Milano, _____ l'appartamento con una ragazza spagnola, Pilar.

8. Se organizziamo un gruppo di viaggio, possiamo _____ le spese.

Soluzione:

1. 'Caterina. È pronto a tavola'. 'Non <u>ho</u> fame, grazie'.

2. Vado a preparare <u>la</u> cena. Stasera ho ospiti.

3. Quando non hai impegni di lavoro, anche <u>sbagliare</u> strada è bello.

4. A volte, è difficile <u>trovare</u> la strada giusta.

5. Finalmente, ho <u>trovato</u> un appartamento da condividere con altre 4 persone.

6. Riccardo aveva <u>affittato</u> l'appartamento dell'ultimo piano a uno studente di medicina.

7. Quando vivevo a Milano, <u>dividevo</u> l'appartamento con una ragazza spagnola, Pilar.

8. Se organizziamo un gruppo di viaggio, possiamo <u>dividere</u> le spese.

Rimetti le parole nell'ordine giusto:

1) a Andiamo una ho cena, pazzesca! fame

   ....

2) abbiamo sbagliato Forse siamo? strada. Dove

   ....

3) cena. Mentre una la preparo ti io doccia, tu fai

   ....

4) trovi ti strada. tua tu che Desidero la

   ....

5) mare. Abbiamo appartamento un trovato bellissimo al vicino

   ....

6) Vorrei all'università. vicino stanza una affittare

   ....

7) con un dividere appartamento piacerebbe Mi colleghi. altri molto

   ....

8) tutte viaggio insieme, le Quando un dividiamo spese. facciamo

   ....

Soluzione:

1) Andiamo a cena, ho una fame pazzesca!

2) Dove siamo? Forse abbiamo sbagliato strada.

3) Mentre tu ti fai una doccia, io preparo la cena.

4) Desidero che tu ti trovi la tua strada.

5) Abbiamo trovato un bellissimo appartamento vicino al mare.

6) Vorrei affittare una stanza vicino all'università.

7) Mi piacerebbe molto dividere un appartamento con altri colleghi.

8) Quando facciamo un viaggio insieme, dividiamo tutte le spese.

Appendix B 229

Inventa una frase per ciascuna combinazione:

1. AVERE FAME

....

2. PREPARARE LA CENA

....

3. SBAGLIARE STRADA

....

4. TROVARE LA STRADA

....

5. TROVARE UN APPARTAMENTO

....

6. AFFITTARE UNA STANZA

....

7. DIVIDERE UN APPARTAMENTO

....

8. DIVIDERE UNA SPESA

....

Appendix C
Phraseological competence test
Test

Data: _____

Nome (cinese e italiano): _____

Codice studente: _____ Codice del corso: _____

Scegli l'opzione corretta.

1. In estate vorrei…
a. fare viaggio
b. fare la viaggio
c. fare un viaggio
d. nessuna di queste

2. Mi sono trasferito per…
a. avere nuove esperienze
b. fare le nuove esperienze
c. fare nuove esperienze
d. nessuna di queste

3. Molti italiani…
a. innamorano lo sport
b. amano sport
c. prendono sport
d. nessuna di queste

4. Quando ci sono i saldi, moltissime persone…
a. fanno shopping
b. fanno il shopping
c. hanno shopping
d. nessuna di queste

5. Prima di uscire di casa…
a. vestiamo la giacca
b. ci mettiamo la giacca
c. ci vestiamo la giacca
d. nessuna di queste

6. Nei pomeriggi di primavera è piacevole…
a. fare la passeggiata
b. fare passeggiata
c. fare una passeggiata
d. nessuna di queste

7. In estate, a molte persone piace…
a. spendere il sole
b. avere il sole
c. prendere il sole
d. nessuna di queste

8. Un'attività molto comune è...
a. ascoltare la musica
b. prendere la musica
c. prendere musica
d. nessuna di queste

9. Le foto sono belle per...
a. ricordare un'esperienza
b. commemorare esperienze
c. commemorare il esperienza
d. nessuna di queste

10. Ogni settimana, dal lunedì al venerdì, ...
a. abbiamo lezione
b. abbiamo la lezione
c. abbiamo una lezione
d. nessuna di queste

11. Se qualcuno ci chiede la nostra età, possiamo rispondere...
a. sono 25 anni
b. faccio 25 anni
c. ho 25 anni
d. nessuna di queste

12. Quando una persona è contenta...
a. fa un sorriso
b. dà un sorriso
c. mette un sorriso
d. nessuna di queste

13. Claudio vuole...
a. fare l'artista
b. fare artista
c. fare un artista
d. nessuna di queste

14. Dopo una lunga passeggiata, spesso...
a. siamo fame
b. abbiamo fame
c. facciamo fame
d. nessuna di queste

15. Quando ci svegliamo la mattina...
a. prendiamo la colazione
b. facciamo una colazione
c. mettiamo la colazione
d. nessuna di queste

16. Dopo molte ore di studio, è una buona idea...
a. prendere aria
b. dare aria
c. avere aria
d. nessuna di queste

17. Ai nonni piace spesso...
a. dire una storia
b. raccontare una storia
c. dire storia
d. nessuna di queste

18. Nel fine settimana, molte persone...
a. fanno la gita
b. hanno una gita
c. fanno una gita
d. nessuna di queste

19. Diventare amico o amica di una persona significa...
a. ritirare amicizia
b. fare amici
c. fare amicizia
d. nessuna di queste

20. Una persona sportiva...
a. fa sport
b. fa lo sport
c. ha sport
d. nessuna di queste

21. Chi vuole diventare musicista deve...
a. studiare le musiche
b. studiare musica
c. studiare la musica
d. nessuna di queste

22. La biblioteca è il posto perfetto per...
a. leggere il romanzo
b. leggere romanzo
c. leggere un romanzo
d. nessuna di queste

23. Per comprare qualcosa che costa molto, bisogna...
a. salvare soldi
b. risparmiare soldi
c. salvare i soldi
d. nessuna di queste

24. Nel tempo libero, molti studenti...
a. suonano chitarra
b. giocano la chitarra
c. giocano una chitarra
d. nessuna di queste

25. Andiamo al cinema per...
a. guardare il film
b. vedere film
c. vedere il film
d. nessuna di queste

26. Per andare all'università, alcuni studenti devono...
a. prendere l'autobus
b. prendere autobus
c. avere autobus
d. nessuna di queste

27. La settimana scorsa, io e i miei amici abbiamo...
a. guardato la città
b. guardato città
c. visitato la città
d. nessuna di queste

28. Quando visito un posto nuovo, mi piace...
a. godere i cibi del posto
b. gustare i cibi del posto
c. godere cibi del posto
d. nessuna di queste

29. Viaggiare significa...
a. imparare conoscenze
b. imparare la conoscenza
c. ampliare le conoscenze
d. nessuna di queste

30. Una persona che studia pittura, spesso...
a. dipinge le pitture
b. dipinge quadri
c. dipinge pitture
d. nessuna di queste

31. Quando torniamo a casa la sera...
a. prepariamo cena
b. cuciniamo cena
c. prepariamo la cena
d. nessuna di queste

32. Se vediamo qualcosa di bello, possiamo...
a. fare il foto
b. prendere foto
c. fare una foto
d. nessuna di queste

Appendix C 233

Scrivi il verbo che manca.

1. Tra poco, il film al cinema inizierà. _____ una doccia e andiamo.

2. Appena arrivo ti _____ un messaggio.

3. Ho deciso di _____ casa e trovarmi un posto con un terrazzino.

4. Abbiamo un giorno e una notte per _____ una soluzione.

5. Possiamo creare un gruppo di viaggio e _____ le spese, così risparmiamo e non perdiamo molto tempo per il viaggio.

6. Non mi sembra di essere adatto a _____ consigli sentimentali.

7. Ho bisogno di consigli per _____ un viaggio.

8. Non _____ dubbi, quasi mai. Sapeva come raggiungere un obiettivo.

9. Abbiamo _____ la spesa al supermercato, poi abbiamo mangiato e adesso facciamo una passseggiata.

10. Alcuni venivano costretti a fare pulizia e a _____ i letti.

11. Mi compro un nuovo vestito. _____ soldi mi dà soddisfazione.

12. In alcuni Paesi, quando uno studente decide di iscriversi all'università, deve _____ un esame di ammissione.

13. Mi piacerebbe moltissimo _____ un appartamento con altre persone, per avere uno scambio più intenso.

14. D'inverno, doveva _____ il treno ogni giorno per andare a scuola in città.

15. Il romanzo 'Fontamara' ha _____ successo in tutto il mondo.

16. C'è molta gente fuori che _____ la fila per entrare. Vogliono entrare tutti.

17. Era molto riservato e non _____ i consigli degli altri.

18. Ma qui dove siamo? Forse ho _____ strada.

234   *Appendix C*

19. Per il mio compleanno, le mie amiche hanno _____ una festa a sorpresa.

20. Tommaso, sei uno sciocco; su questo non ho _____ opinione.

21. Dopo essermi perso, ho finalmente _____ la strada.

22. Sono entrata in un negozio di dischi, perché volevo _____ un regalo a Diego.

23. Voglio _____ tanti auguri di buon compleanno a Marco.

24. Non bisogna passare il fine settimana a _____ la casa.

25. _____ le valigie e andiamo via.

26. Litigavamo e facevamo pace. E poi ci piaceva _____ la musica a tutto volume.

27. Se hai bisogno di un posto dove stare, ti posso _____ una stanza a casa mia.

28. Se pensate di _____ un'idea buona per migliorare il mondo in cui viviamo, cercate di realizzarla.

29. Di solito non _____ consigli per scegliere i libri, ma leggo tutto quello che trovo.

30. Lo stimavo come artista, quindi è bastato poco per _____ amici, e scoprire le cose che avevamo in comune.

31. Sono innamorati e vogliono vivere insieme, ma è difficile _____ casa per una coppia con poco lavoro.

32. Aspettiamo da mezz'ora! _____ fretta, dobbiamo andare a lavorare!

Appendix D
End-of-course student questionnaire (DDL group)

Lezioni con Luciana: come sono state?
跟Luciana学意大利语：感觉如何？

Grazie mille per aver partecipato alle mie lezioni! Rispondendo alle domande qui sotto, mi aiuterai a migliorarle per il futuro.
非常感谢大家参加了我的课程！请回答以下的问题，来帮助我提高以后的教学水平。

1= totalmente in disaccordo 完全不赞同

2= in disaccordo 不赞同

3= parzialmente in disaccordo 部分不赞同

4= parzialmente d'accordo 部分赞同

5= d'accordo 赞同

6= totalmente d'accordo 完全

	1	2	3	4	5	6
	totalmente in disaccordo 完全不赞同	*in disaccordo* 不赞同	*parzialmente in disaccordo* 部分不赞同	*parzialmente d'accordo* 部分赞同	*d'accordo* 赞同	*totalmente d'accordo* 完全赞同
1. Studiare le combinazioni di parole è stato utile. 学习词语组合非常有用。						
2. Lavorare con gli altri compagni di classe ha rallentato il mio apprendimento. 和班上其他同学的分组合作减慢了我的学习。						
3. I commenti sui compiti per casa mi hanno aiutato a scrivere meglio. 家庭作业上的批语帮助我写的更好。						
4. Fare esercizi su otto combinazioni in un'ora è stato troppo impegnativo. 一个小时完成八个词语组合的练习太费劲了。						
5. Leggere molte frasi con la stessa combinazione mi ha confuso. 阅读同一词组的很多例句会让我混淆。						
6. Osservare molte frasi con la stessa combinazione mi ha aiutato a capire come usare quella combinazione in futuro. 观察同一个词组在不同例句中的应用帮助我明白之后如何使用该词组。						

	1	2	3	4	5	6
	totalmente in disaccordo 完全不赞同	*in disaccordo* 不赞同	*parzialmente in disaccordo* 部分不赞同	*parzialmente d'accordo* 部分赞同	*d'accordo* 赞同	*totalmente d'accordo* 完全赞同
7. I gruppi di frasi mi aiuteranno a fare meno errori in futuro. 句子群体的练习会让我以后出现更少的错误。						
8. Una nuova applicazione per cellulari con un elenco di frasi per ogni combinazione di parole sarebbe inutile. 如果有一个新的手机软件能够给每个词组都配备一系列的例句应该没什么用。						

Che cosa ti è piaciuto di più del corso? 你喜欢该课程的哪些部分呢？

Che cosa ti è piaciuto di meno del corso? 该课程的哪些部分你不喜欢呢？

Descrivi il corso con tre aggettivi: 用三个形容词来描述这个课程：

Altre idee e suggerimenti: 其它想法和建议：

GRAZIE!

Appendix E
End-of-course student questionnaire (non-DDL group)

Lezioni con Luciana: come sono state?
跟Luciana学意大利语：感觉如何？

Grazie mille per aver partecipato alle mie lezioni! Rispondendo alle domande qui sotto, mi aiuterai a migliorarle per il futuro.
非常感谢大家参加了我的课程！请回答以下的问题，来帮助我提高以后的教学水平。

1= totalmente in disaccordo 完全不赞同
2= in disaccordo 不赞同
3= parzialmente in disaccordo 部分不赞同
4= parzialmente d'accordo 部分赞同
5= d'accordo 赞同
6= totalmente d'accordo 完全

	1	2	3	4	5	6
	totalmente in disaccordo 完全不赞同	in disaccordo 不赞同	parzialmente in disaccordo 部分不赞同	parzialmente d'accordo 部分赞同	d'accordo 赞同	totalmente d'accordo 完全赞同
1. Studiare le combinazioni di parole è stato utile. 学习词语组合非常有用。						
2. Lavorare con gli altri compagni di classe ha rallentato il mio apprendimento. 和班上其他同学的分组合作减慢了我的学习。						
3. I commenti sui compiti per casa mi hanno aiutato a scrivere meglio. 家庭作业上的批语帮助我写的更好。						
4. Fare esercizi su otto combinazioni in un'ora è stato troppo impegnativo. 一个小时完成八个词语组合的练习太费劲了。						

Che cosa ti è piaciuto di più del corso? 你喜欢该课程的哪些部分呢？

Che cosa ti è piaciuto di meno del corso? 该课程的哪些部分你不喜欢呢？

Descrivi il corso con tre aggettivi: 用三个形容词来描述这个课程：

Altre idee e suggerimenti: 其它想法和建议：

GRAZIE!

Index

Note: Page numbers in **bold** indicate tables; those in *italics* indicate figures.

Academy of Fine Arts 104, 123
adjacency of collocations 117, 119
Akaike Information Criterion (AIC), DDL study: DDL effects over time 144; L1-L2 congruency 151; phraseological knowledge, dimensions of 154; semantic transparency 148
Alliance of Digital Humanities Organizations (ADHO) 106n3
Altenberg, B. 114
annotators 79
AntConc 70, 104
Aquinas, T. 86–87
Association for Computers in the Humanities (ACH) 87
Association for Literary and Linguistic Computing (ALLC) 87
audio recording of search strategies 74
authenticity of examples 2, 15; debate 33–34; language theories 19; learner attitudes 122; response to DDL 49–51, 53; transferable knowledge 122
authority, as source of knowledge 61–62

background questionnaires 72–73
Bacon, F. 62
Balboni, P.E. 90
Baldwin, T. **113**
Barr, D.J. 144
Bax, S. 24
BELI (*Bibliografia dell'Educazione Linguistica in Italia*) 90–92, **91**, **92**
Bennett, G. 27
Bernardini, S. 50–51

between-groups study design 76; control groups 77; DDL study 121, 157–158
Bibliografia dell'Educazione Linguistica in Italia see BELI
Biblioteca di italiano e oltre 88
Biskup, D. 161–162
BNClab 32
Boers, F. 81n5, 119
Bond, F. **113**
book chapters on Italian L2 learning and teaching 29
books on DDL 27
Booth, W.C. 64, 80
Boulton, A. 4–5, 24–28, 30, 32, 42–45, 47–48, **48**, 59, 75–78, 121, 157–159, 182–183, 191, 193
Bratankova, L. 101, 119
Braun, S. 32–34
Brown corpus of American written English 85
Bulté, B. 114
Busa, R. 86–87
Busa Award 87

CAEL (Computerizzazione delle Analisi Ermeneutiche Lessicologiche) 86–87
CAIL2 (*Corpus di Apprendenti di Italiano L2*) 101, **102**, 119
CALICO 97
CALL 24
Candlin, C. 27
Capel, A. 27
Carter, R. 19
Ceccotti, M.L. 30
CELI 101, **103**; exams 107n32
CELTA 54

Centro Nazionale di Calcolo Elettronico 87
Chalmers, A. 63
Chambers, A. 4, 24, 49–52, 74
chapters on Italian L2 learning and teaching 29
Cheng, W. 50–51
Chiari, I. 31, 89
Chinese L1 learners of Italian: DIY corpora 104; L2 corpora 101; phraseological competence development 120; *see also* data-driven learning study
Choi, S. 117
Chomsky, N. 21
Christensen, L. 60–62
Chujo, K. 4, 26, 43–44, **47–48**, 48, 159, 182–183
CLIPS (*Corpora e Lessici dell'Italiano Parlato e Scritto*) **95**, 98
CNR – Istituto di Linguistica Computazionale di Pisa 87
Cobb, T. 4, 22, 24, 26, 32, 43–45, **47–48**, 48, 76, 157, 159, 182–183, 190
COBUILD project 20, 27
COCA (*Corpus of Contemporary American English*) 24
coding procedures 78–79
Cohen, J. 43
Cohen's *d* 43–44
CoLFIS (*Corpus e Lessico di Frequenza dell'Italiano Scritto*) **94**, 97
COLI (*Corpus of Chinese Learners of Italian*) 101, **102**
Collins COBUILD Concordance Sampler 27
collocations *see* phraseological units and collocations
comparison groups 76–77, 81n5
competence tests 74; DDL study 128–131, 162, 181, 193, 230–234
complexity theory 24
computer-based DDL: effectiveness 45–46, 159; etic data collection tools 74; reluctance to use 32–33; research methodology 71–72; response to 50–52
concordances: AntConc 104; cotext vs. context debate 34; DDL pedagogy 15–16; DDL research and SLA research evidence, need to connect 190; DDL study 121–122, 127–128, 158–159, 170, 179–180, 182–183; effectiveness 46; frequency effects 192; future research 196; input-enhancement 23–24; involvement load hypothesis 24; L1 background 159; Lancsbox 105; presentation 16; reading 33; research methodology 70–72; response to 50–52; *viso* 15–16, *16*; Voyant Tools 105
Concordances in the Classroom (C. Tribble and G. Jones) 27
conference proceedings 29, 30
confounding variables 77
congruency: collocations 117; L1-L2 *see* L1-L2 congruency; teaching context 118
consent forms 73
Conservatorium of Music 104, 123
constructionist theories of language 20–21
constructivist learning theory 22, 23, 190
context vs. cotext debate 34, 50–52
contextual theory of meaning 18–19, 114
control groups 76–77, 81n5
convenience sampling 66, 68, 69
Copestake, A. **113**
C-ORAL-ROM (*Integrated Reference Corpora for Spoken Romance Languages*) **94**, 98
CORDIC **95**, 98
Corino, E. 31
CORIS/CODIS (*Corpus di Italiano Scritto – Corpus dinamico di italiano scritto*) **94**
CORITE (*CORpus del Italiano de los Españoles*) 100–101, **103**
corpora: ad hoc 33; apprenticeship in use of 55; data limitations 51; data relevance 33; direct use of *see* data-driven learning; DIY 104–105; empirical evidence, need for 59; exploration difficulties 51; future directions 196–197; for linguistics and for learners, gap between 31; mental 21; pedagogical value 12–13; preliminary training myth 33; research methodology 70–72; results interpretation difficulties 52; sampling criteria 1; teacher/learner-friendly 32; teachers unsure how to use 53; time demands 53; uses 1–4, *3*

242 Index

Corpora and Language Education
 (L. Flowerdew) 27
Corpora e Lessici dell'Italiano Parlato e Scritto see CLIPS
Corpus, Concordance, Collocation
 (J.M. Sinclair) 19
CORpus del Italiano de los Españoles see CORITE
Corpus di Apprendenti di Italiano L2 see CAIL2
Corpus di Italiano Scritto – Corpus dinamico di italiano scritto see CORIS/CODIS
Corpus e Lessico de Frequenza dell'Italiano Scritto see CoLFIS
Corpus for Schools project 28, 32, 71
corpus linguistics 85; *see also* Italian corpus linguistics
Corpus of Chinese Learners of Italian see COLI
Corpus of Contemporary American English (COCA) 24
cotext vs. context debate 34, 50–52
Cotos, E. 76
Craft of research, The (W.C. Booth et al.) 80
Cramer, D. 42, 78–79
Cresti, E. 89
Croce, B. 89

Daskalovska, N. 76
data analysis 79–80, 193; DDL study 130–133, **132–133**, 166
data coding 78–79
data collection 72–76, 193; DDL study 122, **123**, 128–130, 166; future research 196
data-driven learning (DDL): debates 32–34; defined 2, 4; effectiveness 42–49, 54–56, 121; evolution 25–28; normalisation 5, 24, 27, 54, 59, 69, 182–183, 196; origins 12–15; pedagogy 15–18; pedagogy theories 18–25; publications on Italian L2 learning and teaching 28–31, *29*; resources and affordances 93–105, **94–96, 102–103**; response of learners 49–52, 121, 133, 166–185, **167–173**, *175–178*, 188–189, 196; response of teachers 52–54; terminology 4; *see also* data-driven learning effects over time; data-driven learning study; research into DDL

data-driven learning effects over time 120–121, 130–131, 140, 156–158, 160, 187–188; descriptive overview 140–142, *141, 143*, **144**; modelling 142–147, *145, 146, 147, 147*
data-driven learning study (DDL study) 187–189; data analysis 130–133, **132–133**; DDL effects over time 140–148; design 122, **123**, 157–158; dimensions of phraseological knowledge 152–156; findings 140–163; L1-L2 congruency 149–152; length 156–157, 182, 194; operationalising the DDL construct 124–128, **126–127**; participants 157; phraseological competence test 122, **123**, 123, 128–131, 162, 171, 181, 193, 230–234; population and participant sample 122–124, *124*, **125**; rationale, research questions, and hypotheses 120–122; reflecting on 193–194; research questions 130–133, 140; sample control lesson plan and activities (week 4) 216–229; sample experimental lesson plan and activities (week 4) 200–215; semantic transparency 148–149; student questionnaire 129–130, 235–239
data interaction modalities 71
data interpretation 80
data types 78
De Mauro, T. 87
definitional knowledge: DDL research and SLA research evidence, need to connect 190; DDL study 121–122, 131–133, 140, 152, 155, *155*, 162, 188
dependent variables 77
descriptive statistics 79–80
DICI – A project 119, 125
dictionaries: of collocations or word combinations 119; vs. DDL 50, 52, 55
discourse competence 45
discovery-based approach 51
DIY corpora 104–105
Dörnyei, Z. 75, 130
dual-route model of language processing 116
Ducati, R. 31
Durrant, P. 118–119, 161

effect sizes 42–43; *see also* Cohen's *d*; unbiased *d*

emic dimension 73, 78; data collection 73–75; DDL research and SLA research evidence, need to connect 190; DDL study 129–130, 193–194; within-groups study design 158
empiricism, as source of knowledge 62–63
Enciclopedia Italiana 87
English corpus linguistics 85
English language pedagogy 195; DDL empirical research methods 194; DDL research 5–7; effectiveness of DDL 43–47, **47–48**; evolution of DDL 25, 26; origins of DDL 12–15; semantic transparency/opacity 160–161
Erman, B. 114
etic dimension 73, 78; data collection 73–75; DDL study 128–129, 140, 193–194; gamified language assessment 181; language gains according to proficiency level 183
Eurac Research 100–101
European Association for Digital Humanities 106n3
explicit vs. implicit knowledge 60
explicit vs. implicit language 191
Exploring Academic English (J. Thurstun and C. Candlin) 27
externalised vs. internalised language 21
extracting instances from corpora 15
eye-tracking studies 74, 196

Facebook 87
Fare i conti con le parole (S. Spina) 88–89
Farr, F. 53
Firth, J.R. 18–19, 114
FLAX 32
Flickinger, D. **113**
Flowerdew, L. 27, 190–191
focus groups 75
formulaic language *see* phraseology
formulaic units/sequences *see* phraseological units and collocations
Forti, L. 31, 54, 93, 159, 161–162, 182–183
Francis, G. 20
Frankenberg-Garcia, A. 53, 76
French language, Belgian L1 learners of 159
frequency effects 192
frequency lists *see* word lists

frequency-of-encounters effect 118
frequency of phraseological units and collocations 113–114, 117–118
Friginal, E. 32
From Corpus to Classroom (A. O'Keeffe) 27
From Printout to Handout (T. Johns) 14
Fundación Tomás de Aquino 86

Gablasova, D. 28, 32, 71
Gabrielatos, C. 24
gamified language assessment 181
gap-fill tasks 14
Gass, S.M. 73
Giacalone Ramat, A. 100
Gilquin, G. 4, 117–118
Goldberg, A.E. 20–21
Goodale, M. 27
grammatical items 44
Granger, S. 2–4
Gries, S.T. 80
Guide to Patterns and Usage in English, A (A.S. Hornby) 20
guided discovery 14
Guidetti, M.G. 31
Gulpease 98
Gyllstad, H. 117, 160–161

Halliday, M.A.K. 19–20
Hasselgren, A. 115
Henriksen, B. 115, 119
Hirvela, A. 50–52
Hoey, M. 21
Hornby, A.S. 20
Horst, M. 76
Housen, A. 114
Howitt, D. 42, 78–79
how-to guides 27
Hunston, S. 20
hypotheses: DDL study 121–122; empirically testable 64; formulation 63–64; sample and population 65

IBM 86, 87
idiom principle, language use 19, 112–113
implicit vs. explicit knowledge 60
implicit vs. explicit language 191
incidental learning 192
Incorporating corpora project 28, 32
independent variables 77–78
Index Thomisticum Online 86–87

244 Index

inductive approach of DDL 51
inferential statistics 79–80
input enhancement 23–24
Integrated Reference Corpora for Spoken Romance Languages see C-ORAL-ROM
internalised vs. externalised language 21
interviews 75
Introduzione ai corpora dell'italiano (E. Cresti and A. Panunzi) 89
Introduzione alla linguistica computazionale (I. Chiari) 89
intuition, as source of knowledge 61
involvement load hypothesis 24
Italian corpora: DIY 104–105; L1 93–99, **94–96**; L2 99–104, **102–103**
Italian corpus linguistics: contributing to 195; DDL resources and affordances 93–105, **94–96, 102–103**; history 85–89; in Italian L2 landscape 90–93, **91, 92**
ItTenTen16 **95**
ItTenTen20 98
Ivanovska-Naskova, R. 31

Jablonkai, R. 31
Jaèn, M.M. 118, 129
Jiang, N. 118–119, 162
Johns, T. 2, 14–16, 22, 28, 71, 197
Jones, G. 27
judgment sampling 66, *68*, 69; DDL study 123, *124*, 194
justtheword 32

Kahoot 181
Karpenko-Seccombe, T. 32
Kavanagh, B. 54
Kennedy, C. 30, 54–56, 92
key-logging 74, 75, 196
Key Word in Context (KWIC) format 16, 23, 160
kibbitzers 22, 28
KIParla **96**, 99
knowledge: implicit vs. explicit 60; nature of 59–64; scientific 63–64; sources 60–63; *see also* definitional knowledge; phraseological knowledge, dimensions of; productive knowledge; receptive knowledge; transferable knowledge
KOLIPSI 100, **103**
Koya, T. 118
KWIC format 16, 23, 160

L1-L2 congruency: DDL research and SLA research evidence, need to connect 189–190; DDL study 120–122, 131, **132–133**, 140, 149–152, **152**, *153*, **153**, 159–162, 188; phraseological competence development 117
Lancaster-Oslo-Bergen Corpus 114
Lancaster University 32
Lancsbox 70, 105
language learning and teaching theories 21–25
language theories 18–21
languaging 23
Larsen-Freeman, D. 24
learner-centred learning 16–18
learning aims 69–70; as confounding variable 77; DDL research and SLA research evidence, need to connect 189; DDL study 120–121, 124–125, **126–127**, 194; phraseology 112
Least a second language acquisition theory needs to explain, The (M.H. Long) 191
Lee, H. 4, 26–27, 43, 45–47, **47–48**, 49, 52, 157, 159, 182–183
Leech, G. 2
Lenci, A. 89
Leone, P. 31
LEONIDE (*Longitudinal LEarner COrpus iN Italiano, Deutsch, English*) 101, **103**
Lessico dell'italiano parlato da stranieri see LIPS
Lessico di Frequenza (LIF) 87
Lessico di frequenza dell'italiano parlato see LIP
Levshina, N. 80
Levy, R. 144
lexical priming 21
lexicogrammar 19; competence 45
Licui, Z. 117
LIF (*Lessico di Frequenza*) 87
LIP (*Lessico di frequenza dell'italiano parlato*) 93, **94**, 97
LIPS (*Lessico dell'italiano parlato da stranieri*) 100, **102**
listening skills 45
lists of words *see* word lists
literature review 64; learning aims 69–70
Lo Cascio, V. 119

LOCCLI (*Longitudinal Corpus of Chinese Learners of Italian*) 101, 103; DDL study 124, 128–129
London-Lund Corpus 114
Long, M.H. 191
long-term effects of DDL 75–76
Longitudinal Corpus of Chinese Learners of Italian see LOCCLI
Longitudinal LEarner COrpus iN Italiano, Deutsch, English see LEONIDE
Lorge, I. 12
Lyding, V. 31

Mackey, A. 73
Manning, C.D. 113, **113**
manuals: DDL 27; history of Italian corpus linguistics 88–89; statistics 79–80
Marco Polo programme 122–123, *124*, 156
Marcoulides, G.A. 142
Marello, C. 31
Masini, F. 114
matching-type activities 118
McKay, S. 13–14, 25
Mental Corpus, The (J.R. Taylor) 21
MERLIN (*Multilingual Platform for the European Reference Levels: interlanguage exploration in context*) 93, 101, **102**
meta-analyses 4; call for 59; data collection 76; DDL research and SLA research evidence, need to connect 189; effectiveness of DDL 42–49, **47–48**, 159; evolution of DDL 26–27; future 194; interaction modalities 71; learning aims 69; length of exposure to DDL 157; response to DDL 49–52; semantic transparency/opacity 161; study design 121
Meunier, F. 2
Miceli, T. 30, 54–56, 92
Micro-concord (T. Johns) 14
mixed DDL: effectiveness 45–46; research methodology 71–72
mixed-effects modelling 79; DDL study 130, 142, 145–146, 148, 194
Mizumoto, A. 4, 26, 43–44, **47–48**, 48, 75, 129, 159, 182–183
Morris, M. 73
Mukherjee, J. 53

Multilingual Platform for the European Reference Levels: interlanguage exploration in context see MERLIN
multiword units/expressions *see* phraseological units and collocations

n-grams 104
Nation, P. 118
Nesselhauf, N. 160
neuroimaging 74
non-probability sampling 65–66, 68, 69
normalisation of DDL 5, 24, 27, 54, 59, 69, 182–183, 196
noSketch Engine 97–98
noticing hypothesis 22, 191
numerosity of examples 50–51, 53

O'Keeffe, A. 22–25, 27, 191
O'Sullivan, Í. 52
online resources 28
open-choice principle, language use 19; phraseology 112–113
open educational resources 59
open-ended interviews 75
Oswald, F.L. 43–45

Paisà 31, 93, **95**, 98
Palermo, M. 100
Panunzi, A. 89
paper-based DDL 32, 195; DDL study 125, 127, 158, 187; effectiveness 45–46; research methodology 71–72
Parkinson, J. 117–118
Parole in rete (S. Spina) 88
part-of-speech patterns 24
participant effects, as confounding variable 77
Pattern Grammar (S. Hunston and G. Francis) 20
patterning of language 20–21
Pavia Project 99–100, **102**
PEC (*Perugia corpus*) **95**, 98–99; DDL study 125, 127, 128, 179
Pedagogic use of spoken corpora, The 30–31
Pérez-Paredes, P. 24
Perugia corpus see PEC
phrasal frequency 161–162
phrasal items 44
phraseological competence: international perspective 116–119; Italian perspective 119; tests 122, **123**, 124, 128–131, 162, 171, 181,

193, 230–234; *see also* data-driven learning study
phraseological knowledge, dimensions of: DDL research and SLA research evidence, need to connect 190; DDL study 121–122, 131–133, 140, 152–156, **154**, **155**, **156**, 160, 162, 188, 194
phraseological units and collocations: complexity 114; DDL research and SLA research evidence, need to connect 189–190; DDL study 120, 131, **132**, 167–180, 182–184, 188; dictionaries of 119; dual-route model of language processing 116–117; frequency 113–114, 117–118; graphs/networks 105; holism 114; idiosyncrasy 114; importance in language pedagogy 114–115; 'islands of reliability' and fluency 115; L1-L2 congruency 117–118, 161–162; phraseological competence development 116–119; phraseological knowledge, dimensions of 162–163; prefabrication 114; semantic prosody 115; semantic transparency/opacity 117, 120, 160; unpredictability 113–114; working definitions of 113–114, **113**
phraseology 112; nature of 112–115; role in L2 learning 115–116; *see also phraseological entries*
Plonsky, L. 43–45
Polezzi, L. 6, 30, 104
Poole, R. 32
Popularising corpus consultation by language learners and teachers (A. Chambers) 49–52
population: DDL study 123; and sample 64–66, **65**
Poverty of the Stimulus argument 192
pre-coding 78–79
pre-/post-/delayed-post test design 75–76
pre-/post-test design 75–76
probability sampling 65–66, **67**
production data 74
productive knowledge: DDL study 162; phraseological competence development 118
proficiency levels: DDL research and SLA research evidence, need to connect 189; DDL study 121, 157–159, 183, 188; effectiveness of DDL 44, 46, 49; future directions 196; tests 74
pseudo-randomisation 76; DDL study 122, 123

quasi-randomisation 76
questionnaires: background 72–73; data collection 74–75; DDL study 129–130, 166, 193, 235–239
Quirk, R. 13, 14
quota sampling 66, 68, 69

R (software program) 80
randomisation 76
rationalism, as source of knowledge 62
Raykov, T. 142
Reading concordances (J.M. Sinclair) 18, 71
reading skills 45
receptive knowledge: DDL study 122, 162; phraseological competence development 118
relevance of examples 50–51, 53
reliability of data coding 79
Repubblica, La **94**, 97
Rescher, N. 114
research effects, as confounding variable 77–78
research into DDL 8; challenge of 5–8; debates 32; effectiveness of English language DDL 42–49, **47–48**; effectiveness of Italian language DDL 54–56; empirical research methods, reflecting on 193–194; evolution of DDL 25–27, **26**; future 47–49, 159–160, 194, 196–197; Italian L2 learning and teaching 29; for Italian language pedagogy 6–8; methodology *see* research methodology; need for 4–7, 28, 56; response to DDL 49–54; and SLA research evidence, need to connect 189–190; and SLA theories, need to connect 190–193; *see also* data-driven learning study
research methodology: data analysis 79–80; data coding 78–79; data collection 72–75; data interpretation 80; designing the DDL activities 69–72; developing the study design 75–78; knowledge, nature of 59–64; manuals 60; sample definition 64–69; scientific knowledge, nature of 63–64

research questions, DDL study 130–133, 140
researcher-imposed coding 79
Révész, A. 79
Riazi, A.M. 77–78, 81n5
Römer, U. 2
Routledge handbook of research methods in applied linguistics, The (eds J. McKinley and H. Rose) 79–80

Sabatini, F. 89
Sag, I.A. **113**, 114
sample and sampling: confounding variables 77; data collection 72; DDL study 122–124, *124*, **125**, 194; definition 64–69; future research 196; and population 64–66, *65*; representativeness 65, 66; types 65–66, 67–68
sampling error 66
Sassi, M. 30
scaffolding 18, 23, 51, 179, 190–191
Scheepers, C. 144
Schmitt, N. 116–117
Schütze, H. 113, **113**
scientific knowledge, nature of 63–64
scientific method 60
screen-recording 74, 75, 196
second language acquisition (SLA): research evidence 189–190; theories 5, 190–193
semantic transparency/opacity: DDL research and SLA research evidence, need to connect 189; DDL study 120–121, 131, **132**, 140, 148–149, *150*, **150**, 160–161, 188; phraseological competence development 117
semi-structured interviews 75
Shin, J. 180
Should you be persuaded – Two examples of data driven learning materials (T. Johns) 14–15
Simone, R. 88–89
simple random sampling 66, 67
Sinclair, J.M. 14, 18–20, 50, 71, 112–113
Siyanova, A. 116
Siyanova-Chanturia A. 119
SkELL (*SketchEngine for Language Learning*) 70, 93, **96**, 99, 158, 197; availability 7; KWIC format 16; teacher/learner-friendliness 32; *viso*

concordance 15–16, *16*; *viso* word sketch 16, *17*
SketchEngine 70, 98
SketchEngine for Language Learning see SkELL
snowball sampling 66, 68
sociocultural theory 23, 190
Socrative 181
speaking skills 45
Spina, S. 31, 88, 93, 99, 101, 119
statistical analysis 79–80, 193–194
stimulated recall 74
stratified random sampling 66, 67
Stratton, G.M. 62–63
student questionnaire, DDL study 129–130, 235–239
Supatranont, K. 76
Survey of English Usage 85
Swain, M. 23
systematic random sampling 66, 67

task effects, as confounding variable 77
Taylor, J.R. 21
Teacher's Word Book (E.L. Thorndike) 12–13
Teaching and language corpora (C. Tribble) 25
Teaching the syntactic, semantic and pragmatic dimensions of verbs (S. McKay) 13–14, 25
tenacity, as source of knowledge 60–61
Test of English for International Communication (TOEIC) 43–44
Testo e computer (A. Lenci et al.) 89
tests: DDL study 122, **123**, 123–124, 128–131, 162, 171, 181, 193, 230–234; uses of corpora 2
textbooks on DDL 27
theories: complexity theory 24; constructionist theories of language 20–21; constructivist learning theory 22, 23, 190; contextual theory of meaning 18–19, 114; DDL debates 32; language 18–21; language learning and teaching 21–25; pedagogy 18–25; second language acquisition 5, 190–193; sociocultural theory 23, 190; underpinning DDL pedagogy 18–25
theses 29
think-aloud protocols 74
Thirty years of data-driven learning (A. Boulton and N. Vyatkina) 25

Thomas, C.G. 60, 66
Thompson, G. 27
Thorndike, E.L. 12–13
Thurstun, J. 27
Tiberii, P. 119
Tily, H.J. 144
Towards a Description of English Usage (R. Quirk) 13
training: on corpora prior to DDL activities 180–181; data coding 79; DDL's non-comprehensive inclusion 59; effectiveness of DDL 47; Italian L2 pedagogy 195; materials 29–31; preliminary training myth 33; and response to DDL 52–54
transferable knowledge: DDL research and SLA research evidence, need to connect 190; DDL study 120–122, 131–132, 140, 152, 155, *155*, 162, DDL study 188
translating skills 45
Tribble, C. 25, 27, 53
Turandot programme 122–123, *124*, 157

U-shaped learning curves 119; DDL study 141, 149, 159–160, 187–188
unbiased d (d_{unb}) 44–47
Università Ca' Foscari Venezia 90
Università Cattolica del S. Cuore di Milano 101
University for Foreigners of Perugia 101; *see also* data-driven learning study
University for Foreigners of Siena 100
University of Navarra 87
University of Turin 31, 100
Urzì, F. 119
usage-based theories of language learning 24, 191
Using Corpora in the Language Learning Classroom (G. Bennett) 27

VALICO (*Varietà Apprendimento Lingua Italiana Corpus Online*) 100, 102
validity of data coding 79
Van Patten, B. 191
Varietà Apprendimento Lingua Italiana Corpus Online see VALICO
Varietà di Italiano di Nativi Corpus Appaiato see VINCA

Viganò, P.B. 31
Vilkaitė, L. 117
VINCA (*Varietà di Italiano di Nativi Corpus Appaiato*) **94**, 97–98
'Vision without inversion of the retinal image' (G.M. Stratton) 62–63
visualisation tools: in data analysis 80; DIY corpora 104–105; ItTenTen20 corpus 98; research methodology 70
vocabulary 44–46, 49
Voyant Tools 105
Vyatkina, N. 25, 28, 32, 75, 77–78, 191, 193
Vygotsky, L.S. 23

Wang, Y. 160
Warren, B. 114
Watson, T.J. 86
Webb, S. 119
What is this thing called Science? (A. Chalmers) 63
Whence and whither classroom concordancing? (T. Johns) 14
Widdowson, H. 33, 34
within-groups study design 76–77, 157–158
Wolter, B. 117, 160–161
Wood, D. 23
word clouds 70–71, 105
word combinations *see* phraseological units and collocations
word lists: AntConc 104–105; DDL pedagogy 16; history of Italian corpus linguistics 87; origins of DDL 12; research methodology 70; response to DDL 51; Voyant Tools 105
word sketches: research methodology 70; *viso* 16, 17
word units/expressions *see* phraseological units and collocations
working memory 180
Wray, A. 113, **113**, 114, 116
writing skills 45, 55

Yamashita, J. 118, 162
Yang, J.-S. 76
Yoon, H. 50–52

Zampolli, Antonio 87
Zipf's law 87
Zorzi, D. 30–31

Printed and bound by CPI Group (UK) Ltd, Croydon, CR0 4YY
01/12/2024
01797780-0013